THE NAVARRE BIBLE

The Gospel of Saint Mark

THE NAVARRE BIBLE
Saint Mark's Gospel

in the Revised Standard Version and New Vulgate
with a commentary by members of the
Faculty of Theology of the University of Navarre

FOUR COURTS PRESS

This volume consists of the text of St Mark's Gospel in the Revised
Standard Version Catholic Edition and in the New Vulgate edition, with
introduction, commentaries and apparatus made or selected by members
of the Faculty of Theology of the University of Navarre under the
direction of Professor José María Casciaro and published in the original
Navarre edition — *Sagrada Biblia: Santos Evangelios*. Quotations from
Vatican II documents are based on the translation in *Vatican Council II: The
Conciliar and Post Conciliar Documents*, ed. Austin Flannery, OP (Dublin 1981).

Nihil obstat: Stephen J. Greene, *censor deputatus.*
Imprimi potest: Desmond, Archbishop of Dublin, 12 August 1988.

The typesetting of this book was produced by Gilbert Gough Typesetting.
The book, designed by Jarlath Hayes, is published by
Four Courts Press, Kill Lane, Blackrock, Co. Dublin, Ireland.

First edition 1988
Second impression (with corrections) 1989
Second edition 1992, reprinted 1994, 1997

A catalogue record for this book
is available from the British Library

ISBN 1-85182-092-2

Printed in Ireland
by Colour Books Ltd, Dublin

Contents

Preface

In providing both undergraduate and postgraduate education, and in the research it carries out, a university is ultimately an institution at the service of society. It was with this service in mind that the theology faculty of the University of Navarre embarked on the project of preparing a translation and commentary of the Bible accessible to a wide readership—a project entrusted to it by the apostolic zeal of the University's founder and first chancellor, Monsignor Josemaría Escrivá de Balaguer.

Monsignor Escrivá did not live to see the publication of the first volume, the Gospel according to St Matthew; but he must, from heaven, continue to bless and promote our work, for the volumes, the first of which appeared in 1976, have been well received and widely read.

This edition of the Bible avoids many scholarly questions, discussion of which would over-extend the text and would be of no assistance to the immense majority of readers; these questions are avoided, but they have been taken into account.

The Spanish edition contains a new Spanish translation made from the original texts, always taking note of the Church's official Latin text, which is now that of the New Vulgate, a revision of the venerable Latin Vulgate of St Jerome: on 25 April 1979 Pope John Paul II, by the Apostolic Constitution *Scripturarum thesaurus*, promulgated the *editio typica prior* of the New Vulgate as the new official text; the *editio typica altera*, issued in 1986, is the Latin version used in this edition. For the English edition of this book we consider ourselves fortunate in having the Revised Standard Version as the translation of Scripture and wish to record our appreciation for permission to use that text, an integral part of which are the RSV notes, which are indicated by superior letters.

The introductions and notes have been prepared on the basis of the same criteria. In the notes (which are the most characteristic feature of this Bible, at least in its English version), along with scriptural and ascetical explanations we have sought to offer a general exposition of Christian doctrine—not of course a systematic exposition, for we follow the thread of the scriptural text. We have also tried to explain and connect certain biblical passages by reference to others, conscious that Sacred Scripture is ultimately one single entity; but, to avoid tiring the reader, most of the cross-references etc. are given in the form of marginal notes (the marginal notes in this edition are, then, those of the Navarre Bible, not the RSV). The commentaries contained in the notes are the result of looking up thousands of sources (sometimes reflected in explicit references given in our text)—documents of the Magisterium, exegesis by Fathers and Doctors of the Church, works by important spiritual writers (usually saints, of every period) and writings of the founder of our University. It would have been impertinent of us to comment on the Sacred Bible using our own expertise alone. Besides, a basic principle of exegesis is that Scripture should be interpreted in the context of Sacred Tradition and under the guidance of the Magisterium.

From the very beginning of our work our system has been to entrust each volume to a committee which then works as a team. However, the general editor of this edition takes ultimate responsibility for what it contains.

It is our pleasant duty to express our gratitude to the present chancellor of the University of Navarre, Bishop Alvaro del Portillo y Diez de Sollano, for his continued support and encouragement, and for reminding us of the good our work can do for the Church and for souls.

"Since Sacred Scripture must be read and interpreted with its divine authorship in mind,"[1] we pray to the Holy Spirit to help us in our work and to help our readers derive spiritual benefit from it. We also pray Mary, our Mother, Seat of Wisdom, and St Joseph, our Father and Lord, to intercede that this sowing of the Word of God may produce holiness of life in the souls of many Christians.

---

1   Vatican Council II, Dogm. Const. *Dei Verbum*, 12.

Abbreviations and Sources

1. BOOKS OF SACRED SCRIPTURE

Acts	Acts of the Apostles	2 Kings	2 Kings
Amos	Amos	Lam	Lamentations
Bar	Baruch	Lev	Leviticus
1 Chron	1 Chronicles	Lk	Luke
2 Chron	2 Chronicles	1 Mac	1 Maccabees
Col	Colossians	2 Mac	2 Maccabees
1 Cor	1 Corinthians	Mal	Malachi
2 Cor	2 Corinthians	Mic	Micah
Dan	Daniel	Mk	Mark
Deut	Deuteronomy	Mt	Matthew
Eccles	Ecclesiastes (Qohelet)	Nah	Nahum
Esther	Esther	Neh	Nehemiah
Eph	Ephesians	Num	Numbers
Ex	Exodus	Obad	Obadiah
Ezek	Ezekiel	1 Pet	1 Peter
Ezra	Ezra	2 Pet	2 Peter
Gal	Galatians	Phil	Philippians
Gen	Genesis	Philem	Philemon
Hab	Habakkuk	Ps	Psalms
Hag	Haggai	Prov	Proverbs
Heb	Hebrews	Rev	Revelation (Apocalypse)
Hos	Hosea	Rom	Romans
Is	Isaiah	Ruth	Ruth
Jas	James	1 Sam	1 Samuel
Jer	Jeremiah	2 Sam	2 Samuel
Jn	John	Sir	Sirach (Ecclesiasticus)
1 Jn	1 John	Song	Song of Solomon
2 Jn	2 John	1 Thess	1 Thessalonians
3 Jn	3 John	2 Thess	2 Thessalonians
Job	Job	1 Tim	1 Timothy
Joel	Joel	2 Tim	2 Timothy
Jon	Jonah	Tit	Titus
Josh	Joshua	Tob	Tobit
Jud	Judith	Wis	Wisdom
Jude	Jude	Zech	Zechariah
Judg	Judges	Zeph	Zephaniah
1 Kings	1 Kings		

Alphonsus Mary Liguori, St
The Love of our Lord Jesus Christ reduced to practice
Sermons for all the Sundays of the Year

Ambrose, St
Expositio Evangelii sec. Lucam

Augustine, St
Against Faustus
Confessions
Contra Epist. Fundamenti
De consensu Evangelistarum
De doctrina christiana
De Genesi ad litteram
In Ioann. Evangel. tractatus
Letters
On the Psalms 36, 1
Sermons

Bede, St
In Marci Evangelium expositio
Sermon *Super qui audientes gavisi sunt*

Benedict XII
Const. *Benedictus Deus*, 29 January 1336

Code of Canon Law
Codex Iuris Canonici (Vatican City 1983)

Escrivá de Balaguer, J.
Christ is passing by (followed by section no.)
Conversations (do.)
Friends of God (do.)
Holy Rosary
The Way
The Way of the Cross

Eusebius
Ecclesiastical History

Flavius Josephus
Jewish Antiquities
The Jewish War

Florence, Council of
Decree *Pro Armeniis*

Francis de Sales, St
Treatise on the Love of God

Gregory the Great, Pope St
In Evangelia homiliae

Irenaeus, St
Against heresies

Jerome, St
Ad Nepotianum
Comm. in Marcum
Comm. in Matth.
On famous men

John Chrysostom, St
Adversus Iudaeos
II Hom. de proditione Iudae
Homilies on St Matthew
In Gen. hom.

John Paul II
Enc. *Dives in misericordiae*, 30 November 1980
Enc. *Laborem exercens*, 14 September 1981
Enc. *Redemptor hominiis*, 4 March 1979
Apos. Const. *Scripturarum thesaurus*, 25 April 1979
Apos. Exhort. *Catechesi tradendae*, 16 October 1979
Apos. Exhort. *Familiaris consortio*, 22 November 1981
Homily on Boston Common, 1 October 1979
Address to penitentiaries of the four major basilicas in Rome, 30 January 1981

Justin, St
Apology
Against Tryphon

Luis de Leon, Fray
The Names of Christ

Leo XIII
Providentissimus Deus, 18 November 1893

Missal, Roman
Missale Romanum ex decreto sacrosancti oecumenici concilii Vatican I instauratum auctoritate Pauli PP. VI promulgatum, editio typica altera (Vatican City 1975)

New Vulgate
Nova Vulgata Bibliorum Sacrorum editio typica altera (Vatican City 1986)

Origen
In Matth. Comm.

Paul IV
Const. *Cum quorumdam*, 7 August 1555

Paul VI
Apos. Exhort. *Evangelii nuntiandi*, 8 December 1975
Enc. *Populorum progressio*, 26 March 1967
Enc. *Sacerdotalis coelibatus*, 24 June 1967

Pius V, St
Catechism of the Council of Trent

Pius X, St
Enc. *Acerbo nimis*, 15 April 1905
Enc. *Communium rerum*, 21 April 1909
Catechism of Christian Doctrine

Pius XI
Enc. *Casti Connubii*, 31 December 1930

Pontifical Biblical Commission
Inst. *Sancta Mater Ecclesia*, 21 April 1964
Enchiridion Biblicum, 4th ed. (Naples-Rome 1961)

Teresa, St
Exclamations of the Soul to God
Mansions

Tertullian
  Against Marcion
  Scorpiace
Theophylact
  Enarratio in Evangelium Marci
Thomas Aquinas, St
  Commentary on St Matthew
  Summa theologiae
Thomas More, St
  De tristitia Christi
Trent, Council of
  Decree *De libris sacris et de traditionibis recipiendis*

Trent, Council of (contd.)
  Decree *De sacramento matrimonii*
  Decree *De S. Missae sacrificio*
  Doctrina de peccato originali
  Doctrina de sacramento extremae unctionis
Vatican II
  Dogm. Const. *Dei Verbum*
  Dogm. Const. *Lumen gentium*
  Const. *Sacrosanctum Concilium*
  Past. Const. *Gaudium et spes*
  Decree *Ad gentes*
  Decree *Apostolicam actuositatem*
  Decree *Presbyterorum ordinis*
  Decree *Dignitatis humanae*

3. OTHER ABBREVIATIONS

A.D.	*anno domini*, after Christ	f	and following (*pl.* ff)
ad loc.	*ad locum*, commentary on this passage	Hom.	homily
		ibid.	*ibidem*, in the same place
Exhort.	Exhortation	*in loc.*	*in locum*, commentary on this passage
Apost.	apostolic		
B.C.	before Christ	*loc.*	*locum*, place or passage
can.	canon	n.	number (*pl.* nn.)
chap.	chapter	p.	page (*pl.* pp.)
cf.	*confer*, compare	*pl.*	plural
Const.	Constitution	par.	and parallel passages
Decl.	Declaration	Past.	Pastoral
Dz-Sch	Denzinger-Schönmetzer, *Enchiridion Symbolorum*	SCDF	Sacred Congregation for the Doctrine of the Faith
Dogm.	Dogmatic	sess.	session
EB	*Enchiridion Biblicum*	v.	verse (*pl.* vv.)
Enc.	Encyclical		

General Introduction to the Bible

WHAT IS THE BIBLE?

The Bible or Sacred Scripture is the collection of books which, written under the inspiration of the Holy Spirit, have God as their author, and have been entrusted as such to the Church.[1]

Therefore, in order to understand what these sacred books essentially are, in the first place we should realize that they have two unique characteristics. Firstly, they are of divine origin, the result of a special action which is called "divine inspiration" of Holy Scripture; and, secondly, the Bible has been entrusted by God to his Church as a sacred deposit and a divine gift which she has to keep, interpret and expound to all men so that, by knowing and loving God in this life, they can obtain eternal happiness thereafter.

We should bear in mind that the reading of Holy Scripture, apart from giving us a knowledge of God as he is in himself, ought also produce in us an increase of love of God and of our neighbour; moreover, we can say that if one does not achieve this increase of charity one has not fully understood Holy Scripture: "everybody who knows that the purpose of the law is love that issues from a pure heart and a good conscience and a sincere faith (cf. 1 Tim 1:5), preferring all knowledge of the divine Scripture to other things, let him dedicate himself with confidence to expounding the divine books. If anybody thinks that he has understood the divine Scriptures or any part of them, and with this knowledge does not build up the double love of God and of his neighbour, then he has not yet understood them."[2]

Before explaining these two characteristics in more detail we should like to outline a few ideas about divine Revelation.

DIVINE REVELATION

The word "revelation" literally means to remove a veil that is hiding something. In religious language it means God's manifestation to mankind of his own being and of those other truths necessary for or helpful to salvation. God makes himself known to man in two ways. One is through the things he has created, like an artist through his work; this is our natural knowledge of God, described with great poetic feeling in the Old Testament Book of Wisdom: "For all men

---

1   Vatican Council I, Dogm. Const. *Dei Filius*, ch. 2.
2   St Augustine, *De doctrina christiana*, 1, 36, 40; 1, 40, 44.

who were ignorant of God were foolish by nature; and they were unable from the good things that are seen to know him who exists; nor did they recognize the craftsman while paying heed to his works; but they supposed that either fire or wind or air, or the circle of the stars, or turbulent water, or the luminaries of heaven were the gods that rule the world. If through delight in the beauty of these things men assumed them to be gods, let them know how much better than these is their lord, for the author of beauty created them. And if men were amazed at their power and working, let them perceive from them how much more powerful is he who formed them. For from the greatness and beauty of created things comes a corresponding perception of their Creator" (Wis 13:1-5). This is what the Apostle St Paul points out to the Romans when he says that the invisible perfections of God become visible to our intelligence through created things, especially his eternal power and his divinity (cf. Rom 1:20).

But God has not been content for man to have just this natural knowledge; he has also made himself known directly: "In many and various ways God spoke of old to our fathers through the prophets; but in these last days he has spoken to us through a Son, whom he appointed the heir of all things, through whom he created the world" (Heb 1:1-2). This action of God is supernatural or divine Revelation.

God chose the people of Israel in order to reveal himself gradually, through the prophets, in the Old Testament. This Revelation reaches its fulness in Christ, the Son of God made man, who has communicated to us all truth: "God has graciously arranged that what he had revealed for the salvation of all nations would abide perpetually in its full integrity and be handed on to all generations. Therefore, Christ the Lord, in whom the entire revelation of the most high God is brought to completion, commissioned the Apostles to preach to all men that Gospel which is the source of all saving truth and moral teaching, and to impart to them heavenly gifts. This Gospel had been promised in former times through the prophets, and Christ himself had fulfilled it and promulgated it with his lips. This commission was faithfully fulfilled by the Apostles who by their oral preaching, by example and by observances handed on what they had received from the lips of Christ, from living with him, and from what he did, or what they had learned through the prompting of the Holy Spirit. The commission was fulfilled, too, by those Apostles and other men associated with the Apostles who, under the inspiration of the same Holy Spirit, committed the message of salvation to writing."[3] And so in the Church, side by side with holy Scripture, there exists sacred Tradition. Both constitute the deposit of God's Revelation on matters of faith and morals, entrusted by Christ to the Apostles and by them in turn to their successors down to our day.

In this way Tradition and Holy Scripture are the means by which we receive God's saving Revelation: "There exists a close connexion and communication between sacred Tradition and sacred Scripture. For both of them, flowing from

3   Vatican Council II, Dogm. Const. *Dei Verbum*, 7.

the same divine well-spring, in a certain way merge into a unity and tend toward the same end."[4]

Thanks to Tradition, the Church knows the canon of the sacred books and understands them ever more deeply. For this reason Holy Scripture cannot be understood without Tradition.

This Tradition is contained chiefly in the teaching of the universal Magisterium of the Church, in the writings of the Fathers, and in the words and actions of the sacred liturgy.

Both Tradition and Scripture have been entrusted to the Church, and within the Church, only the Magisterium has the role of interpreting them authentically and of preaching them with authority. And so both have to be received and interpreted with equal devotion.[5]

THE DIVINE INSPIRATION OF THE BIBLE

How does the divine action of inspiration influence the human authors of the sacred books?

Divine inspiration enlightens their intellect so that they can rightly conceive all that, and only that, which God wants them to write; it is also an infallible motion which moves the will of the sacred writer or hagiographer, though without impairing his freedom, to write faithfully what he has conceived in his intellect; and finally, it also consists in effective assistance to the sacred writer to find the correct language and expressions for describing aptly and with infallible truth all that he has conceived and has wanted to write.[6]

Thus, God is the principal author of Holy Scripture, and the sacred writers are also true, though subordinate, authors, intelligent and free instruments in the hands of God.[7]

According to this, the inspired book is the result of an action of God and of the hagiographer, in such a way that all the concepts and all the words of the sacred text can be attributed simultaneously to God and to his instrument, the hagiographer. There is nothing, then, in the Bible, that is not inspired by God.

THE MESSAGE OF THE BIBLE

The Bible does not speak about God as other books do; rather, in it *God speaks to us about himself*—which is something quite different. Both the Old and New Testament are the Word of God, a word at once living and life-giving. Apart from the narration of historical facts, the Bible contains a whole marvellous collection of teachings from which there derive a profound philosophy and a complete system of ethical principles; but all this treasure of truths is communicated by being linked to real events, God's intervention in history: for example, the first chapters of Genesis, when describing the origin of the

4   *Dei Verbum*, 9.
5   Cf. Council of Trent, Decree *De libris sacris et de traditionibus recipiendis*, sess. IV.
6   Cf. Leo XIII, Encyclical *Providentissimus Deus*, 18 November 1893.
7   Cf. *ibid.* and *Dei Verbum*, 11.

world and of man, also give us some very fundamental teaching about not only supernatural truths but also natural truths such as the creation by God of all things out of nothing. When we read that God created the heavens and the earth we see that God is the Creator and that he transcends the world, and that man is God's creature.

The Bible contains the most important events of human history relevant to our salvation; throughout this history, like an internal motor driving it, there is something else to be seen, also historical but less perceptible, namely, the impulses, forces and sentiments which God has placed in the protagonists of that history or in the sacred authors who wrote down these events. There is, then, within human history yet another history, as it were, wrought by God on behalf of man—for us and with our cooperation or indeed in spite of us. Fundamentally the Bible is the History of Salvation, or better, the history of the salvation of men by God. And in its midst we find the key to understanding all that history, namely, the death and resurrection of Jesus: the cross is the great explanation of that history: to save the world God becomes man and allows himself to be nailed to the cross like a criminal, but on the third day he rises from the dead. This is how God saves humanity from the slavery of sin, from death and from the devil. This Incarnation-Death-Resurrection, or, saying it another way, this mysterious God-Man, Jesus Christ, is the very centre of the Bible; from the opening pages of Genesis to the last pages of the Apocalypse everything at first tends towards, then afterwards derives from, Christ dead and risen again. Once the cross has been raised on Calvary and in the centre of history, neither history nor the world can have any meaning independently of it. At that moment the history of salvation reaches its climax. The great and all-powerful Love of God, humbling himself unto death, gains victory over death, over evil and over the powers of the devil. This is the mystery of the cross: to live one must die; to conquer, one must perish. Before the coming of Jesus, from the time of the original fall of our first parents, everything is promise, preparation, waiting. Afterwards everything is fulfilment, fact, although in hope and in faith, until the end of the world.

Biblical history also has a beginning, but, unlike secular history which speaks only of events that have already taken place, it also has a future ending which to a certain extent is already written. The beginning is the creation of man and his immediate elevation to a state of justice, holiness and happiness, all this later being dramatically lost. The end is the vision of heaven under the image of heavenly Jerusalem, the future holy city of God. This biblical history unfolds in time and space; in it we can distinguish different periods, along the following lines:

1. After the loss of Paradise time passed slowly. Immediately after the original sin of our first parents, God promised a Saviour who would come from the lineage of the Woman (cf. Gen 3:15, the so-called "proto-evangelion", i.e. "first gospel" or good news of salvation). Afterwards came the centuries in which God did not completely abandon mankind: he showed mercy to the patriarchs, like Enoch, and especially Noah, with whom he formed a special

16

relationship or covenant. In his speech to the Athenians in the Areopagus, St Paul referred to this period as the "times of ignorance" (Acts 17:29-30), and, in his Letter to the Romans, as the "times of God's patience" (cf. Rom 3:26). In his speech to the citizens of Lycaonia he mentions that in those days God "allowed" the nations to follow their own devices (Acts 14:16). During this period God "has patience" and allows mankind to experience the dreadful consequence of sin and of ignorance of the true God.

2. At a certain moment God intervenes more decisively in human history: when he calls Abraham, to whom he makes the *promise*: "In you [in your descendants] all the tribes of the earth will be blessed" (Gen 12:3). This is the "time of the promise" mentioned by St Stephen (cf. Acts 7:17). From here on mankind is divided: on the one hand, the race born of Abraham, and on the other the great mass of mankind, the Gentiles. Human life outside the chosen people was governed by the principles engraved by God in the individual conscience (cf. Rom 2:12-15); these could be saved by fulfilling the natural law, for God does not deny his grace to anyone who does what he can. But the great majority of people drowned the voice of their conscience and lived in sin (cf. Rom 1:18-32).

3. A new divine intervention marks the start of a third period, the "time of the Law". God chooses Moses, reveals his own intimacy to him in the episode of the burning bush (Ex 3:14-17) and establishes a pact, the Covenant of Sinai (cfr. Ex 19-24; Deut 29), in which God gives the Hebrews the Law which they have to fulfil to show their faithfulness to the Covenant. In this manner God constitutes the Hebrew clans as "his people", the people of God. From then on (thirteenth century B.C.) until Jesus Christ, biblical history is simply the history of the Old Covenant, the history of the Old Testament.

The Covenant and the Law given to Moses, the starting point of the chosen people, is the centre of rebirth to which they return again and again after their crises and their falls, to remain faithful to their vocation as the people of God. On occasions of special solemnity or gravity the Old Testament is renewed. Different periods can be distinguished: the conquest of Canaan under the leadership of Joshua (end of thirteenth century B.C.); the period of the separate tribes (twelfth century and first half of eleventh), united partially and occasionally under the judges; the long centuries of the Hebrew monarchy (eleventh to sixth centuries) in which the prophets exercise a transcendental religious ministry and continually exhort the people and their rulers to return to the genuine spirit of the Covenant and of the Law; the great national and religious crisis of the Babylonian exile (sixth century B.C.), the terrible trial in which the soul of the people of Israel is re-forged thanks to the prophets and to certain deeply religious leaders like Nehemiah and Ezra; and finally the long post-exilic period (fifth to first century B.C.) not without its dangerous and difficult moments, such as the forced hellenization which the Seleucid kings of Syria sought to inflict on the Jews and against which they revolted under the leadership of the Maccabees (second century B.C.).

During these long centuries the religion and the history of Israel were being forged simultaneously. Under the impulse of the Holy Spirit the judges, the kings and other leaders defended the nation's independence, a necessary pre-condition for conserving of the monotheistic purity of the revealed religion of the Old Testament. Under the impulse of the same Spirit the prophets taught the truths of Revelation: some stressed the moral and social responsibility of the people of God (for example, Amos); others, the infinite and intimate love of God for his people (for example, Hosea); or the ineffable transcendence of God's majesty (for example, Isaiah); or the need for limitless confidence in God (for example, Jeremiah); or individual responsibility as opposed to the anonymity of the crowd (Ezekiel); etc. Meanwhile hope grew steadily to form the backbone of the prophets' preaching around the messianism of the Old Testament, which was to have its fulfilment in the Person and in the work of Jesus, the Christ or Messiah. At the same time, and more so especially in the latter centuries of Old Testament history and also under the influence of the same Holy Spirit, there took place the gradual development of Hebrew *wisdom*: gifted individuals, chosen by God and educated in the meditation of the Law and in the teachings of the prophets and trained to reflect on life, gradually fashion, under the inspiration of the Holy Spirit, the so-called *wisdom* literature of the Old Testament, which completes Revelation and prepares men for the coming of the messianic Saviour in the "fullness of the times" (cf. Gal 4:4).

4. Finally, the "fullness of the times": the Incarnation of the Word of God, Jesus Christ. By his life on earth and by his sacrifice on the cross followed by his glorious resurrection, Jesus gains victory over the powers and forces that have enslaved mankind. Jesus brings a new and definitive creation, quite distinct from the former one. He is the new Adam, to use St Paul's image, first-born of the renewed creation; he is the head of the new people of God, the Church, based not on "flesh and blood" but on the spirit and the charity of the New Covenant in Jesus' own blood. By his resurrection and ascension into heaven the humanity of Jesus, united to his divinity in the self-same one Person of the Word (the hypostatic union), receives from the Father lordship over all creation, visible and invisible, earthly and heavenly: the "last times" of history have begun.

THE BOOKS WHICH MAKE UP THE BIBLE

Given that the divine inspiration of the Bible is a supernatural grace, only God can reveal which books specifically are inspired by him. The list of inspired books is called the Canon of the Bible. The revealed fact of the biblical canon is to be found in the faith of the Church from her beginnings. The most important documentary evidence that we have of this faith are the decrees of the councils of Carthage (*c*. A.D. 400) and some other documents of the ordinary Magisterium from the fifth century onwards. The Council of Florence (1441) in due course witnessed to this Tradition of the Church. This truth of faith was solemnly defined by the Council of Trent (1546). The First Vatican Council

(1870) repeated in a solemn manner the definition of Trent, which Vatican II also adopted (cf. *Dei Verbum*, 11).

The concept of "canonicity" presupposes that of inspiration: a book is canonical when, having been written under divine inspiration, it is recognized and proclaimed as such by the Church. The Church does not define as canonical any book that has not been inspired. The criterion which the Magisterium of the Church has used in order to define exactly which books are inspired and canonical is Sacred Tradition, which stems from Jesus and the Apostles, interpreted with the assistance of the Holy Spirit.

The books of the biblical canon are those which are to be found in Catholic editions of the Bible.

CONSERVATION OF THE SACRED BOOKS

Once we have discussed the question of *what* the Bible is and *which* books it comprises, a third question arises, namely, what relationship do the present-day versions of Scripture have with the original writings as they came from the hands of the inspired authors? Or, in other words, do they conserve and reproduce the original inspired text?

We should point out in the first place that the original manuscripts or autographs (that is, written by the author himself) are no longer extant; instead we have only copies, either direct or indirect. The same is true of the other literary works of ancient times.

The books of the Old Testament were written originally in Hebrew, with the exception of the book of Wisdom and the second book of Maccabees which were composed in Greek; in addition some small fragments of other books were written originally in Greek or in Aramaic. The New Testament, on the other hand, was originally composed entirely in Greek with the single exception of the first redaction of the Gospel of St Matthew which was written in Aramaic.

Insofar as the dates of composition are concerned, the Old Testament began to be written down possibly towards the end of the thirteenth century B.C. and was finished at the beginning of the first century B.C., thus spanning a long period of twelve centuries. The New Testament, by contrast, was completed in the short period of fifty years, A.D. 50-100 approximately.

The Bible, and especially the New Testament, is far and away the best-documented literary production of antiquity: in the case of Homer's *Iliad* and *Odyssey* and certain works of Plato and of Aristotle (for which the most manuscripts are extant) the number of manuscripts never exceeds one thousand; indeed at most there are twenty or thirty and of a rather late date (tenth to fifteenth centuries); but for the Bible we have over 6,000 manuscripts in the original languages (Hebrew and Greek) and over 40,000 in other very early versions (Coptic, Latin, Armenian, Aramaic etc.).

Hence we see that the Bible, quite apart from its divine authority, also possesses a historico-critical character immeasurably superior to any other ancient literary work.

"We can know the authentic meaning of Holy Scripture only through the Church, because only the interpretation given by the Church is guaranteed free from error."[8] And from the definition of Holy Scripture given by the First Vatican Council we get another of the essential conditions for interpretation of the Bible, namely, that only the Church, through her Magisterium, is the authentic interpreter of Holy Scripture. This has to be understood in both the positive and the negative sense: we have to accept as a biblical meaning one that has been proposed as such by the Church Magisterium (either directly or indirectly); and we have to reject as false any interpretation that does not agree with the meaning proposed by the Magisterium. Hence Holy Scripture cannot be understood by somebody who does not have the Christian faith. Something similar occurs with the Bible as occurs with the figure of Jesus Christ: the person who does not have faith recognizes Jesus only as a unique and extraordinary man, but falls very far short of the truth and therefore cannot comprehend that he is the Incarnate Son of God, the second Person of the Blessed Trinity, the only Saviour and Redeemer of mankind.

Likewise, the Bible, in its deeper sense, cannot be understood by somebody who does not believe in its divine inspiration and that it has God as its principal author. This fact is a necessary condition for correct interpretation of the Bible, and its absence cannot be compensated for by any human technique, whether literary, historical, philosophical or of any other kind.

St Augustine, having explained some difficulties in interpretation of Scripture, replies to a friend: "Let him who asks these things become a Christian, lest in trying to solve all the questions about the holy books he should end his life before having passed from death to life. There are innumerable problems that cannot be solved before believing, at the risk of ending this life without faith. Once faith has been accepted then they can be studied in detail as an exercise for the pious enjoyment of the faithful mind."[9]

Insofar as the Bible is also a human book of notable antiquity, our understanding of it is helped by certain explanations of a historical or literary character, as is the case with any ancient work.

At this point we should like to recall the comparison St Augustine offers: when the Israelites left Egypt they took with them valuables of gold, silver, precious stones, garments etc. which the Egyptians used either as personal ornaments or for idolatrous worship. But from these very same precious objects the Hebrews made ornaments for use in the worship of the one true God. The saintly bishop of Hippo applies this idea to the use of human sciences (philosophy, history, literature etc.) in the understanding of the Scriptures, provided they are used properly in the service of Scripture, that is to say, with humility and reverence and the invocation of divine grace: "He who applies himself to the study of Holy Scripture [. . .] should not forget to consider that

8   *St Pius X Catechism*, 887.
9   *Letter* 102, 6, 38.

apostolic maxim: knowledge puffs up, but love builds up (1 Cor 8:1); because he will realize that although he has emerged rich from Egypt, if he does not celebrate the Pasch he cannot be saved."[10]

TRUTHFULNESS AND INERRANCY OF THE BIBLE

Everything that the hagiographer affirms, states or implies, ought to be taken as affirmed, stated or implied by God who can neither deceive nor be deceived. Truthfulness has to do with agreement between what one expresses and what one thinks or feels; inerrancy means absolute freedom from error. Consequently, in Holy Scripture there can be no errors whatsoever because, since all of it is inspired, God himself is the author of all its parts.

In the things of nature, proper to the physical sciences, God has not wished to make any supernatural revelation about the inner constitution of the visible world; hence neither have the sacred authors revealed anything on this matter. What they do teach, however, are the truths necessary for salvation: the creation of the world and of man by God, the providence and government of the world by God and his freedom and omnipotence to perform miracles. It is normal to quote two reasons of convenience that help us to understand why God has not revealed the inner constitution of the visible world: firstly, the knowledge of these things does not affect directly the doctrine of salvation; and secondly, God has left precisely these matters to the free investigation of human science. And so the hagiographers allude to the events of nature using the expressions and concepts of their own time and cultural surroundings. Because they were writing in a period long before the development of the natural sciences, the sacred authors speak about things in the manner in which they are immediately apprehended by the senses and according to the common descriptions of all ages: the sun rises, the moon sets, etc. The attitude of those writers, especially in the last century, who felt that the sacred authors ought to have spoken about the most up-to-date scientific theories (often abandoned later) is superficial and unreasonable. We should thank God that the sacred writers have spoken in simple language so that anyone can understand them by applying a little common sense.

In historical matters it is another question altogether. If the explanation of the happenings of nature is a matter in which divine Revelation has no part to play, human history nevertheless has in many ways a close connexion with revealed truth. The reason is because biblical revelation is concerned not only with abstract truths, but also with the merciful intervention of God in certain events of human history. The foundations of Christian Revelation and the major dogmas are very firmly rooted in history. For example, the creation of the world by God underlies the whole of Revelation about the notion of God, of the world and of man. The birth of Jesus Christ of the Blessed Virgin Mary and the power of the Holy Spirit without the intervention of a man, is an event that has really taken place in history and which is at the centre of the Christian faith. The death

10   St Augustine, *De doctrina christiana*, 2, 9, 14.

and resurrection of Jesus Christ in the time of Pontius Pilate is the crucial historical event of salvation history and cannot be changed nor denied, nor can it be understood in a way that denies its real historical character.

CHRISTIAN READING OF THE BIBLE

"Here we are going to read the words, not of a lord of this world, but of the Prince of Angels. If we prepare ourselves in this manner, the grace of the Holy Spirit will guide us with all certainty and we will reach the very throne of the King, and we will attain all good things through the grace and love of our Lord Jesus Christ, to whom be the glory and the power, with the Father and the Holy Spirit, now and forever. Amen."[11]

St John Chrysostom calls the Holy Scriptures letters sent by God to men.[12] Given that this is so, the first thing that we have to do on reading the Holy Scripture is to foment in ourselves a holy desire and longing to know and to meditate the content of these divine letters. And so St Jerome exhorted his friend: "Read very often the divine Scriptures; nay, never abandon the sacred reading."[13]

The Second Vatican Council "earnestly and especially urges all the Christian faithful [...] to learn by frequent reading of the divine Scriptures 'the surpassing knowledge of Jesus Christ' (Phil 3:8). For ignorance of the Scriptures is ignorance of Christ (St Jerome). Therefore they should gladly go to the sacred text itself, whether in the liturgy, rich in the divine words, or in spiritual reading. [...] Let them remember that prayer should accompany the reading of sacred Scripture, so that God and man may talk together; for "we speak to him when we pray; we hear him when we read the divine sayings' (St Ambrose)."[14] And St Pius X affirms that "whereas the reading of the Bible is not required of all Christians because they are already taught by the Church, it is nevertheless very useful and is recommended to everybody."[15]

For faithful reading we have to start necessarily from *the obedience of faith of the one Church of Jesus Christ*; faith, to be precise, in all that the Church professes and teaches about the canon of the sacred books, their divine inspiration, their inerrancy and truthfulness, their historicity and their authenticity; in brief, faith that God is the principal author of the sacred books and that they contain the truth of salvation without any error.

Piety and *holiness of life* are also needed for the understanding of Holy Scripture. As one grows in the understanding of the written Word of God, one needs to prepare oneself through prayer to receive the insights that are freely given by the Holy Spirit. The person who reads, meditates or studies the Bible needs to have recourse to constant prayer, to contact with God, for the

11   St John Chrysostom, *In Matt. hom.*, 1, 8.
12   Cf. *In Gen. hom.*, 2, 2.
13   *Ad Nepotianum*, 7, 1.
14   *Dei Verbum*, 25.
15   *St Pius X Catechism*, 884.

comprehension of this holy word. The secrets of Holy Scripture are not unlocked only with the aid of linguistics, archaeology, sociology, psychology or any other human science, but rather by a desire to achieve personal holiness, and therefore in the light of God.

It is also necessary to have the virtue of humility which makes us like children before our Father God. Only in this way will the words of Christ be fulfilled in us: "I thank you, Father, Lord of heaven and of earth, because thou hast hidden these things from the wise and understanding and revealed them to babes" (Mt 11:25).

This humility and piety are manifested in the Christian by his prudence in not allowing or accepting wanton opinions that are opposed to the constant teaching of the Magisterium of the Church and Tradition; and also, by the firm conviction that we shall never manage to demonstrate truths of the supernatural order and that therefore we do not discover for ourselves, but rather accept joyfully, what God has revealed and precisely as the Church Magisterium proposes it. Faced with the grandeur of the divine mysteries, the Christian ought to experience humble joy at the fact that his intelligence cannot comprehend them. How can I, small and finite that I am, comprehend the infinity and grandeur of God? Hence Pope St Pius X quoted a passage from St Anselm: "The desire for knowledge will move our reason, and humility will subdue it when it fails to understand. No Christian ought to discuss whether something that the catholic Church believes in her heart and confesses with her mouth is indeed as she says or not; but rather, always maintaining and loving the same faith without doubting, and living in accordance with it, he will humbly investigate, as far as he is able, why it is so. If he understands let him thank God, and if he cannot, let him not lower his horns to attack but bow his head to adore."[16]

Finally, let the reader embark with these dispositions on the reading of the Holy Bible, knowing that, if he does so, in them he will find Christ, in the words of St Augustine: "Divine Scripture is like a field in which we are going to build a house. We cannot be lazy and be happy to build just on the surface: we have to dig down until we reach the living rock, and this rock is Christ."[17]

16 Encyclical *Communium rerum*, 21 April 1909.
17 *In Ioann. Evang. tractatus*, 23, 1.

Introduction to the Books of the New Testament

What "New Testament" primarily means is the new and definitive stage in salvation history brought about by Jesus Christ, which replaced and completed the Revelation and structures of the "Old Testament"; both expressions have been in use among Christian writers since the first century.

God's promise of salvation, given in paradise after the fall of our first parents (cf. Gen 3:15), was ratified by the covenant he made with the patriarch Abraham (cf. Gen 17) and renewed with Isaac and with Jacob (cf. Gen 26; 28:12-15); later Moses sealed this covenant by offering victims (cf. Ex 24:1-11). In the New Testament God keeps his promise : Jesus, by his death on the cross, establishes the New and Eternal Covenant. The expression "New Testament" is taken from the words Jesus uses when instituting the eucharistic Sacrifice (cf. Mt 26:28; Mk 14:24; Lk 22:20; 1 Cor 11:25). The sacrifice which Christ offers on the cross is the new and definitive Covenant, also known as the New Alliance or New Testament.

This first meaning of the expression led to a special meaning: from the end of the second century the words "New Testament" were more and more taken also to designate the collection of divinely inspired books containing the full and definitive Revelation given by our Lord Jesus Christ.

THE BOOKS OF THE NEW TESTAMENT

The New Testament is made up of twenty-seven books, all of them written in the second half of the first century. These are often divided into three groups: (i) historical books: the four Gospels and the Acts of the Apostles; (ii) didactic books : the fourteen letters of St Paul and the seven "catholic" letters; (iii) the prophetic book of the Apocalypse of St John.

These writings exactly as we have them today were from the beginning accepted by the Church as being the *new* sacred books and were placed alongside the books of the Old Testament—which the Church also accepted as God's gift. Together these two collections constitute the Bible or Sacred Scripture.

Just as Christ fulfilled the promises made by God through the patriarchs and prophets of the Old Covenant or Testament, so the books of the New Testament record the fulfillment of these promises which themselves were recorded in the sacred books of the Old Alliance : the whole Old Testament can be seen as a promise or prophecy of the New Testament, and the New Testament as the keeping of that promise.

THE GREAT RESPECT DUE THE NEW TESTAMENT

Since God is the author of the New Testament and salvation its purpose, it should be read with great respect and veneration. As the Second Vatican Council says: "The word of God, which is the power of God for salvation to everyone who has faith (cf. Rom 1:16), is set forth and displays its power in a most wonderful way in the writings of the New Testament. For when the time fully came (cf. Gal 4:4), the Word became flesh and dwelt among us full of grace and truth (cf. Jn 1:14). Christ established on earth the kingdom of God, revealed his Father and himself by deeds and words; and by his death, resurrection and glorious ascension, as well as by sending the Holy Spirit, completed his work. Lifted up from the earth he draws all men to himself (cf. Jn 12:32), for he alone has the words of eternal life (cf. Jn 6:68). This mystery was not made known to other generations as it has now been revealed to his apostles and prophets by the Holy Spirit (cf. Eph 3:4-6), that they might preach the Gospel, stir up faith in Jesus Christ and the Lord and bring together the Church. The writings of the New Testament stand as a perpetual and divine witness to these realities."[1]

The New Testament contains the Good News, that is, the Gospel of Jesus Christ (cf. Mk 1:1)—the Gospel which our Lord himself preached and commanded his Apostles to preach. God wanted the books of the New Testament to be written, so that by their being preached and authentically explained by the Church they would provide people in every generation with an excellent means of getting to know Jesus Christ, the *Way* for all men, *Truth* for our intellects and *Life* for our souls (cf. Jn 14:6).

DOCTRINAL CONTENT OF THE NEW TESTAMENT

The New Testament proclaims the gifts and also the commands of God, Almighty Father, who sent his only-begotten Son into the world to save us ("for us men and for our salvation he came down from heaven", in the words of the Nicene-Constantinopolitan Creed in the Mass). The New Testament reveals to us the unfathomable mystery of God, one and triune, a mystery which was hinted at but not clearly revealed in the Old Testament.

In Jesus Christ, the Son of God, we can see the Father : "All things have been delivered to me by my Father; and no one knows the Son except the Father, and any one to whom the Son chooses to reveal him (Mt 11:27). "Philip said to him, 'Lord, show us the Father, and we shall be satisfied.' Jesus said to him, 'Have I been with you so long, and yet you do not know me, Philip? He who has seen me has seen the Father'" (Jn 14:8-9).

1   Vatican Council II, Dogm. Const. *Dei Verbum*, 17.

Jesus' teaching came not only from himself but also from the Father who had sent him : "He who does not love me does not keep my words; and the word which you hear is not mine but the Father's who sent me" (Jn 14:24).

Jesus came in obedience to his Father's command: "For I have come down from heaven, not to do my own will, but the will of him who sent me" (Jn 6:38). The Father wants him to lead men to divine sonship and to the vision of the glory of God : "he has granted us his precious and very great promises, that through these you may . . . become partakers of the divine nature" (2 Pet 1:4).

Jesus is, then, the Saviour : in him is revealed God's tender loving-kindness towards us. Jesus is the Christ (the Messiah), the Lord, the Son of God. He not only offers man the way to satisfy his deepest yearnings : he brings something that is on an entirely different plane—supernatural grace, which makes us adoptive sons and daughters of God.

The books of the New Testament, together with those of the Old, are all part of one, single, ornate plan : "In many and various ways God spoke of old to our fathers by the prophets; but in these last days he has spoken to us by a Son, whom he appointed the heir of all things, through whom also he created the world. He reflects the glory of God and bears the very stamp of his nature, upholding the universe by his word of power. When he had made purification for sins, he sat down at the right hand of the Majesty on high" (Heb 1:1-3).

The Old Testament, then, bore witness to Christ by announcing his coming: its books, whether historical, prophetical or wisdom books, prophesied the future Christ. The Gospels, by God's design, deal with Jesus' life on earth, his words and actions, his redemptive death and his glorious resurrection. Through Christ we have been freed from sin, from death and from the power of the devil, and enabled to live in the glorious liberty of the children of God (cf. Rom 8:21). The Acts of the Apostles reports the coming of the Holy Spirit on the day of Pentecost; we see him promote the early spreading of the Church among Jews and Gentiles. The letters of the Apostles teach us how to practise the Christian faith, whatever our circumstances. And, finally, the Apocalypse or Book of Revelation consoles and strengthens us in the midst of difficulties and keeps alive our hope of final victory (in this connexion it foretells the second coming of Christ).

Jesus established the Kingdom of God on earth, but it will not take final shape until, at the end of the world, Jesus returns in glory to judge the living and the dead and deliver the Kingdom to the Father (cf. 1 Cor 15:24). In the meantime, "some of his disciples are pilgrims on earth, others have died and are being purified, while still others are in glory, contemplating 'in full light, God himself triune and one, exactly as he is'."[2] In the Beatitudes (cf. Mt 5:1-12) our Lord promises Christians fulfilment : in heaven that fulfilment will be complete, but even on earth, whether in the midst of affliction and sorrow or joy and prosperity, in honour or in dishonour, in scarcity or in plenty, in sickness or in health, a Christian always realizes that he is God's son, redeemed by Christ's death, and destined to eternal life with Christ in God. Buoyed up by

2   Vatican Council II, Dogm. Const. *Lumen gentium*, 49.

this hope he can face any tribulation with the serenity of a son of God, identifying himself with Christ his Saviour.

WHEN WERE THE BOOKS OF THE NEW TESTAMENT WRITTEN?

Jesus did not command his Apostles to write books; he commanded them to teach : "Go therefore and make disciples of all nations, baptizing them in the name of the Father and of the Son and of the Holy Spirit, teaching them to observe all that I have commanded you; and lo, I am with you always, to the close of the age" (Mt 28:19-20). The Spirit trained the Apostles for this mission; and then he gave the Church another gift : he stirred some of them, and a few of their immediate disciples, to put into writing, under God's inspiration, everything that, taken in conjunction with the Old Testament and with Sacred Tradition, would constitute the deposit of Revelation.

This writing took place more or less in the period A.D. 50-100. No book in the New Testament gives its date of composition; but scholars have managed to assign dates : some of these can be taken as certain; others are quite probable or at least approximate. The chronological table given below outlines the dates deduced; we would like to point out three things about it. (i) A date given in brackets is a second hypothesis, less probable than the first but certainly possible. (ii) Most of St Paul's epistles were written before the three Synoptic Gospels, with the exception of the early Hebrew or Aramaic version of St Matthew. (iii) Question marks in parentheses indicate that the date is unclear in Christian tradition or has been questioned by scholars on good grounds.

Date of Composition	Canonical Writing	Author	Written in
51-52	1 and 2 Thess	Paul	Corinth
50-55	[Early Aramaic Gospel]	Matthew	Palestine (?)
50-60	Jas	James	Jerusalem (?)
54	Gal	Paul	Ephesus (?)
57 (spring)	1 Cor	Paul	Ephesus
57-58 (autumn)	2 Cor	Paul	Macedonia
57-58 (winter)	Rom	Paul	Corinth
60 (?) (64-70)	Mk	Mark	Rome (?)
62 (?) (54-57)	Phil	Paul	Rome (Ephesus)
62	Col, Philem, Eph	Paul	Rome
62 (?) (67-70)	Lk	Luke	Rome (Achaia)
63 (75)	Acts	Luke	
64	1 Pet	Peter	Rome
64 (80)	2 Pet	Peter (?)	Rome (?)
65	1 Tim and Tit	Paul	Macedonia
65 (?) (80)	Heb	Paul (?)	Rome (?) Athens (?)
66	2 Tim	Paul	Rome
68-70	Mt	Matthew	Syria (?)
70 (?)	Jude	Jude Thaddeus	(?)
85-95	Rev	John	Patmos
95-100	1, 2 and 3 Jn	John	Ephesus (?)
98-100	Jn	John	Ephesus (?)

Introduction to the Holy Gospels

WHAT ARE THE GOSPELS?

The climax of God's Revelation to mankind is the incarnation of the Son of God. Jesus Christ perfected Revelation "by the total fact of his presence and self-manifestation—by words and works, signs and miracles, but above all by his death and glorious resurrection from the dead, and finally by sending the Spirit of truth."[1] By this Christ "accomplishes the saving work which his Father gave him to do."[2] The account of this saving work of the Lord, which was taught orally by the Apostles and is continually being handed on in the Sacred Tradition of the Church, was also written down under the inspiration of the Holy Spirit, in the books of the New Testament, where the word of God is given its fullest written expression.

The New Testament opens with four books each of which is called a "Gospel"; all the other books of Sacred Scripture are also inspired but these four are of outstanding importance, for "they are our principal source of the Incarnate Word, our Saviour."[3]

These four books were given the name "Gospel" from the beginning of the second century : for example, around the year 150 St Justin Martyr calls them "recollections of the Apostles" or "Gospels."[4] But before this time, the word "gospel" was not used in the sense of book, which it later acquired. How did these books come to be called "gospels"?

The word "gospel" is of Greek origin (*euangelion*) and originally means "good news." It is also used in Greek antiquity to describe the reward given to the bearer of this good news, or the offering made to the gods in thanksgiving for benefits received.

The Romans used the word *evangelios* to describe the contribution made by Emperor Augustus to the world. Among the Jews, the verb "to evangelize", "to announce the good news", obtains special significance when used to refer to the messianic times when God will save his people : "How beautiful upon the mountains are the feet of him who brings good tidings, who publishes peace, who brings good tidings of good, who publishes salvation" (Is 52:7).

When, from the beginning of his public ministry, our Lord invites people to believe in the Gospel, he is referring to the good news of the arrival of the

---

1   Vatican Council II, Dogm. Const. *Dei Verbum*, 4.
2   *Ibid.*
3   *Dei Verbum*, 18.
4   *Apology*, 1, 66.

Kingdom of God which he is announcing and establishing : "The time is fulfilled, and the kingdom of God is at hand; repent, and believe in the gospel" (Mk 1:14). This good news of salvation must be proclaimed to the whole world, which is the mission our Lord entrusts to the Apostles (cf. Mk 13:10).

The preaching of the Twelve concerning Christ and his work of salvation also came to be called "the gospel" : in their preaching "gospel" covers the words and actions of Jesus, but it particularly proclaims that, through his death and resurrection, he has redeemed us from our sins and fulfilled the promises of salvation which God made in the Old Testament. So, the Gospel which the Apostles proclaim is the proclamation of the good news, that is to say, Jesus Christ himself.

Therefore, there is only one Gospel, only one "good news"—that preached by the Apostles, which they in turn received from Christ and which they proclaim with the power of the Holy Spirit. St Paul wrote: "As we have said before, so now I say again, If any one is preaching to you a gospel contrary to that which you received, let him be accursed" (Gal 1:9). The Gospel is immutable; it must be held on to, for it is the only route to salvation.

To sum up : the word "gospel" was first used by Christians to describe the joyous proclamation of the salvation brought by Christ. When this was later expressed in written form, the word was applied to the actual books which contained this preaching : the first four books of the New Testament are called Gospels because they transmit the "gospel" preached by the Apostles, who had received it from Christ himself.

THE CONTENT OF THE GOSPELS

Here is how St Peter, in one of his addresses, describes the life of our Lord: "You know . . . the word which was proclaimed throughout all Judea, beginning from Galilee after the baptism which John preached : how God anointed Jesus of Nazareth with the Holy Spirit and with power; how he went about doing good and healing all that were oppressed by the devil, for God was with him. And we are witnesses to all that he did both in the country of the Jews and in Jerusalem. They put him to death by hanging him on a tree; but God raised him on the third day and made him manifest; not to all the people but to us who were chosen by God as witnesses, who ate and drank with him after he rose from the dead. And he commanded us to preach to the people, and to testify that he is the one ordained by God to be the judge of the living and the dead. To him all the prophets bear witness that every one who believes in him receives forgiveness of sins through his name" (Acts 10:37-43).

The Gospels tell the story of Christ's life along the general lines of the structure of this address by St Peter. St John begins his by going right back to the eternity of the Word in the bosom of the Father and then moves on to describe the incarnation of the Son of God and his life among men (cf. Jn 1:1-14). St Luke and St Matthew start with accounts of the birth of Jesus (Mt

30

12; Lk 1-2). St Mark starts directly with St John the Baptist preaching the need to do penance to prepare for the Messiah.

The four Gospels then describe the prelude to Christ's public ministry : the baptism of Jesus by John in the river Jordan, with a clear Revelation of the Holy Trinity; John bearing witness that Jesus is the Christ; (and the first three Gospels also give accounts of his fasting and being tempted by the devil). In reporting these events the Gospels teach that Christ is incomparably greater than John the Baptist and all the prophets of the Old Testament : Jesus is the Son of God, and his mission is divine : he has come to instal the Kingdom of God (cf. Mt 3:1 - 4:11; Mk 1:1-13; Lk 3:1-4, 13; Jn 1:19-51).

Most of the text of each Gospel has to do with showing us Jesus going about doing good : he healed the sick and freed those possessed by the devil, for God was with him (Acts 10:38); he preached and worked miracles by the power of God (Acts 2:22). And as he did so the Jewish authorities grew to hate him more and more, until eventually they brought about his passion and death. This section of the Gospels covers what is described as Christ's "public life". "Christ established on earth the kingdom of God and revealed his Father and himself by deeds and words."[5] The evangelists report what Jesus was constantly preaching—particularly, how his disciples must conduct themselves (the Sermon on the Mount); the characteristics of the Kingdom of heaven which he has come to establish (the Kingdom parables); the true nourishment of the soul in the new Kingdom (discourse on the bread of life); etc. Our Lord backs up his teaching by performing many miracles, among the most outstanding of which are : changing water into wine at Cana in Galilee (Jn 2:1-11); raising the son of the widow of Naim (Lk 7:11-17) and the daughter of Jairus (Mk 5:21-43; the curing of possessed people (Mk 5:1-20), of lepers (Mk 8:22-26), and people suffering from other diseases (Mk 1:29-31 and parallel passages in other Gospels; 2:1-12 and par.; 3:7-12 and par.); the multiplication of the loaves and fish (Mk 6:32-44 and par.). The Gospels also tell, at this point, about Jesus' choice of the Apostles (Mk 3:13-19 and par.) : they are to be direct witnesses of his miracles and he will give them a detailed explanation of what his doctrine means; with God's grace, they eventually manage to recognize him as the Messiah and Son of God : this is a key stage in the whole Gospel narrative (cf. Mt 16:13-20; Mk 8:27-30; Lk 9:18-21; Jn 6:67-71).

From this point forward the Gospels concentrate on the lead-up to Christ's passion and death. In this section, to which St Luke gives much more space than the others, we see the hostility of the Jewish authorities growing to the point where they decide to put him to death (Mk 11:18 and par.; Jn 11:53) : God has mysteriously planned that events should take this turn, and three times Jesus prophesies what will happen on the last days of his life on earth (Mk 8:31-33 and par.; Mk 9:30-32 and par.; Mk 10:32-34 and par.; Jn 10:17-18). He also manifests his divinity more clearly to his disciples (cf. Mk 9:2-10 and par.; Jn 12:28- 30).

As regards Jesus' activity in Judea immediately prior to his triumphant entry

5   *Dei Verbum*, 17.

into Jerusalem (Mk 11:1-11 and par.; Jn 12:12- 19), what stand out are the miracles of the raising of Lazarus (Jn 11:1-45) and the curing of the blind man, Bartimaeus (Mk 10:46-52). The narrative of the last days of his ministry in Jerusalem (Mt 21-25 and par.; Jn 12:12-50) conclude the Gospels' account of his public life. In this account the evangelists have passed on to us the most important things our Lord said and did, the reason why he died on the cross and rose in triumph : all of which constitute the core of the Gospel as preached by the Apostles.

The accounts of our Lord's passion describe how he died, and they are followed by the witness of disciples who have seen the risen Christ, have eaten with him, have listened to his words and touched his glorified body. Before ascending into heaven, the risen Christ sends out the Apostles to preach the Gospel and baptize all nations for the forgiveness of sins (Mt 28:18-20; Mk 16:15; Lk 24:27; cf. Jn 20:21-23).

The Gospels are "a perpetual and divine witness"[6] to all this. They were written to help fulfil Christ's commandment to preach the Gospel, the "good news", to all mankind. St John expressly states this at the end of his text : "Now Jesus did many other signs in the presence of the disciples, which are not written in this book; but these are written that you may believe that Jesus is the Christ, the Son of God, and that believing you may have life in his name" (Jn 20:30-31). God has given us the written Gospels to help ground us in the truths we already hold (cf. Lk 1:4) : they are sincere, truthful accounts of the sayings and doings of Jesus Christ, true God and true Man.[7]

WHO WROTE THE GOSPELS?

God, who is the principal author of all Sacred Scripture, is therefore the principal author of the four Gospels officially recognized by the Church. To compose them, "God chose certain men who, all the while he employed them in this task, made full use of their powers and faculties so that, though he acted in them and by them, it was as true authors that they consigned to writing whatever he wanted written, and no more."[8] In other words, the Holy Spirit used each evangelist as a living and intelligent instrument; he did not suspend his faculties, he raised them and applied them to compose the books : in such a way that, under divine inspiration, everything the evangelists affirm, state or imply in their writings, must be regarded as affirmed, stated or implied by the Holy Spirit.[9]

We know the names of the four evangelists through the testimony of Christian tradition, which from the beginning unanimously attributed these four books respectively to St Matthew, St Mark, St Luke and St John. In addition to Tradition, critical analysis of the literary features of the text and historical references in each Gospel support the unanimous, precise testimony of Tradition.

6 *Dei Verbum*, 17.   7 Cf. *Dei Verbum*, 19.   8 *Dei Verbum*, 11.
9   *Replies* of the Pontifical Biblical Commission, 18 June 1915, para. 1—*Dz.-Sch.*, 3629; *EB*, 415.

32

The earliest Christian writings which cite the Gospels go back to the last years of the first century. Thus St Clement of Rome (between 92 and 101) and St Irenaeus of Antioch (who died around 107) speak of the four books but do not refer to their authors. It is Papias, bishop of Hierapolis in Asia Minor, who around 130 refers to Matthew and Mark as the authors of the first two Gospels: this is reported in Eusebius of Caesarea's *Ecclesiastical History*[10] (around the middle of the fourth century). At the end of the second century (between the years 178 and 188), St Irenaeus attests to the authenticity of the four Gospels in his book *Against heresies*[11] (Irenaeus had wide experience of the Church; a native of Asia Minor, he lived for a time in Rome and became Bishop of Lyons in Gaul : hence the importance of what he has to say). From around the same time we have the statements in the *Muratorian Canon*, a document of Roman origin. Around the start of the third century Clement of Alexandria, writing in Alexandria, in Egypt, and Tertullian, who represents the tradition of the churches of the north of Africa (Carthage), give the four saints as the recognized authors of the four Gospels.

From the fourth century onwards, given the rapid spread of the Church, so many ecclesiastical writers give the same four authors that it would be tedious to list them here.

What tradition tells us is corroborated by evidence in the text of the Gospels themselves. In St John's Gospel it says that "the disciple whom Jesus loves" (cf. Jn 21:20-24) is its author. But this must be St John, as can be deduced from the text of the Gospels as a whole. As regards the Synoptics, certain evidence as to authorship can be gleaned, but nowhere are we told who precisely the human authors are. Thus, for example, we can notice that the First Gospel has a more Jewish ring about it than the others; that the Second seems to be written for people in Rome and that it treats the figure of St Peter in a very particular way; and that the Third has the same style as the Acts of the Apostles : it is as if it were the first part of a two-volume work.

Data of this type support the arguments based on Christian Tradition, which attributes the First Gospel to St Mathew, who wrote it for Palestinian Christians of Jewish origin; the Second to St Mark, who wrote it in Rome and who was the disciple of St Peter; and the Third to the Antiochene physician and disciple of St Paul, St Luke, who also wrote the Acts of the Apostles.

In the early centuries it was extremely necessary for the Church to identify which were the true Gospels and who wrote them, for there were already many apocryphal books in circulation which heretics used to help spread their errors. In replying to heresy the Christian apologists put forward the genuine apostolic tradition, making it quite clear that the Gospels officially used in the Church came either from Apostles themselves—St Matthew and St John—or from their immediate disciples, so-called "apostolic men"—St Mark and St Luke.

So the Gospels' apostolic origin and authenticity—that is, that they were written precisely by those to whom they are attributed—are something that has

10   III, 39.
11   III, 1, 1.

been held in all parts of the Church from the first centuries.[12] In his book *Against Faustus*[13] St Augustine presents the clinching argument: "You should believe that this is Matthew's because the Church has preserved this book ever since the time when Matthew lived, through an uninterrupted series of generations, in an unfailing succession, down to our own day."

WHEN WERE THE GOSPELS WRITTEN?

Christian Tradition is unanimous in attesting that St Matthew was the first to put the Gospel in writing in the Hebrew tongue. The earliest testimony to this effect is that of Papias, bishop of Hierapolis, part of whose book *An explanation of the sayings of the Lord* has been preserved for us by the quotations taken from it by Eusebius in his *Ecclesiastical History*.[14] Early tradition also says that some years later St Mark, in Rome, wrote down what he heard St Peter say in his preaching. Some Fathers say that he wrote it immediately after St Peter's death;[15] others, during the Apostle's lifetime.[16] Of St Luke, Tradition states that, being a disciple of St Paul, he wrote down what he heard Apostles say or what he had picked up indirectly and verified.[17] All concur in suggesting that St John was the last to write his Gospel, the so-called "spiritual" Gospel.[18]

Tradition clearly states that St Matthew was the first to write; but this text written in the language of the Jews has not come down to us. Our copy of the Gospel of St Matthew is the Greek edition, substantially the same as the original Hebraic and definitely later than the Gospel according to St Mark, as we shall see later when we discuss the connexion among the first three Gospels.

We do not know the exact year in which each Gospel was written : it was not literary practice at the time for writings to carry the author's name or the date; but we can certainly establish limits within which the Gospels must have been written—by inferring from the data of tradition and from the texts themselves. We have already noted that some early ecclesiastic authors say that St Mark wrote in Rome, a little before or a little after the death of St Peter, which occurred in the year 64 (or 67 at the latest). Added to this there is the fact that the first three Gospels speak prophetically of the destruction of Jerusalem, which had not yet taken place : they mention that it will happen but they are imprecise about when it will happen. There are grounds, therefore, for thinking, as the Pontifical Biblical Commission indicated,[19] that the first three Gospels could have been written before the year 70, that is, before the destruction of the Holy City.

---

12 Cf. *Replies* of the Pontifical Biblical Commission, 29 May 1907, 19 June 1911, 26 June 1912— *EB*, 187-189; 383-389; 390-398—and *Dei Verbum*, 18.
13 28, 2.
14 III, 39.
15 *Against heresies*, III, 2, 1.
16 Clement of Alexandria, as quoted by Eusebius, *Ecclesiastical History*, VI, 14.
17 Cf. *Against heresies*, III, 1, 1.
18 *Ecclesiastical History*, VI, 25.
19 In its *Replies*, 19 June 1911 and 26 June 1912, *EB*, 386 and 395.

34

Another argument which confirms this is an inference drawn from the Acts of the Apostles : this goes up as far as St Paul's imprisonment in Rome, which lasted from 61 to 63, and it seems more than reasonable to deduce that Acts was composed immediately after this imprisonment or fairly soon after it. Then, if, as we have said, the Third Gospel contains features which make it look like volume one of a work extending to the Acts of the Apostles, we must conclude that Luke wrote his Gospel sometime before he wrote the Acts. These arguments point to dates prior to the year 70.

However, the Gospel of St John is in a different position. Tradition attests that it was written by the Apostle St John in Ephesus after his exile on the island of Patmos, that is, around the year 100, perhaps a very short time before he died.[20] For more documentation on this subject see the special introduction provided for each Gospel.

HOW WERE THE GOSPELS WRITTEN?

We have seen what the Gospels are, their general content, who wrote them, and when. At this point we should ask about how God arranged for the Gospel of Jesus Christ to be written down in the first books the Church possesses. The evangelists, whom the Holy Spirit chose for this work, were direct witnesses of Jesus (in the case of St Matthew and St John) or indirect (in the case of St Mark and St Luke, disciples respectively of St Peter and St Paul). Before being written down, the content of these was handed on orally, starting on the day of Pentecost.[21]

We can distinguish three stages in the shaping of the Gospels : (i) our Lord's preaching; (ii) the preaching and catechesis of the Apostles; (iii) the work of writing done by the evangelists under the inspiration of the Holy Spirit.

(i) The Sower of the word, the divine Master who chose the Apostles, instructed them in his teaching, made them the pillars, the foundation, of his Church, with St Peter at their head, and sent them out to preach the Gospel to the whole world. Our Lord took pains to get his teaching across to them in such a way that they could easily grasp it and be able to remember it. The net result was that, even before the Resurrection, the Apostles already understood that one of the reasons Jesus performed miracles was to move people to have faith in him. Our Lord not only proclaimed the Gospel : he actually carried it out through his presence on earth, through what he said and did and expecially through his death, resurrection, ascension into heaven and sending of the Holy Spirit.[22]

When our Lord arose from the dead the Apostles clearly realized his divinity: thus, Thomas confesses his faith by saying to Jesus, "My Lord and my God!" The risen Jesus opened their minds and explained to them the

20 *Against heresies*, III, 1, 1.
21 *Dei Verbum*, 19.
22 Cf. *Dei Verbum*, 17; Pontifical Biblical Commission, Instruction *Sancta Mater Ecclesia* (21 April 1964), 2.

Scriptures—the Old Testament—causing their hearts to burn when he showed how what the prophets had foretold, and what he himself had foretold, had been fulfilled in him (Lk 24:44-48). Now they grasped the inner meaning of everything they had heard and seen Jesus do. When passing on to us our Lord's words "Destroy this temple, and in three days I will raise it up," in which he refers to his death and resurrection, St John comments that "when he was raised from the dead, his disciples remembered that he had said this, and they believed the scripture and the word which Jesus had spoken" (Jn 2:19, 22).

(ii) The Holy Spirit, the Spirit of Truth whom our Lord promised to send, reminded the Apostles of everything Jesus said, and enabled them to understand the whole truth concerning Christ and his saving mission, and the meaning of his words and miracles, which prior to this they had failed to grasp fully (Jn 14:26; 16:13). And in addition to this the Holy Spirit constantly guided the Apostles in their teaching and moved them boldly to preach the truth concerning Christ (cf. Acts 2:36).

"The Apostles proclaimed particularly the death and resurrection of the Lord; in bearing witness to Christ they accurately described his life and repeated his words suiting them to the capacity of their audiences to understand what he meant" (cf. Acts 2:33-36).[23] As well as this *first preaching* aimed at the conversion of both Jews and Gentiles, which proclaimed the fact of the death and resurrection of Christ and the main features of his life on earth (cf. Acts 10:36), the Apostles also devoted time to improving the formation of those already converted, to help them deepen their faith and shape their life-style to that faith : this "apostolic catechesis" trained Christians to explain to enquirers the reason for their faith and their hope (1 Pet 2:5).

It is only reasonable to presume that the early Christians were very keen to know as much as possible about our Lord's life, his miracles, his meetings with the crowds and with individuals, the circumstances of his birth, of his passion and death, his appearances after his resurrection, etc. : and the more they learned the more their piety increased. The Apostles were aware that they constituted the foundation on which the Church was built—and that their writings would be read by Christians in every era, and not just their own; however, they did try to meet the needs of their listeners. The faithful "devoted themselves to the Apostles' teaching and fellowship, to the breaking of the bread and the prayers" (Acts 2:42) : this undoubtedly was the setting for which the Apostles' first accounts of Christ were devised. They do not all tell the same things or tell them in the same way; but they do agree on basics, because they were witnesses of the same events and heard the same words spoken by Jesus. St John expressly says this when he writes : "That which was from the beginning, which we have heard, which we have seen with our own eyes, which we have looked upon and touched with our hands, concerning the word of life—. . . we proclaim also to you, so that you may have fellowship with us" (Jn 1:1-3).

Although the Apostles had helpers in this task, it is they who were primarily responsible, as qualified witnesses of Christ and people whom he sent out to

---

23   Pontifical Biblical Commission, Instruction *Sancta Mater Ecclesia*, 2.

continue his saving work. They were very careful to make sure that nothing inaccurate about Jesus was taught, and they made sure to omit nothing important. By continuing Jesus' teaching in this way, they were not only the immediate source of oral Tradition : they were the zealous custodians of that Tradition, and were guided by the Holy Spirit. St Peter, whom our Lord placed at the head of the Apostolic College, took the initiative in preaching the Gospel, as we see in the Acts of the Apostles, and his teaching had a decisive influence on the way our Lord's words and deeds have been passed on to us in the first three Gospels : he preached the Gospel in Jerusalem, Antioch and Rome, the places where the Gospels of Matthew, Luke and Mark, respectively originated.

(iii) What were the evangelists doing when they produced their Gospels, under the inspiration of the Holy Spirit? St Luke gives us the answer to this question at the start of his book : "Inasmuch as many have undertaken to compile a narrative of the things which have been accomplished among us, just as they were delivered to us by eyewitnesses and ministers of the word, it seemed good to me also, having followed all things closely for some time past, to write an orderly account for you, most excellent Theophilus, that you may know the truth concerning the things of which you have been informed" (Lk 1:1-4). The evangelists gave of their very best when writing their books, intent as they were on the good of the Church and seeking to strengthen their readers in the faith and encourage them to do the will of Christ. To this purpose, they used the best sources available—what the Apostles preached, or their own personal recollections. Naturally they availed of any earlier writings which recorded parts of Christ's life or things he said. They collected all the oral and written material they could lay their hands on, and then each author organized it to suit his purpose. They took account of their immediate readership and how best to communicate with it. Depending on their own personal qualities and their readers' needs, they put the emphasis on some or other aspects of our Lord's life and teaching. But in all this process the Holy Spirit was influencing them: God, as we have said, is the principal author of these documents.[24]

We do know that they selected what they considered most important— whether intrinsically more important, or because previous writers had omitted it. We read in John's Gospel that "There are also many other things which Jesus did; were every one of them to be written, I suppose that the world itself could not contain the books that would be written" (Jn 21:25). At other times they provide a summary of what our Lord did, or collect together everything he said about one particular subject or said in one particular place. And sometimes they explain something which readers might otherwise find confusing, or point out the significance of certain events, showing that they were foretold in the Old Testament.[25] The evangelists, therefore, were not merely re-compilers of material which was already being handed on; no: using the material available to them they applied their minds, aided by the Holy Spirit by means of the charism of divine inspiration, in such a way that, although they were

24   Cf. *Dei Verbum*, 11.
25   Cf. *Dei Verbum*, 19.

instruments subordinate to God, the principal author, they themselves were true authors of their books and each left on his book the mark of his own personality.

The first three Gospels have many passages in common, even word for word. But they also contain many striking differences. By setting out their content in three parallel columns we can see these differences and similarities at a glance (*synopsis*), which is why they have come to be called *synoptic* Gospels. They are also said to share a *concordia discors*, a discordant agreement : in general they coincide, but in particulars they can differ. Thus, all three share about 350 verses. St Matthew and St Luke coincide in an *additional* 230-240 verses; St Matthew and St Mark in 170-180 and St Mark and St Luke in about 50. The study of the possible causes of these coincidences and differences is usually called the "synoptic question". Many different and complicated theories have been devised to solve this problem.

Here we can only outline the question in broad terms. Recalling what we said about the date of composition of the Gospels, we know from Church Tradition that the first to write a Gospel was St Matthew who wrote it in the language of the Jews. A little later St Mark and St Luke wrote theirs : if they had access to St Matthew's text at the time this would explain how the three have so many verses in common.

It is also possible that very early on there were in existence certain short texts containing sayings of our Lord, which St Luke would have used and which could also have been used for the Greek edition of St Matthew. If the latter did happen it could explain the similarities (especially in parts where our Lord's words are given) between the Gospel of St Matthew and that of St Luke. Besides, in the production of the Greek edition of St Matthew, the writer must have also had access to the Gospel of St Mark, which would explain why there are verses common to Matthew and Mark not found in Luke (Luke also used St Mark's Gospel, but independently of the Greek Matthew, which would explain why there are verses common to Mark and Luke which are not found in Matthew). But in addition to all this borrowing, each of the three had his own particular sources of inspiration : St Matthew, his personal recollections; St Mark, St Peter's catechesis and very personal accounts; St Luke, who never met Jesus, seems to have been the one who consulted the greatest number of eyewitnesses and written documents : all of which helps us understand the differences and similarities in the synoptic Gospels.

When scholars speak of the "historicity" of the Gospels they mean that the accounts they give are true accounts of what Jesus said and did. In other words, the evangelists are writing real history, they are telling of events which really happened, which people have actually witnessed and which impact on human history; and they are reporting things which were actually said. Although the

Gospels are not a systematic history aiming at covering *all* events referring to Jesus Christ, this does not mean that they are not genuine history.

The Gospels also contain doctrinal teaching : in other words, the evangelists were not only concerned to record mere facts, for posterity; they sought also to explain what those facts meant in God's plan of salvation, and how man is supposed to respond to them.

For example : St Matthew reports that when Joseph was puzzled on finding that Mary was expecting a child, "an angel of the Lord appeared to him in a dream, saying, 'Joseph, son of David, do not fear to take Mary your wife, for that which is conceived in her is of the Holy Spirit; she will bear a son, and you shall call his name Jesus, for he will save his people from their sins'" (Mt 1:20-21). But St Matthew does not stop there; he goes further than just report on the event : "All this took place to fulfil what the Lord had spoken by the prophet : 'behold, a virgin shall conceive and bear a son, and his name shall be called Emmanuel (which means, God with us)'" (Mt 1:22-23). So the description of the event is followed by an explanation of it : God has already foretold through Isaiah the future virginal birth of the Saviour, and now the divine oracle is coming true. Showing that it has come true is obviously not a matter of anecdotal interest : it is a call to the readers to respond in faith and to commit their lives to Jesus Christ.

Hence the special importance of the *historicity* of the Gospels : what was, is and always will be at stake is man's eternal destiny. This, then, is the purpose of the Gospels, as perfectly expressed by the fourth evangelist : "Now Jesus did many other signs in the presence of the disciples, which are not written in this book; but these are written that you may believe that Jesus is the Christ, the Son of God, and that believing you may have life in his name" (Jn 20:30-31).

Since the historicity of the Gospels is so important, we can appreciate how historical sciences can help us go deeper into the text; but we also realise that to decide on the *truthfulness* of what the Gospels contain is not something to be left to the mercy of developments in these sciences or to the opinion of specialists : it is faith that decides that, though faith rests on reason and the way reason works.

The Church, which has by God's command the duty and right of protecting, handing on and interpreting Holy Scripture, "has firmly and with absolute constancy maintained and continues to maintain, that the four Gospels just named, whose historicity she unhesitatingly affirms, faithfully hand on what Jesus, the Son of God, while he lived among men, really did and taught for their eternal salvation."[26] Every effort made to understand the Gospel better is highly praiseworthy, but any interpretation is always subordinate to what the Church, aided by the Holy Spirit, had taught from the very beginning, about this divine treasure entrusted to her by God. For, as St Augustine put it, "I would not believe in the Gospel were I not moved to do so by the authority of the Church."[27]

26 *Dei Verbum*, 19.
27 *Contra Epist. Fundamenti*, 5, 6; cf. *Confessions*, VI, 5, 7; VII, 7, 11.

Down the centuries Christian Tradition shows that the historical character of the Gospels has always been taken as an undisputed truth. Their historicity is, in the first instance, part of our faith : the Gospels are books which narrate history and, like all the books of the Bible, they are inspired by God. Hence, since they have God as their principal author (which is a matter of faith), the history which they contain is, without doubt, true history, for God cannot deceive or be deceived. At the same time, the Church has always maintained that this historicity, which our faith assures us of, has also a solid basis in reason: competent historico-literary critical scholarship, even if pursued on the margin of faith, provided it really uses serious, scientific arguments, fully supports faith in the historical truthfulness of the Gospels.

The Gospels narrate the life of our Lord Jesus Christ, the Son of God become man. And just as the most holy humanity of our Lord can be seen and contemplated with the physical eye, whereas his divinity can be discovered only with the eye of faith, similarly, the Gospel accounts can be checked by historico-critical methods only in those areas which are verifiable by human tools. And just as Jesus' miracles and words were, for those who experienced them, signs of his divine mission, so those Gospel accounts which can be tested by historical science are a guarantee of the veracity of those others which cannot be tested by reason and are accepted on faith.

Let us take some examples. Historical research can show that Christ was crucified in the time of Pontius Pilate; that he preached in Palestine; that he gathered disciples around him; that he founded the Church; that on the third day after his death he began to appear to certain of his disciples and this led to an enormous change in their lives; that he raised Lazarus from the dead; etc. But what history on its own cannot do is provide any ultimate explanations of these historically verifiable facts; only the light of faith can explain them.

On the other hand, many episodes in Jesus' life are so concrete and so tiny in the framework of world history that it is very difficult to check them by referring to non-Christian sources : in fact even the Gospels themselves provide few such checks. This does not mean that they are not historically checkable, that is, theoretically possible to check, but that in practice it is very difficult to find any historical documentation to support them, outside the Gospels themselves. In cases like this, as in so many others in world history, historical science can assess at least the degree of credibility which such accounts merit by critical examination of the testimonies themselves. Historians tend to require (i) that the authors be sincere, that is, that they are striving to tell the truth; and (ii) that they be well-informed on the matters in question. If careful study shows that these or similar requirements are met, then the document is historically acceptable. Well, in the case of the Gospels these requirements are in fact met.

(i) The human authors of the Gospels did write in order to pass on to us the truth about what they had seen and heard (cf. Lk 1:1-4; Jn 21:24). Although they did not write their histories in exactly the same way as modern historians (for example, as far as chronological and topographical exactness goes), they still really did try to tell the facts just as they happened. Thus in the case of St

Matthew and St Luke, when they tell about the temptations Christ underwent in the desert, they give them in a different order but both of them tell us what really happened. It is also true that the evangelists were enlightened by the Holy Spirit when they wrote and that their purpose was to strengthen the faith of their readers : but that did not lead them to falsify events or neglect historical accuracy; on the contrary : the very articles of our faith include some which are historical facts, such as those to do with Christ's life (his incarnation, death, resurrection etc.), which is why St Paul asserts that if Christ had not risen then our faith would be in vain (cf. 1 Cor 15:14, 17). Hence the evangelists do what they set out to do precisely by telling the true story of what happened.

However, each evangelist, under the inspiration of the Spirit, tries to lay special emphasis on particular aspects of Jesus and his work : and to this end each plans his book differently. The evangelists, even those who were witnesses of Jesus' public life, each remember things differently depending on their mentality and the circumstances in which they are operating. The Holy Spirit does help them to remember and to understand everything they have seen and heard (Jn 14:16) but this does not cancel out their human faculties or the use of memory. Also, each evangelist drew on different sources, and these sources had peculiarities of their own—thus explaining the different order in which they narrate words and events in our Lord's life, and the differences which we find between Gospel and Gospel. But this does not in any way take from their historicity; on the contrary, as St Augustine explains, "it is quite likely that the evangelists believed they had a duty to tell things in the order in which God suggested them to their memory, at least in matters where the order in which they were reported in no way took from the truth and authority of the Gospel. For the Holy Spirit distributes gifts to each individually as he wills (1 Cor 12:11). He directed and ruled the minds of the saints [the sacred writers] to ensure that the books would have full authority; in bringing to their minds the things they should write, the Holy Spirit would allow each to plan his narrative as he thought fit and in such a way that anyone who read it carefully and devoutly would be able to read it with God's help."[28]

Another proof of the evangelists' sincerity is their fortitude in bearing persecution, even to the point of giving their lives to bear witness to the truth they pass on to us in their writings. From what has been said, it is clear that the human authors of the Gospels were sincere and strove to tell the truth.

(ii) But investigation into the historicity of the Gospels needs to go further than that : were the writers well-informed about the subject in question, or were they, unintentionally, mistaken or misled? In reply to this question we must say that, humanly speaking, they were very well-informed, because they have been eyewitnesses of the events they describe or had been in contact with eyewitnesses. We should also add that the educational method used by Jesus—which was similar to rabbinical method of the time—consisted in repeating the same teachings time and again, to ensure his disciples got a good grasp of them. This learning method, based on exercising memory, meant that the Apostles

28 *De consensu Evangelistarum*, 2, 21, 51.

could remember many sayings of Jesus which the evangelists later put down in writing. The fact that they sometimes do not pass on exactly the same wording must be due to (a) the fact that Jesus said these things often, on different occasions and in different ways in the course of his preaching in various parts of Palestine; (b) the evangelists being more concerned about getting the meaning right than giving his exact words; (c) differences naturally arising in translations from the original into Greek.

Another factor which gives us the guarantee that the evangelists were not mistaken is that their narratives coincide in essentials with the preaching of St Peter after Pentecost, as reported in the Acts of the Apostles. There are no grounds, therefore, for thinking that the Gospel story was the product of the fertile hyper-imagination of the first generation of Christians : from the very first moment, fifty days after the Resurrection, the very same things were already being proclaimed, and the Apostles, in their zeal to perform the mission of preaching entrusted to them by our Lord, were extremely careful not to pass on anything which was not true. A proof of this is that the Church never accepted as authentic later outpourings of popular imagination such as the apocryphal gospels.

The evangelists, then, were well-informed about the material they were transmitting; and the fact that their books were received by the Church as divinely inspired indicates that their content concurred with what the Apostles, in their preaching about Jesus, had spread all over the world. It is true that the evangelists do not present our Lord's life in the way a modern biography would; but they do give us reliable information about what Jesus, the Son of God, taught and did when he was living among us. They do not tell us everything about Christ, but they have left us a permanent and divine witness to the truth we need to know about our Lord and his teaching.

After the meticulous research the Gospels have been subjected to over the past two centuries, any serious critic must accept that the sacred books are true history. The main difficulty which some people experience is the fact that supernatural phenomena, the miracles of Jesus, appear frequently in the Gospels. Ultimately this involves questions of faith : either one accepts the supernatural or one does not. So in fact we find that one of two things happen: if a person accepts the supernatural and God's direct intervention in human and physical events, that is, the possibility of miracles, the key question of the historical truthfulness of the Gospels is solved in the affirmative; if a person does not accept the possibility of God directly intervening in history in this way, then from the outset he denies the historicity of the Gospels, because if one denies the possibility of miracles one cannot accept as true writings which report miracles even if these documents scientifically merit acceptance as being historical.

Summing up what we have said, we can assert that when our faith tells us that the Holy Gospels "faithfully hand on what Jesus, the Son of God, while he lived among men, really did and taught for their eternal salvation, until the day of his ascension,"[29] this faith is based on a solid, reasonable foundation; it is not a blind option; it is based on certain facts which are part of history and which have been passed down to us in reliable documents (the Gospels) in the bosom of a society which authenticates them (the Church), and which has faithfully conserved them and which offers us a correct interpretation of them. But these historical facts can only be deeply understood and fully accepted if one has the divine gift of faith. As St Augustine puts it referring to people of his own time, who found some passages in the Gospels an obstacle to their conversion : "Let him who asks these things become a Christian, lest in trying to solve all the questions about the holy books he should end his life before having passed from death to life. There are innumerable problems that cannot be solved before believing, at the risk of ending this life without faith. Once faith has been accepted, then they can be studied in detail as an exercise for the pious enjoyment of the faithful mind."[30]

This concludes our general introduction to the four Gospels. The characteristics of each particular Gospel will be dealt with briefly in the introduction which precedes it.

---

29   *Dei Verbum*, 19.
30   *Letter*, 102, 6, 38.

The Dates of the Life of our Lord Jesus Christ

Modern research has succeeded in establishing the dates of our Lord's life with considerable accuracy.

It was Dionysius Exiguus, a monk who died in 556, who fixed the birth of our Lord Jesus Christ as the centre of the history of mankind; using such historical information as was available to him, he placed our Lord's birth in the year 753 after the foundation of Rome and made the following year A.D. 1. This computation, although it is a few years too late, is the one still used in most of the world for dating purposes.

We know from the Gospels that Jesus was born "in the days of Herod the king" (Mt 2:1; cf. Lk 1:5). We now know, from information given by the Jewish historian Flavius Josephus, that Herod died in the year 750 after the foundation of Rome.[1] Therefore, the date of Christ's birth must be brought forward at least by four years from that worked out by Dionysius. Moreover, Herod's death did not occur immediately after the birth of our Lord : to these four years must be added, therefore, the time that elapsed between Christ's birth and Herod's death. In this connexion we should remember that Herod left Jerusalem due to an illness which proved fatal and that he must have been away about six months;[2] whereas when the Magi visited Herod he was still in the Holy City. Therefore, Jesus was born at least six months before Herod's death.

In addition to this we have to take into account what age Jesus would have been when Herod, still in Jerusalem (cf. Mt 2:3), ordered the killing of the Holy Innocents. Presuming that by ordering the slaughter of all children under the age of two Herod was confident that Jesus would be included, the child cannot have been more than two : he must have been less : more or less one year old.

Therefore, the date of Christ's birth assigned by Denis must be brought forward : by four years due to the mistake in fixing the start of the Christian era in relation to the foundation of Rome; by an additional year which would

---

1 Flavius Josephus refers to Herod's death in two of his works : *The Jewish War*, written between A.D. 75 and 79, and *Jewish Antiquities*, written between 93 and 94 (cf. *The Jewish War*, I, 33, 1 and 5, 6 and 8; II, 1, 3; *Jewish Antiquities*, XVII, 6, and 8.

2 When he took ill, Herod went to Jericho. And from there to Callirhoe, for the thermal baths; getting no relief there he returned to Jericho, where he died in the spring of 750. From information in Flavius Josephus it can be inferred that it was in November 749, at the beginning of the cold season in Jerusalem, that he moved to Jericho, where the climate was much warmer.

be Jesus' age when the Innocents were killed, since Herod would have erred on the "generous side" to make sure he caught the Child in his net; and by a further six months, being the period of time Herod's illness lasted. The net result of this is that the very latest date for the birth of Christ was 748 from the foundation of Rome, which is the equivalent of year 6 before the Christian era.

Nor can we bring the date forward very much from 748 from the foundation of Rome, because St Luke tells us that Jesus was about thirty years old when he was baptized by John in the fifteenth year of the reign of Tiberius Caesar (cf. Lk 3:1-2, 21-23) which, as we shall see later would correspond to 780 or 781 (A.D. 27-28). Accordingly, Jesus would have been 32-33 years old when he received baptism from John and began his public ministry, an age which fits in with the information given in Luke 3:23.

Summing up, therefore : Jesus was probably born in the year 748 (6 B.C.) or at the very earliest 746 (8 B.C.).

THE BEGINNING OF HIS PUBLIC MINISTRY

Jesus began his public ministry very soon after being baptized by John the Baptist (cf. Mt 3:13-17; Mk 1:9-11; Lk 3:21-22).

Not very much time can have elapsed between when the Precursor began to preach and when he baptized Jesus (cf. Mt 3:1-13; Mk 1:4-9; Lk 3:1-21; Acts 1:22; 10:37-38). Therefore, the information we get from Luke on when the Baptist began to preach can help us establish when Jesus began his public ministry : in fact, many authors think that Luke gave this data about John precisely to identify when Jesus was baptized and began to preach.

St Luke says that John began to preach "in the fifteenth year of Tiberius Caesar, Pontius Pilate being governor of Judea, and Herod being tetrarch of Galilee, and his brother Philip tetrarch of the region of Ituraea and Trachonitis, and Lysanias tetrarch of Abilene, in the high-priesthood of Annas and Caiaphas" (Lk 3:1-2). This information enables us to establish very tight dating. Tiberius was associated with the Empire by Augustus, to govern the eastern provinces, in the year 765 (A.D. 12); this would mean that the fifteenth year of Tiberius' reign corresponds with 780 (A.D. 27). This would be the year of Christ's baptism and the year in which he began his ministry : Jesus would have been thirty-two years old, which is approximately the age St Luke assigns him.

It is also probable, however, that the fifteenth year of Tiberius' reign should be calculated from the date of Augustus' death, which occurred in August 767 (A.D. 14), in other words one year and eight months after Tiberius was associated with the Empire. But if we remember that it was customary to take as a full year the period between succeeding to the throne and the end of the civil year, we should count as the first year of Tiberius' reign the period August-December 767 (A.D. 14); this would mean that the baptism of Christ would have to be dated a year later (A.D. 28). On this hypothesis, Jesus would have been thirty-three when John baptized him : this is possible but less probable, given what Luke says in 3:23.

46

The datum that Pontius Pilate was procurator of Judea fits in with the first and second hypotheses we have just dealt with : Pilate took up his appointment in Judea in A.D. 26 (779); this date does provide us with another limit : Jesus could not have begun his public ministry before A.D. 26.

Dates connected with the other people St Luke lists do not give us any greater precision—but they do confirm what we have already deduced : Herod Antipas was tetrarch of Galilee from 4 B.C. to A.D. 40; Philip held the tetrarchy of Ituraea from 4 B.C. to A.D. 34; of Lysanias all that is known is that he ceased to rule in A.D. 37. As far as Annas is concerned, Flavius Josephus states that he was elected in the year A.D. 6; he was deposed by the Roman emperor Valerius Gratus in A.D. 15, but in spite of this deposition—by the Romans, not the Jews—he was very powerful, enjoying great moral authority, as is attested by Jewish sources of the period and by the part he played in our Lord's trial (cf. Jn 18:12- 14).[3] Caiaphas, Annas' son-in-law, was elected high priest in the year A.D. 18 and held that position until A.D. 36

Another piece of information which helps establish when Jesus' public ministry began is usually taken from John 2:20: "The Jews then said, 'It has taken forty-six years to build this temple, and will you raise it up in three days?'" According to Jn 2:12-23 this conversation of Jesus with the Jews took place at the Passover of the first year of his public ministry. We know through Flavius Josephus[4] that the rebuilding of the temple began in the year 20-19 B.C. (the eighteenth year of Herod's reign). If we add forty-six years to that we come to the year A.D. 26-27. The conversation in question implies that the Temple was finished, and since Jesus had already been preaching for a year it can be deduced that his public ministry could not have begun before A.D. 25-26, which fits in with Luke 3:1-2.

THE DURATION OF HIS PUBLIC MINISTRY

None of the evangelists expressly says how long Jesus' public ministry lasted; but St John gives us ample information to help us calculate. He refers clearly to three Passovers, corresponding to three different years : the first (Jn 2:13-23) finds Jesus in Jerusalem; the second (Jn 6:4) occurs shortly after the first multiplication of the loaves; the third is the Passover of Christ's passion and death (Jn 11:55; 12:1; 13:1; etc.) This gives us, then, a minimum period for the public ministry : two full years plus the months elapsing between Jesus' baptism and the first Passover.

But in John 5:1 there is a reference to "the feast of the Jews" or rather "*a* feast of the Jews." This expression is somewhat difficult to interpret : the first problem is whether it is *the* feast or *a* feast (some of the oldest manuscripts say one thing, some the other). If it is *the* feast then it would seem to refer to the Passover; if it is *a* feast, it does not exclude the Passover but it suggests, rather,

3   The dates given here are, of course, according to the official count which, as we have shown, is 6-8 years out.
4   *Jewish Antiquities*, XV, 11, 1.

one of the other Jewish feasts (Tabernacles, Pentecost, Dedication of the Temple, etc). If it does refer to the Passover, then it is a different Passover from the other three mentioned and it means that a year elapsed between the Passovers referred to in 5:1 and 6:4, in which case a year would have to be added on to the length of the public ministry, which would mean, therefore, that it covered three years and a few months.

Quite a number of authors think that what is narrated in John 5 is chronologically later than what is described in chapter 6. If this is so, the feast mentioned in 5:1 could be the same feast of Tabernacles referred to in 7:2 or else the Passover itself which appears in 6:4. In any event, it does not refer to another, different, Passover. To sum up : according to the Passovers mentioned in St John's Gospel it cannot be said with certainty whether our Lord's public ministry lasted two years and some months—or three years and some months.

To help solve this problem we need to work from the date of his baptism and the date of his death. With regard to the baptism which, according to Tradition, took place in January, we have already said that the most likely date is A.D. 27 (780), with A.D. 28 as a less probable option. With respect to his Death, as we shall see, it almost certainly took place in the spring of A.D. 30. Therefore, it is more probable that Jesus' public ministry lasted three years and a few months, but we should not totally reject the other calculation of two years plus some months (the months being the period between his baptism in January, and 7 April, because his death, very probably, took place on 7 April).

THE DATE OF JESUS' DEATH

We know for certain that our Lord died on a Friday (cf Mt 27:62; Mk 15:42; Lk 23:54; Jn 19:31) in the Hebrew month of Nisan, in our month of April. As far as the year is concerned, almost all the indications point to A.D. 30; but 33 cannot be ruled out entirely. As regards the day of the month, our Lord died on 14 or 15 Nisan.

We have said that Jesus' public ministry began, we are almost sure, at the beginning of the year A.D. 27. If it lasted, as we have seen, three years and three months, the year A.D. 30 would be the year of his death. And this year would fit exactly because in that year 14 Nisan fell on a Friday (7 April).

However, if the public ministry lasted only two years three months then Jesus would have died in A.D. 29. But this would not work out very well at all, because in that year neither 14 nor 15 Nisan fell on a Friday (they fell on Tuesday and Wednesday). Therefore, it would seem that A.D. 29 must be excluded as a possible date.

The year 33 has also been proposed for two reasons : the first is based on that hypothesis that our Lord's ministry began in the year A.D. 29 and lasted four years and three months : but that is not at all probable, as we have seen. The second is based on the fact that in that year 14 Nisan was a Friday (3 April); that is so, but the whole theory is unlikely because of the weakness of the first of the two reasons given.

48

Excluding the years 31 and 32, because in neither of them does 14 or 15 Nisan fall on a Friday, this leaves A.D. 30 as almost certainly the year our Lord died.

It is very difficult to establish whether he died on 14 or 15 Nisan, because the information given in the Synoptics, on the one hand, and in St John's Gospel, on the other, have not (despite strenuous efforts) allowed scholars to determine for sure which of these two days was the Friday on which Christ died.

The Synoptics say that our Lord celebrated the Last Supper "on the first day of Unleavened Bread, when they sacrificed the passover lamb" (Mk 14:12; cf. Mt 22:26; Lk 22:7).[5] This would correspond to 14 Nisan (Thursday, 7 April). His death would have taken place on 15 Nisan, the day of the Passover (Friday, 8 April), in the early afternoon. However, some details in the Synoptics themselves seem to indicate that the day of our Lord's death could not have been the day of the Passover, 15 Nisan.[6]

But St John's Gospel places our Lord's death on the day before the Passover, the day of Preparation (cf. Jn 18:28; 19:31), which corresponds to 14 Nisan (Friday, 7 April). The only difficulty is that that means Jesus would have celebrated the Last Supper one day before the date given in the official Jewish calendar : that is, the night of 13 to 14 Nisan, taking the fourteenth as the day of the Passover.

In spite of this difficulty, St John's Gospel seems to offer much clearer information than the Synoptics for fixing the date of our Lord's Death and for clearing up certain indicators in the Synoptics (the actions of Simon of Cyrene, Joseph of Arimathea etc), which are difficult to accommodate if the date of our Lord's death is that of the Jewish Passover.

Various explanations can be offered as to why Jesus would celebrate the Last Supper one day before the official Jewish calculation of the correct date : the explanation which is best grounded on Jewish usage at the time and which offers the best explanation for the apparent discrepancy in the four Gospels is this : in the period in question it was not possible to establish the calendar with the same degree of astronomical accuracy as became possible later. This led to an elasticity in coincidence between the day of the month and the day of the week which in modern times would be unthinkable. Thus, the Sadducees used to avoid 15 Nisan falling on a Friday, so as not to have to make the offering of ears of grain on the sabbath;[7] they would make 15 Nisan fall on a sabbath, and

5   The Jewish day started at sunset. This explains why the passover meal took place on the evening of the day which we would call the eve. According to the Synoptics, Jesus celebrated the Last Supper during the first hours of 14 Nisan (this is, according to our calendar, on the evening of Thursday 7 April) and died in the last hours of 14 Nisan (early afternoon of 8 April).

6   For example, it is very unlikely that the rest prescribed for the day of Passover would be infringed—as the actions of Simon of Cyrene who was returning from the fields (Mk 15:21) or of Joseph of Arimathea who buys a sheet (Mk 15:46) or of the devout women who prepare the spices and ointments (Lk 23:56) etc. imply.

7   According to the Sadducees, the feast of Pentecost always had to fall on a Sunday and be celebrated fifty days after the offering of ears of grain, which was done on the Sunday after Passover. Whereas the Pharisees laid it down that the offering of ears of grain had to be done the day after Passover, even if it were a sabbath, and that Pentecost should be celebrated on whatever day it happened to fall.

so the offering would be on the Sunday. The Pharisees, on the other hand, were quite meticulous in celebrating the Passover on whichever day of the week it fell.

In that year the Passover fell on a Friday, 15 Nisan. The Pharisees, with most of the people, began the passover meal on the night of Thursday-Friday, and so did Jesus. But the leading priests, Sadducees almost all of them, celebrated the Passover on the sabbath. This explains the apparent discrepancies between the Synoptics (which would have mentioned the Pharisee use) and St John (which would have followed the Sadducees).

To sum up: Jesus celebrated his Last Supper on the night of Thursday-Friday and died on the Friday. For the Pharisees this Friday would have been 15 Nisan and the day of the Passover (8 April) : the Synoptics follow this calculation. For the Sadducees this Friday was 14 Nisan (7 April) and the following day, a sabbath, Passover : St John's Gospel is following this computation when it says that the chief priests had not yet celebrated the Passover on the Friday (cf. Jn 18:28); but in positioning the Last Supper one day before the passover meal of the chief priests, it is implicitly indicating that Jesus was following the Pharisees' computation, and thus is in agreement with the Synoptics.

TABLE OF DATES IN THE LIFE OF JESUS CHRIST

	YEAR			DATE		
	Christian	*Roman Era*		*Christian*	*Jewish*	
Birth	6 B.C.	748		25 December	Tebeth	
Baptism and start of public ministry	A.D. 27 A.D. 28*	780 781		January	Tebeth	
	A.D. 30	783		6 April	13 Nisan (Sadducees) 14 Nisan (Pharisees)	
Last Supper (Thursday)	A.D. 33*	786		2 April	13 Nisan (Sadducees) 14 Nisan (Pharisees)	
	A.D. 30	783		7 April	14 Nisan (Sadducees) 15 Nisan (Pharisees)	
Death (Friday)	A.D. 33*	786		3 April	14 Nisan (Sadducees) 15 Nisan (Pharisees)	

*Alternative but less likely date

Dispositions for Reading the Gospel[1]

This is the love of Christ which each of us should try to practise in his own life. But to be Christ himself, we must *see ourselves in him*. It's not enough to have a general idea of the spirit of Jesus' life; we have to learn the details of his life and, through them, his attitudes. And, especially, we must contemplate his life, to derive from it strength, light, serenity, peace.

When you love someone, you want to know all about his life and character, so as to become like him. That is why we have to meditate on the life of Jesus, from his birth in a stable right up to his death and resurrection. In the early years of my life as a priest, I used to give people presents of copies of the Gospel and books about the life of Jesus. For we need to know it well, to have it in our heart and mind, so that at any time, without any book, we can close our eyes and contemplate his life, watching it like a film. In this way the words and actions of our Lord will come to mind in all the different circumstances of our life.

In this way we become involved in his life. It is not a matter of just thinking about Jesus, of recalling some scenes of his life. We must be completely involved and play a part in his life. We should follow him closely as Mary his Mother did, as closely as the first twelve, the holy women, the crowds that pressed about him. If we do this without holding back, Christ's words will enter deep into our soul and will really change us. For "the word of God is living and active, sharper than any two-edged sword, piercing to the division of the soul and spirit, of joints and marrow, and discerning the thoughts and intentions of the heart" (Heb 4:12).

If we want to bring other men and women to our Lord, we must first go to the Gospel and contemplate Christ's love. We could take the central events of his passion, for, as he himself said: "Greater love has no man that this, that a man lay down his life for his friends" (Jn 15:13). But we can also look at the rest of his life, his everyday dealings with the people he met.

In order to bring men his message of salvation and show them God's love, Christ, who was perfect God and perfect man, acted in a human and divine way. God comes down to man's level. He takes on our nature completely, except for sin.

It makes me very happy to realize that Christ wanted to be fully a man, with flesh like our own. I am moved when I contemplate how wonderful it is for God to love with a man's heart.

1   Taken from J. Escrivá, *Christ is passing by*, 107-8.

Introduction to the Gospel according to St Mark

THE AUTHOR

Christian tradition has always attributed the Second Gospel to St Mark, disciple of St Peter, St Paul and St Barnabas. Written testimonies of this attribution date back to around the year 125, with a text of Papias, bishop of Hierapolis (Asia Minor), preserved for us by Eusebius, the great Church historian.[1] St Justin Martyr (*c*.155)[2] gives the same report, as does an ancient document, Roman in origin, called the *Muratorian Canon* (written *c*.180), and various references in St Irenaeus' *Against heresies*[3] (written around the end of the second century). From the third century onwards so many writings—from both east and west—bear similar witness that it would be tedious to cite them. The authenticity of the Gospel of St Mark has also been stated by the Magisterium of the Church. The Pontifical Biblical Commission, in its reply of 26 June 1914,[4] expressly teaches that Mark is the author.

As we shall see later the internal evidence in the Gospel itself corroborates this attribution.

The New Testament gives us a certain amount of information about St Mark. He is called Mark in Acts 15:39 and John Mark in Acts 12:12 and 15:37, whereas in Acts 13:5-13 he is referred to as John. This double naming was common practice among the Jews at the time. Thus he used one Jewish name, John (Yohannan) and another hellenized Latin name, *Marcus*, Markos. Compare St Paul: Saul-Paul (the Latin name eventually prevailing).

We can be sure that Mark knew Jesus Christ personally, although he was not one of the twelve Apostles : most ecclesiastical writers see in Mk 14:51-52, the episode of the young man who leaves his sheet behind him as he flees from the garden when Jesus is arrested, as Mark's own veiled signature to his Gospel, since only he refers to this episode. If this were the only reference it would be ambiguous, but it is supported by other circumstantial evidence : Mark was the son of Mary, apparently a well-to-do widow, in whose house in Jerusalem the first Christians used to gather (cf. Acts 12:12). An early Christian text[5] states

---

1   Cf. *Ecclesiastical History*, III, 39, 15.
2   Cf. *Dialogue with Tryphon*, 106.
3   Cf. *Against heresies*, III, 1, 1; III, 10, 5.
4   *EB*, 390-398.
5   Cf. *Acta Sanctorum*, 2, 1867, 434.

that this was the same house as the Cenacle, where our Lord celebrated the Last Supper and instituted the Holy Eucharist. It also seems probable that the Garden of Olives belonged to this same Mary; which would explain Mark's presence there.

We also know from the Acts of the Apostles that Mark was a cousin of Barnabas, one of the great evangelizers of the early days, though not one of the Twelve.

THE APOSTOLIC FIGURE OF ST MARK

From his early youth, Mark shared the vibrant, intimate life of the first Christians of Jerusalem, close to the Blessed Virgin and the Apostles : Mark's mother and her family were among the first to help Jesus and the Twelve. It was quite natural for Barnabas to choose Mark, his cousin, to initiate him into the task of spreading the Gospel, in company with and under the direction of himself and St Paul. Thus, Barnabas took him with him after visiting Jerusalem with St Paul to bring the first collection for the members of the mother church (cf. Acts 12:25); Mark went back with them to Antioch in Syria. When Paul and Barnabas were sent by the Holy Spirit on the first missionary journey, they brought Mark along with them (cf. Acts 13:1-6). But at the end of the first phase of evangelization in Cyprus, it seems that Mark was not very keen on the discomforts of such adventurous apostolic work; he left them and returned home (cf. Acts 13:13). Paul was not at all pleased by Mark's lack of commitment. When the second missionary journey was being planned Barnabas wanted to bring Mark with them again, but St Paul would not agree to this, given his previous experience. The result of this difference of opinion was that Paul and Barnabas decided to divide the work that lay ahead of them, Barnabas taking Mark as his assistant and sailing to Cyprus to visit the communities established there earlier (cf. Acts 15:36-39).

Some ten years later we find Mark in Rome, this time helping St Peter as "interpreter". This is also easy enough to explain because Peter, after being miraculously freed from prison by an angel, made his way precisely to the house of Mary, Mark's mother (cf. Acts 12:11-17). Peter calls Mark his son (cf. 1 Pet 5:13), which implies a long-standing and deep relationship. Mark's stay in Rome as St Peter's co-worker must have been shortly before St Paul arrived in the city, under arrest, to appeal his case to Caesar (the year 61, cf. Acts 25:11-12; 28:11-15). Tradition attributes to Mark this position of being "Peter's interpreter", which is very relevant to his writing his Gospel, as we shall see later when we discuss the Gospel in more detail.

St Paul's letters tell us more things about Mark in the years that follow : Mark, therefore, must have stayed on in Rome, and around the year 62 we find him again as an aide of St Paul (cf. Philem 24), to whom he is a source of great consolation (cf. Col 4:10ff), because of his fidelity. Later still, around the year 66, St Paul asks Timothy to come to him bringing Mark, because he is very useful to him in spreading the Gospel (cf. 2 Tim 4:11).

That is what we know about Mark's apostolic itinerary : in contrast to his softness in the early years, we find him later on as a faithful and effective co-worker of prominent Apostles (Peter, Paul, Barnabas), one of their most constant and valuable assistants, in all spheres of apostolic work. Among his most outstanding contributions is his work as "interpreter of St Peter in Rome", which probably consisted of translating into Greek and Latin (many latinisms are noticeable in the Greek of his Gospel) the oral Galilean-Aramaic preaching and teaching of the head of the Apostles in the capital of the Empire. This was the way the Holy Spirit chose to train Mark, whom he would inspire later to write the second canonical Gospel, a Gospel which would faithfully reflect the preaching and vivid account of Christ's life given by St Peter in Rome.

Mark's progress in Christian holiness should be a great encouragement to us. Despite our weaknesses, despite failures in years past, we too can be confident that God's grace, the care we receive from our Mother the Church and the self-sacrificing service we render her in the future will enable us to do fruitful apostolic work.

From the year 66 onwards (Mark would have been a little over fifty years old), the information we have about him is less reliable but it is in line with what we know of his earlier life. For example, Eusebius (around the middle of the fourth century) in his *Ecclesiastical History* (II, 16) and St Jerome (towards the end of the same century) in his *On famous men* (chap. VIII) pass on the tradition that Mark founded the church of Alexandria in Egypt, a tradition which is also supported by the fact that the liturgy of that church is associated with his name; another ancient tradition, mentioned in various documents (some of which go back to the fifth century), claims that Mark died a martyr in the town of Bucoli, very near Alexandria, and that in 825 his relics were devoutly transferred from Alexandria to Venice, which adopted him as patron and later erected the huge basilica dedicated to him.

DATE OF COMPOSITION

St Mark does not indicate when he wrote his Gospel. The Fathers of the Church and the ecclesiastical authors did their best to fix a date, on the basis of information given in documented tradition and on the likely biographical dates of the author. They also noted the relationships his Gospel holds to other texts in the New Testament, especially the Gospels of St Matthew and St Luke, and the Acts of the Apostles and some of St Paul's letters.

A first approximation indicates the decade 60-70, or perhaps 58-68. The Magisterium of the Church has indicated that it must be dated earlier than the year 70, inferring from interpretation of chapter 13 : the passages reporting Jesus' words about the future destruction of the temple of Jerusalem in that chapter are to be taken as a true prophecy, written before the event (*ante eventum*).[6] This Magisterium teaching also takes account of other data in Christian tradition and of internal evidence in the Gospel.

6   *Reply* of the Pontifical Biblical Commission, 26 July 1912: *EB*, 395.

Taking account of the data of tradition, from which it can be inferred that the Gospel of St Mark is prior to that of St Luke, and that both were written before the year 70, scholars deduce, as a second approximation, that the latest date for this Gospel would be around the year 67.

A third line of research takes 63 as a base year—the most probable date of the redaction of the Acts, "the second book" of St Luke (Acts 1:1), written after his Gospel. This approach suggests that St Luke's Gospel should be dated around the year 62, in which case Mark's would be a little earlier, which would bring us to around the year 60. This date fits in with the biography of St Mark: by that time he would have been in Rome and have worked as St Peter's interpreter.

The scholars who suggest that Mark's Gospel was composed around 64-67 also place the Acts later, around 70. They draw support for this by referring to the passage in St Irenaeus[7] which says: "After his departure [the death of St Peter], Mark, the disciple and interpreter of Peter, transmitted to us in writing what Peter had preached."

To sum up : it should be taken as certain that the Gospel of St Mark was written before the year 70; and the two possible more precise dates are: around the year 60, or else between 64 and 67.

PLACE OF COMPOSITION & IMMEDIATE READERSHIP

Ancient tradition states that St Mark wrote his Gospel in Italy (cf., for example, Clement of Alexandria, +211; the ancient *Latin Prologue*, second to third century; the *Monarchian Prologue*, fourth century); or, more specifically, in Rome itself (this can be inferred from Irenaeus' *Against heresies*, around 175-189; Tertullian, who died in 220, in his *Against Marcion*, and many other writers expressly make the same claim : Clement of Alexandria, St Jerome, etc.).

Internal examination of the text corroborates what tradition says: it uses many Latin words, simply translating them from Greek (census, centurion, denarius, legion, *speculator* or watch tower, flagellum, etc.); it says that Simon of Cyrene was the father of Alexander and Rufus, who were prominent among the Christians in Rome (cf. Rom 16:13); the narrative generally is so vivid and, we might say, so characteristic that scholars are in agreement in claiming to hear St Peter's voice in such phrases as: "then we arrived, we saw, we went, he tells us, etc." These words were transcribed by St Mark with simply a change of first person singular to third person plural. The content fits in perfectly with the Gospel preaching of St Peter, as can be seen from his teaching in the Acts of the Apostles: St Mark's is the Gospel which most closely follows the structure of Peter's addresses as reported in Acts. The way in which the author treats the figure of St Peter is also very characteristic : he gives us a more detailed account than the other evangelists of Peter's less happy interventions, which must clearly indicate Peter's humility in wanting to see them recorded.

7   *Against heresies*, III, 1, 1.

And, on the other side, he omits some episodes which highlight the greater dignity Jesus conferred on Peter, such as the promise of the primacy (cf Mt 16:17-18) and his dedication to the Church (cf. Jn 21:15-17).

All this ties in with the tradition that Mark wrote his Gospel "on the insistence of the Christians of Rome" (Clement of Alexandria, according to a text preserved by Eusebius in his *Ecclesiastical History*, VI, 15, 5). This, of course, does not detract from the Second Gospel's divine inspiration, since the Holy Spirit, as well as internally moving the Evangelist's will, could also stimulate the faithful to ask him to write (which fitted in very well with Mark's circumstances at the time).

It is very reasonable, therefore, to say, in keeping with ancient tradition reaffirmed by recent scholarship, that St Mark wrote in the first instance for the faithful in Rome, though of course his Gospel has perennial value for the whole Church. Internal evidence also supports this view : he explains Jewish rites and customs with which Gentiles would be unfamiliar (cf. for example Mk 7:1-5), and he translates Aramaic words used by Jesus (cf Mk 5:41; 7:34).

THE STRUCTURE OF THE GOSPEL

The Second Gospel is basically a detailed development of St Peter's discourses in the Acts of the Apostles (cf. Acts 2:22-26; 3:12-26; 10:36-43). In it we can distinguish six major sections, as follows:

1. *Prelude to the public ministry of Jesus* (1:1-13).
    St Mark's account, shorter than in the other Synoptics, covers:
        The ministry of John the Baptist. (1:1-8).
        Jesus is baptized (1:9-11).
        The tempting of Jesus (1:12-13).

2. *Jesus' Galilean ministry* (1:14-6:6)
    Mark's report on this section is fairly extensive. From it we can deduce that this ministry certainly lasted some months, with the city of Capernaum, on the shore of Lake Gennesaret acting as the centre of Jesus's activity throughout Galilee.

    The healing and miracles performed by our Lord, his preaching, a number of disputes with Pharisees, his teaching in parables : all combine to increase his following; however, Jesus wants to wean the people away from earth-bound messianism; he wants them to recognize his as a divine and transcendent messianism. He acts very prudently in this regard.

    In the meantime he gathers a group of disciples around him. His popularity provokes envy on the part of Pharisees and Herodians, who begin to plot against him. This fact, and his rejection by people of his hometown, Nazareth, leads him to make a number of evangelical journeys into border areas.

3. *Jesus journeys with his Apostles* (6:6-9:50)
    Jesus now concentrates on training the Twelve. He initiates them into their

mission of evangelization. He leads them north and then east, away from the borders of Galilee—to where the multiplication of the loaves and other miracles take place. He journeys to the Phoenician region of Tyre (6:6-7:37).

He then turns back and follows the western shore of Lake Gennesaret; the second multiplication of the loaves and other miracles; new plots are hatched by the Pharisees; other apostolic journeys (8:1-21).

Jesus heads towards Syria, via the Golan region; in Caesarea Philippi a significant event occurs : Peter, speaking for the Twelve, acknowledges Jesus' divinity (8:27-30). This episode constitutes, as it were, a central point dividing St Mark's Gospel into two parts.

Then Jesus foretells his death for the first time : from this point onwards he prepares his disciples for his passion, though they fail to understand him; Peter is severely reprimanded (8:31-9:1).

The Transfiguration. Return to Galilee (9:2-50).

4. *Making for Judea and Jerusalem* (10:1-12:44).

Journey to Jerusalem, with a detour to Perea and Jericho; teaching on marriage and its indissolubility; episodes about the demands involved in following Jesus. The faith of the blind man, Bartimaeus (10:1-52).

5. *Eschatological discourse* (13:1-37)

Our Lord predicts the destruction of Jerusalem; he speaks about the end of the world and calls for vigilance.

6. *Passion, death and resurrection of Jesus* (14:1-16:20)

The Sanhedrin decide to dispose of Jesus. Judas' betrayal. The Last Supper and the institution of the Blessed Eucharist (14:1- 26).

Jesus' prayer in the Garden of Olives. His arrest. Interrogations. Peter's denials. The trial before Pilate (14:26- 15:15).

The Way of the Cross. Crucifixion and death. Burial (15:16-47).

The risen Jesus. The angel's announcement to the holy women. Appearances to Mary Magdalen, to the disciples at Emmaus and to the Twelve. The commandment to the Apostles to preach the Gospel to the whole world. Jesus' ascension.

DOCTRINAL CONTENT

We could say that the special characteristic of St Mark's Gospel is that it gives us a direct picture of Jesus : the main episodes in his life are reported in a straightforward way, without any further explanation; unlike the other Gospels there are no long discourses in Jesus' words, no detailed explanations of his teachings. For example, St Mark does not give us the great Sermon on the Mount which we find in chapters 5-7 of St Matthew (half of the content of which is to be found in various places in St Luke); in his fourth chapter, he does give the parables discourse, but quite briefly by comparison with chapter 13 of Matthew; he omits many of the rulings and teachings on the life of the Church, which we are given in Matthew 18; etc. St Mark's Gospel contains only two of Jesus' great discourses, properly speaking : the one on the parables, which we have just mentioned (Mk 4:1-34) and the eschatological discourse (Mk 13:1-37), which is the equivalent of Mt 24:1-44 and Luke 21:5-38. To compensate for these omissions Mark has left us something different but quite delightful—his vivid description of episodes of Jesus' life with his disciples. Revelation through Mark allows us to see aspects of Jesus which fill out the picture given by the other evangelists.

St Mark's Gospel takes us out into the little towns on the shore of Lake Gennesaret; we can sense the hubbub of the crowd of people following Jesus and almost exchange remarks with some of them; we can see Christ's loving gestures, the somewhat over-spontaneous reactions of the Twelve [. . .] : we can watch the Gospel story unfold before our very eyes. This is not to say that Mark's account is naive : he has achieved what he set out to do; he has managed to make Jesus attractive to us; Jesus, who is both serene and demanding, exercises on us the same kind of influence the Apostles felt when they lived with him. St Mark is passing on to us what St Peter communicated in his preaching, a preaching which, as the years went by, must have grown in emotion, depth, insight and love. Mark is the living mirror, we could say, of St Peter's preaching, of which St Luke also has left us faithful records in the Acts of the Apostles (cf. Acts 2:22-26; 3:12-26; 10:36-43).

LITERARY STYLE

St Mark's vocabulary and sentence-structure are simple and effective. There is a predominance of *parataxis*—phrases linked together by the continuous use of the conjunction "and" or, occasionally, "then" or "immediately". Also, very often he uses direct speech in the middle of his narrative : in addition to making it vivid, this gives us very many phrases of Jesus which are a literal translation into Greek of the very words our Lord used in the Palestinian Aramaic dialect of his time. Another feature is his use of the historical present tense ("he comes", "he says", "they go"), which occurs over 150 times and his unexpected jumping from one tense to another within the same passage, but this is not reflected in the RSV.

A particular feature of St Mark is the fine detail he gives in certain episodes which are more soberly covered by St Matthew or St Luke (for example, the curing of the paralytic, Mk 2:1:3, compared with Mt 9:1-8 and Lk 5:17-26; the curing of the possessed man at Gerasa, Mk 5:1-20, Mt 8:28-34, Lk 8:26-29). Also St Mark is the only one to give us other little pieces of information: for example, only he tells us that during the storm on the lake Jesus was in the stern asleep on a cushion (Mk 4:38); or that he named the sons of Zebedee "sons of thunder" (Mk 3:17); or that the blind man of Jericho was named Bartimaeus (Mk 10:46). These things must surely reflect not simply Mark's preference for detail but also St Peter's vivid oral account of these events.

In perfect harmony with the other three Gospels, St Mark's depicts Jesus as the Messiah (Mk 14:61-62). Jesus required people to follow him, and being his disciple means accepting that he is the Messiah (Mk 8:27-30). Also, whenever people asked him to do anything for them, he required them to believe that he could do it; whether it was a matter of the instantaneous curing of a paralytic and the forgiving of his sins (Mk 2:5-12) or the raising of Jairus' daughter (Mk 5:35-36), etc, these were powers which Jesus exercised in his own name, by his word alone.

However, as regards making known that he was the Messiah, Jesus acted very prudently. He wanted to make sure that people did not confuse him with some sort of nationalistic, political leader who would liberate the Jews from Roman domination. Thus, when addressing crowds he preferred to call himself 'the Son of man' (Mk 2:10; 2:28; 8:31, 38 etc). This expression, to be found in the prophecies of Daniel (cf. Dan 7:13-14), left no scope for a nationalistic interpretation : it clearly had a very transcendental religious meaning. Other messianic titles, such as "Son of David", or simply "Messiah" (Christ), could, at the time, have led to an interpretation of Jesus' mission as one of predominantly earthly messianism.

By acting in this way Jesus revealed himself gradually, preparing his disciples to recognize him as the Saviour who would redeem men and reconcile them to God, not through force of violence or political power, but through his Sacrifice on Calvary, "for the Son of man also came not to be served but to serve, and to give his life as a ransom for many" (Mk 10:45).

JESUS, THE SON OF GOD

The first words of St Mark's Gospel clearly assert the divinity of Christ : "The beginning of the gospel of Jesus Christ, the Son of God" (Mk 1:1). In many passages his divinity is confessed in an implicit way (cf., for example, Mk 2:11; 4:41). In others it is formally revealed, as when Jesus is baptized: "a voice came from heaven, 'Thou art my beloved Son'" (Mk 1:11); the same revelation is made again at the Transfiguration (Mk 9:7).

We can be quite sure that the assertion that Jesus is the Son of God, made by St Mark at the very beginning of his Gospel, is a summary of everything he plans to tell us in his book; and also it provides the reader with a key to understand everything he is going to find there : if we do not believe that Jesus is the Messiah and the Son of God, we will not be able to understand the Gospel. Therefore St Mark points out at the very beginning that in Jesus Christ we must see someone who is fully God and fully man. (In the last analysis every form of heterodoxy falls into one or other of these extremes—denying Christ's divinity or denying his humanity.) The Holy Spirit has wanted to preserve those words of the Roman officer on Calvary—which also provide a sort of summary of the Gospel according to St Mark: "When the centurion, who stood facing him, saw that he thus breathed his last, he said, 'Truly this man was the Son of God!'" (Mk 15:39).

The Gospel of our Lord Jesus Christ
according to St Mark

ENGLISH AND LATIN VERSION, WITH NOTES

THE PRELUDE TO THE
PUBLIC MINISTRY OF JESUS

The ministry of John the Baptist

¹The beginning of the gospel of Jesus Christ, the Son of God.ᵃ

Mt 3:1-12
Lk 3:3-18
Jn 1:19-34

---

¹Initium evangelii Iesu Christi Filii Dei. ²Sicut scriptum est in Isaia propheta:

---

1. With these words St Mark gives us the title of his book and emphasizes that Jesus is the Messiah foretold by the prophets and that he is the only Son of the Father, whose nature he shares. The title summarizes the content of the Second Gospel: Jesus Christ, true God and true Man.

The word "gospel" means good tidings, the good news God sends to mankind through his Son. The content of this good news is, in the first place, Jesus Christ himself, his words and his actions. "During the Synod [the 1974 Synod of Bishops], the Bishops very frequently referred to this truth: Jesus himself, the Good News of God (Mk 1:1, Rom 1:13), was the very first and the greatest evangelizer: he was so through and through, to perfection and to the point of the sacrifice of his earthly life" (Paul VI, *Evangelii nuntiandi*, 7). The Apostles, who were chosen by our Lord to be the basis of his Church, fulfilled his commandment to present to Jews and Gentiles, by means of oral preaching, the witness of what they had seen and heard—the fulfilment in Jesus Christ of the prophecies of the Old Testament, and the forgiveness of sins, adoptive sonship and inheritance of heaven offered by God to all men. For this reason the word "gospel" can also be used in the case of the Apostles' preaching.

Later, the evangelists, inspired by the Holy Spirit, wrote down part of this oral teaching; and thus, through Sacred Scripture and apostolic Tradition, the voice of Christ is perpetuated throughout the centuries to reach all generations and all nations.

The Church, which carries on the mission of the Apostles, must make the "gospel" known. This it does, for example, by means of catechesis: "The primary and essential object of catechesis is, to use an expression dear to St Paul and also to contemporary theology, 'the mystery of Christ.' [. . .] It is therefore to reveal in the Person of Christ the whole of God's eternal design reaching fulfilment in that Person. It is to seek to understand the meaning of Christ's actions and words and of the signs worked by him, for they simultaneously hide and reveal his mystery. Accordingly, the definitive aim of catechesis is to put people not only in touch but in communion, in intimacy, with Jesus Christ: only he can lead us to the love of the Father in the Spirit and

---

ᵃOther ancient authorities omit *the Son of God*

Mal 3:1
Mt 11:10
Jn 3:28
Is 40:3
²As it is written in Isaiah the prophet,ᵇ
"Behold, I send my messenger before thy face,
    who shall prepare the way;
³the voice of one crying in the wilderness:
Prepare the way of the Lord,
    make his paths straight—"

Acts 19:4
⁴John the baptizer appearedᶜ in the wilderness, preaching a baptism of repentance for the forgiveness of sins. ⁵And there went out to him all the country of Judea, and all the

---

"Ecce mitto angelum meum ante faciem tuam, qui praeparabit viam tuam; ³vox clamantis in deserto: 'Parate viam Domini, rectas facite semitas eius'," ⁴fuit Ioannes Baptista in deserto praedicans baptismum paenitentiae in remissionem peccatorum. ⁵Et egrediebatur ad illum omnis Iudaeae regio et Hierosolymitae

---

make us share in the life of the Holy Trinity" (John Paul II, *Catechesi tradendae*, 5).

2-3. The Gospel quotes Isaiah in particular perhaps because he was the most important of the prophets who foretold the coming of the Messiah: that is why St Jerome called Isaiah the "Evangelist of the Old Testament".

4. St John the Baptist presents himself to the people after spending five years in the desert. He invites the Israelites to prepare for the coming of the Messiah by doing penance. The figure of St John points to the continuity between the Old and New Testaments: he is the last of the prophets and the first of the witnesses to Jesus. Whereas the other prophets announced Jesus from afar, John the Baptist was given the special privilege of actually pointing him out (cf. Jn 1:29; Mt 11:9-11).

The baptism given by the Precursor was not Christian Baptism: it was a penitential rite; but it prefigured the dispositions needed for Christian Baptism—faith in Christ, the Messiah, the source of grace, and voluntary detachment from sin.

5. "Confessing their sins": by seeking John's baptism a person showed that he realized he was a sinner: the rite which John performed announced forgiveness of sins through a change of heart and helped remove obstacles in the way of a person's acceptance of the Kingdom (Lk 3:10-14).

This confessing of sin was not the same as the Christian sacrament of Penance. But it was pleasing to God because it was a sign of interior repentance and the people performed genuine penitential acts (Mt 3:7-10; Lk 3:7-9). In the Sacrament of Penance, in order to obtain God's forgiveness one must confess one's sins orally. In this connexion John Paul II has said: "And keep in mind

ᵇOther ancient authorities read *in the prophets*
ᶜOther ancient authorities read *John was baptizing*

people of Jerusalem; and they were baptized by him in the
river Jordan, confessing their sins. [6]Now John was clothed
in camel's hair, and had a leather girdle around his waist,
and ate locusts and wild honey. [7]And he preached, saying,
"After me comes he who is mightier than I, the thong of
whose sandals I am not worthy to stoop down and untie. [8]I
have baptized you with water, but he will baptize you with
the Holy Spirit."

2 Kings 1:8

Acts 13:25

Jesus is baptized

[9]In those days Jesus came from Nazareth of Galilee and was

Mt 3:13-17
Lk 3:21-22

---

universi et baptizabantur ab illo in Iordane flumine confitentes peccata sua. [6]Et
erat Ioannes vestitus pilis cameli, et zona pellicea circa lumbos eius, et locustas
et mel silvestre edebat. [7]Et praedicabat dicens: "Venit fortior me post me, cuius
non sum dignus procumbens solvere corrigiam calceamentorum eius. [8]Ego
baptizavi vos aqua; ille vero baptizabit vos in Spiritu Sancto." [9]Et factum est

---

that the teaching of the Council of Trent on the need for confession of all mortal
sins still holds and will always hold (sess. XIV, chap. 5 and can. 7). The norm
taught by St Paul and by the same Council of Trent, according to which the
worthy reception of the Eucharist must be preceded by the confession of sins
when one is conscious of mortal sin, is and always will be in force in the Church
(sess. XIII, chap. 7 and can. 11)" (*Address to penitentiaries of the four major
basilicas in Rome*, 30 January 1981).

8. "Baptizing with the Holy Spirit" refers to the Baptism Jesus will institute
and shows how it differs from the baptism of John. In John's baptism, as in the
other rites of the Old Testament, grace was only signified, symbolized. "By the
baptism of the New Law men are baptized inwardly by the Holy Spirit, and this
is accomplished by God alone. But by the baptism of John the body alone was
cleansed by the water" (St Thomas Aquinas, *Summa theologiae*, III, q.38, art.2
ad 1). In Christian Baptism, instituted by our Lord, the baptismal rite not only
signifies grace but is the effective cause of grace, i.e. it confers grace. "Baptism
confers the first sanctifying grace and the supernatural virtues, taking away
original sin and also personal sins if there are any, together with the entire debt
of punishment which the baptized person owes for sin. In addition, Baptism
impresses the Christian character in the soul and makes it able to receive the
other sacraments" (*St Pius X Catechism*, 295). The effects of Christian Baptism,
like everything to do with the sanctification of souls, are attributed to the Holy
Spirit, the "Sanctifier". It should be pointed out, however, that like all the *ad
extra* actions of God (i.e. actions external to the intimate life of the Blessed
Trinity), the sanctification of souls is the work of all three divine Persons.

9. Our Lord's hidden life takes place (apart from his birth at Bethlehem and

Jn 1:31-34
Mk 9:7
Ps 2:7
Is 42:1
Mt 4:1-7
Lk 4:1-13
Jn 1:51

baptized by John in the Jordan. [10]And when he came up out of the water, immediately he saw the heavens opened and the Spirit descending upon him like a dove; [11]and a voice came from heaven, "Thou art my beloved Son;[d] with thee I am well pleased."

---

in diebus illis, venit Iesus a Nazareth Galilaeae et baptizatus est in Iordane ab Ioanne. [10]Et statim ascendens de aqua vidit apertos caelos et Spiritum tamquam columbam descendentem in ipsum; [11]et vox facta est de caelis: "Tu es Filius

---

the time he was in Egypt) in Nazareth of Galilee from where he comes to receive John's baptism.

Jesus had no need to receive this baptism of conversion. However, it was appropriate that he who was going to establish the New Alliance should recognize and accept the mission of his Precursor by being baptized with his baptism: this would encourage people to prepare to receive the Baptism which *was* necessary. The Fathers comment that our Lord went to receive John's baptism in order to fulfil all righteousness (cf. Mt 3:15), to give us an example of humility, to become widely known, to have people believe in Him and to give life-giving strength to the waters of Baptism.

"Ever since the Baptism of Christ in the water, Baptism removes the sins of all" (St Augustine, *Sermon* 135).

"There are two different periods of time which relate to Baptism—one the period of its institution by the Redeemer; the other the establishment of the law regarding its reception. [. . .] The second period to be distinguished, that is, the time when the law of Baptism was made, also admits of no doubt. Holy writers are unanimous in saying that after the Resurrection of our Lord, when he gave to his Apostles the command to go and 'make disciples of all nations, baptizing them in the name of the Father and of the Son and of the Holy Ghost' (Mt 28:19) the law of Baptism became obligatory on all who were to be saved" (*St Pius V Catechism*, Part II).

10. The visible presence of the Holy Spirit in the form of a dove marks the beginning of Christ's public ministry. The Holy Spirit will also appear, in the form of tongues of fire, on the occasion when the Church begins its mission to all the world on the day of Pentecost (cf. Acts 2: 3-21).

The Fathers usually interpret the dove as a symbol of peace and reconciliation between God and men. It first appears in the account of the flood (Gen 8: 10-11) as a sign that God's punishment of mankind has come to an end. Its presence at the beginning of Christ's public ministry symbolizes the peace and reconciliation he will bring.

11. At the very beginning of his public life the mystery of the Holy Trinity is made manifest: "The Son is baptized, the Holy Spirit descends in the form

---

[d]Or *my Son, my (or the) Beloved*

The tempting of Jesus

¹²The Spirit immediately drove him out into the wilderness.   Job 5:22f
¹³And he was in the wilderness forty days, tempted by
Satan; and he was with the wild beasts; and the angels
ministerd to him.

---

meus dilectus; in te complacui." ¹²Et statim Spiritus expellit eum in desertum.
¹³Et erat in deserto quadraginta diebus et tentabatur a Satana; eratque cum

---

of a dove and the voice of the Father is heard" (St Bede, *In Marci Evangelium
expositio, in loc.*). "The Holy Spirit dwells in him," the same author goes on,
"but not from the moment of his Baptism, but from the moment he became
man." In other words, Jesus did not become God's son at his Baptism; he is the
Son of God from all eternity. Nor did he become the Messiah at this point; he
was the Messiah from the moment he became man.

Baptism is the public manifestation of Jesus as Son of God and as Messiah,
ratified by the presence of the Blessed Trinity.

"The Holy Spirit descended visibly in bodily form upon Christ when he was
baptized so that we may believe him to descend invisibly upon all those who
are baptized afterwards" (St Thomas Aquinas, *Summa theologiae*, III, q. 39, a.
6 ad 3).

13. St Matthew (4: 1-11) and St Luke (4: 1-13) relate the temptations of
Jesus in more detail. By submitting to temptation, Jesus wanted to show us that
we should not be afraid of temptations: on the contrary, they give us an
opportunity to progress in the interior life.

"Yet the Lord sometimes permits that souls, which are dear to him, should
be tempted with some violence, in order that they may better understand their
own weakness, and the necessity of grace to prevent them from falling [. . .];
God permits us to be tempted, that we may be more detached from the things
of earth, and conceive a more ardent desire to behold him in heaven [. . .]; God
also permits us to be tempted, in order to increase our merits. [. . .] When it is
disturbed by temptation, and sees itself in danger of committing sin, the soul
has recourse to the Lord and to his divine Mother; it renews its determination
to die rather than offend God; it humbles itself and takes refuge in the arms of
divine mercy. By this means, as is proved by experience, it acquires more
strength and is united more closely to God" (St Alphonsus Mary de Liguori,
The Love of our Lord Jesus Christ reduced to practice, chap. 17).

Besides, as in our Lord's own case, we will always have God's help to
overcome temptation: "Jesus has stood up to the test. And it was a real test [...].
The devil, with twisted intention, quoted the Old Testament: 'God will send his
angels to protect the just man wherever he goes' (Ps 91:11). But Jesus refuses
to tempt his Father; he restores true meaning to this passage from the Bible.
And, as a reward for his fidelity, when the time comes, ministers of God the
Father appear and wait upon him [. . .]. We have to fill ourselves with courage,
for the grace of God will not fail us. God will be at our side and will send his

JESUS BEGINS HIS MINISTRY IN GALILEE

Jesus begins to preach and calls his first disciples

Mt 4:12-17
Lk 4:14-15

Gal 4:4

Mt 4:18-22
Lk 5:1-11

¹⁴Now after John was arrested, Jesus came into Galilee, preaching the gospel of God, ¹⁵and saying, "The time is fulfilled, and the kingdom of God is at hand; repent, and believe in the Gospel."

¹⁶And passing along by the Sea of Galilee, he saw Simon

---

bestiis, et angeli ministrabant illi. ¹⁴Postquam autem traditus est Ioannes, venit Iesus in Galilaeam praedicans evangelium Dei ¹⁵et dicens: "Impletum est tempus, et appropinquavit regnum Dei; paenitemini et credite evangelio." ¹⁶Et

---

angels to be our travelling companions, our prudent advisers along the way, our cooperators in all that we take on" (J. Escrivá, *Christ is passing by*, 63).

14-15. "The gospel of God": this expression is found in St Paul (Rom 1:1; 2 Cor 11:7; etc.) where it means the same as "the gospel of Jesus Christ" (2 Thess 1:8; etc.), thereby implying the divinity of Jesus Christ. The imminence of the Kingdom requires a genuine conversion of man to God (Mt 4:17; Mk 6:12; etc.). The prophets had already spoken of the need for conversion and for Israel to abandon its evil ways (Jer 3:22; Is 30:15; Os 14:2; etc.).

Both John the Baptist and Jesus and his Apostles insist on the need for conversion, the need to change one's attitude and conduct as a prerequisite for receiving the Kingdom of God. John Paul II underlines the importance of conversion for entry into the Kingdom of God: "Therefore, the Church professes and proclaims conversion. Conversion to God always consists *in discovering his mercy*, that is, in discovering that love which is patient and kind (cf. 1 Cor 13:4) as only the Creator and Father can be; the love to which the 'God and Father of our Lord Jesus Christ' (2 Cor 1:3) is faithful to the uttermost consequences in the history of his covenant with man: even to the Cross and to the death and resurrection of the Son. Conversion to God is always the fruit of the 'rediscovery' of this Father, who is rich in mercy.

"Authentic knowledge of the God of mercy, the God of tender love, is a constant and inexhaustible source of conversion, not only as a momentary interior act but also as a permanent attitude, as a state of mind. Those who come to know God in this way, who 'see' him in this way, can live only in a state of being continually converted to him. They live, therefore, *in statu conversionis* and it is this state of conversion which marks out the most profound element of the pilgrimage of every man and woman on earth *in statu viatoris*" (John Paul II, *Dives in misericordia*, 13).

16-20. In these verses the evangelist describes how Jesus called some of those who would later form part of the Apostolic College (3:16ff). From the

and Andrew the brother of Simon casting a net in the sea; for they were fishermen. [17]And Jesus said to them, "Follow me and I will make you become fishers of men." [18]And immediately they left their nets and followed him. [19]And going on a little farther, he saw James the son of Zebedee and John his brother, who were in their boat mending the nets. [20]And immediately he called them; and they left their father Zebedee in the boat with the hired servants, and followed him.

Mt 13:47

Jesus in the synagogue of Capernaum

[21]And they went into Capernaum; and immediately on the sabbath he entered the synagogue and taught. [22]And they

Lk 4:31-37
Mt 4:13
Mt 7:28-29

---

praeteriens secus mare Galilaeae vidit Simonem et Andream fratrem Simonis mittentes in mare; erant enim piscatores. [17]Et dixit eis Iesus: "Venite post me, et faciam vos fieri piscatores hominum." [18]Et protinus, relictis retibus, secuti sunt eum. [19]Et progressus pusillum vidit Iacobum Zebedaei et Ioannem fratrem eius, et ipsos in navi componentes retia, [20]et statim vocavit illos. Et, relicto patre suo Zebedaeo in navi cum mercenariis, abierunt post eum. [21]Et ingrediuntur Capharnaum. Et statim sabbatis ingressus synagogam docebat. [22]Et stupebant

---

start of his public ministry in Galilee the Messiah seeks co-workers to help him in his mission as Saviour and Redeemer. He looks for them among people used to hard work, people for whom life is a struggle and whose life-style is plain. In human terms they are obviously at a disadvantage *vis-à-vis* many of those to whom they will preach; but this in no way prevents their self-surrender from being generous and free. The light lit in their hearts was enough to lead them to give up everything. A simple invitation to follow the Master was enough for them to put themselves completely at his disposal.

It is Jesus who chooses them: he interfered in the lives of the Apostles just as he interferes in ours, without seeking our permission: he is our Lord. Cf. note on Mt 4:18-22.

21. "Synagogue" means meeting, assembly, community. It was—and is— used by the Jews to describe the place where they met to hear the Scriptures read, and to pray. Synagogues seem to have originated in the social gatherings of the Jews during their exile in Babylon, but this phenomenon did not spread until much later. In our Lord's time there were synagogues, in Palestine, in every city and town of any importance; and, outside Palestine, wherever the Jewish community was large enough. The synagogue consisted mainly of a rectangular room built in such a way that those attending were facing Jerusalem when seated. There was a rostrum or pulpit from which Sacred Scripture was read and explained.

Mk 5:7

were astonished at his teaching, for he taught them as one who had authority, and not as the scribes. [23]And immediately there was in their synagogue a man with an unclean spirit; [24]and he cried out, "What have you to do with us, Jesus of Nazareth? Have you come to destroy us? I know who you are, the Holy One of God." [25]But Jesus rebuked him saying, "Be silent, and come out of him!" [26]And the unclean spirit, convulsing him and crying out with a loud voice, came out of him. [27]And they were all

---

super doctrina eius: erat enim docens eos quasi potestatem habens et non sicut scribae. [23]Et statim erat in synagoga eorum homo in spiritu immundo et exclamavit [24]dicens: "Quid nobis et tibi, Iesu Nazarene? Venisti perdere nos? Scio qui sis: Sanctus Dei." [25]Et comminatus est ei Iesus dicens: "Obmutesce et exi de homine!" [26]Et discerpens eum spiritus immundus et exclamans voce magna exivit ab eo. [27]Et mirati sunt omnes, ita ut conquirerent inter se dicentes:

---

22. Here we can see how Jesus showed his authority to teach. Even when he took Scripture as his basis—as in the Sermon on the Mount—he was different from other teachers, for he spoke in his own name: "But I say to you" (cf. note on Mt 7:28-29). Our Lord speaks about the mysteries of God, and about human relationships; he teaches in a simple and authoritative way because he speaks of what he knows and testifies to what he has seen (Jn 3:11). The scribes also taught the people, St Bede comments, about what is written in Moses and the prophets; but Jesus preached to them as God and Lord of Moses himself (cf. St Bede, *In Marci Evangelium expositio, in loc.*). Moreover, first he does and then he preaches (Acts 1:1)—not like the scribes who teach and do not do (Mt 23:1-5).

23-26. The Gospels give us many accounts of miraculous cures, among the most outstanding of which are those of people possessed by the devil. Victory over the unclean spirit, as the devil is usually described, is a clear sign that God's salvation has come: by overcoming the Evil One, Jesus shows that he is the Messiah, the Saviour, more powerful than the demons: "Now is the judgment of this world, now shall the ruler of this world be cast out" (Jn 12:31). Throughout the Gospel we see many accounts of this continuous and successful struggle of our Lord against the devil.

As time goes on the devil's opposition to Jesus becomes ever clearer; in the wilderness it is hidden and subtle; it is noticeable and violent in the case of possessed people; and radical and total during the Passion, the devil's "hour, and the power of darkness" (Lk 22:53). And Jesus' victory also becomes ever clearer, until he triumphs completely by rising from the dead.

The devil is called unclean, St John Chrysostom says, because of his impiety and withdrawal from God. In some ways he does recognize Christ's holiness, but this knowledge is not accompanied by charity. In addition to the historical

amazed, so that they questioned among themselves, saying, "What is this? A new teaching! With authority he commands even the unclean spirits, and they obey him." [28]And at once his fame spread everywhere throughout all the surrounding region of Galilee.

The curing of Peter's mother-in-law
[29]And immediately he[e] left the synagogue, and entered the house of Simon and Andrew, with James and John. [30]Now Simon's mother-in-law lay sick with a fever, and immediately they told him of her. [31]And he came and took her by the hand and lifted her up, and the fever left her; and she served them.

Mt 8:14-16
Lk 4:38-41

Acts 28:8

"Quidnam est hoc? Doctrina nova cum potestate; et spiritibus immundis imperat, et oboediunt ei." [28]Et processit rumor eius statim ubique in omnem regionem Galilaeae. [29]Et protinus egredientes de synagoga venerunt in domum Simonis et Andreae cum Iacobo et Ioanne. [30]Socrus autem Simonis decumbebat febricitans; et statim dicunt ei de illa. [31]Et accedens elevavit eam apprehensa

---

fact of this cure, we can also see, in this possessed man, those sinners who must be converted to God and freed from the slavery to sin and the devil. They may have to struggle for a long time but victory will come: the Evil One is powerless against Christ (cf. note on Mt 12:22-24).

27. The same authority that Jesus showed in his teaching (1:22) is now to be seen in his actions. His will is his command: he has no need of long prayers or incantations. Jesus' words and actions already have a divine power which provokes wonder and fear in those who hear and see him.

Jesus continues to impress people in this way (Mk 2:12; 5:20-42; 7:37; 15:39; Lk 19:48; Jn 7:46). Jesus of Nazareth is the long-awaited Saviour. He knows this himself and he lets it be known by his actions and by his words; according to the gospel accounts (Mk 1:38-39; 2:10-11; 4:39) there is complete continuity and consistency between what he says and what he does. As Vatican II teaches (*Dei Verbum*, 2) Revelation is realized by deeds and words intimately connected with each other: the words proclaim the deeds and clarify the mystery contained in them; the deeds confirm the teaching. In this way Jesus progressively reveals the mystery of his Person: first the people sense his exceptional authority; later on, the Apostles, enlightened by God's grace, recognize the deepest source of this authority: "You are the Christ, the Son of the living God" (Mt 16:16).

[e]Other ancient authorities read *they*

73

Jesus cures many sick people

Lk 4:41
Acts 16:17-18

³²That evening, at sundown, they brought to him all who were sick or possessed with demons. ³³And the whole city was gathered together about the door. ³⁴And he healed many who were sick with various diseases, and cast out many demons; and he would not permit the demons to speak, because they knew him.

Jesus goes to a lonely place to pray

Lk 4:42-44

³⁵And in the morning, a great while before day, he rose and

---

manu; et dimisit eam febris, et ministrabat eis. ³²Vespere autem facto, cum occidisset sol, afferebant ad eum omnes male habentes et daemonia habentes; ³³et erat omnis civitas congregata ad ianuam. ³⁴Et curavit multos, qui vexabantur variis languoribus, et daemonia multa eiecit et non sinebat loqui daemonia, quoniam sciebant eum. ³⁵Et diluculo valde mane surgens egressus

34. Demons possess a supernatural type of knowledge and therefore they recognize Jesus as the Messiah (Mk 1:24). Through the people they possess they are able to publish this fact. But our Lord, using his divine powers, orders them to be silent. On other occasions he also silences his disciples (Mk 8:30; 9:9), and he instructs people whom he has cured not to talk about their cure (Mk 1:4; 5:43; 7:36; 8:26). He may have acted in this way to educate the people away from a too human and political idea of the Messiah (cf. note on Mt 9:30). Therefore, he first awakens their interest by performing miracles and gradually, through his preaching, gives them a clearer understanding of the kind of Messiah he is.

Some Fathers of the Church point out that Jesus does not want to accept, in support of the truth, the testimony of him who is the father of lies. Cf. note on Jn 8:44.

35. Many passages of the New Testament make reference to Jesus praying. The evangelists point to him praying only on specially important occasions during his public ministry: Baptism (Lk 3:1), the choosing of the Twelve (Lk 6:12), the first multiplication of the loaves (Mk 6:46), the Transfiguration (Lk 9:29), in the garden of Gethsemane prior to his passion (Mk 26:39) etc. Mark for his part, refers to Jesus' prayer at three solemn moments: at the beginning of his public ministry (1:35), in the middle of it (6:46), and at the end, in Gethsemane (14:32).

Jesus' prayer is prayer of perfect praise to the Father; it is prayer of petition for himself and for us; and it is also a model for his disciples. It is a prayer of perfect praise and thanksgiving because he is God's beloved Son in whom the Father is well pleased (cf. Mk 1:11). It is a prayer of petition because the first spontaneous movement of a soul who recognizes God as Father is to ask him for things. Jesus' prayer, as we see in very many gospel passages (e.g. Jn 17:9ff)

went out to a lonely place, and there he prayed. [36]And Simon and those who were with him followed him, [37]and they found him and said to him, "Every one is searching for you." [38]And he said to them, "Let us go on to the next towns, that I may preach there also; for that is why I came out." [39]And he went throughout all Galilee, preaching in their synagogues and casting out demons.

Mt 4:23

---

est et abiit in desertum locum ibique orabat. [36]Et persecutus est eum Simon et, qui cum illo erant; [37]et cum invenissent eum, dixerunt ei: "Omnes quaerunt te!" [38]Et ait illis: "Eamus alibi in proximos vicos, ut et ibi praedicem: ad hoc enim veni." [39]Et venit praedicans in synagogis eorum per omnem Galilaeam et

---

was a continuous petition to the Father for the work of redemption which he, Jesus, had to achieve through prayer and sacrifice (cf. notes on Mk 14:32-42 and Mt 7:7-11).

Our Lord wants to give us an example of the kind of attitude a Christian should have: he should make a habit of addressing God as son to Father in the midst of and through his everyday activities—work, family life, personal relationships, apostolate—so as to give his life a genuinely Christian meaning, for, as Jesus will point out later on, "apart from me you can do nothing" (Jn 15:5).

"You write: 'To pray is to talk with God. But about what?' About what? About him, about yourself: joys, sorrows, successes and failures, noble ambitions, daily worries, weaknesses! And acts of thanksgiving and petitions: and love and reparation. In a word: to get to know him and to get to know yourself: 'to get acquainted!'" (J. Escrivá, *The Way*, 91; cf. notes on Mt 6:5-6; 7:11; and 14:22-23).

38. Jesus tells us here that his mission is to preach, to spread the Good News. He was sent for this purpose (cf. also Lk 4:43). The Apostles, in turn, were chosen by Jesus to be preachers (Mk 3:14; 16:15). Preaching is the method selected by God to effect salvation: "it pleased God through the folly of what we preach to save those who believe" (1 Cor 1:21). This is why St Paul says to Timothy: "Preach the word, be urgent in season and out of season, convince, rebuke, and exhort, be unfailing in patience and teaching" (2 Tim 4:1-2). Faith comes from hearing, we are told in Romans 10:17, where St Paul enthusiastically quotes Isaiah: "How beautiful are the feet of those who preach good news!" (Rom 10:15; Is 52:7).

The Church identifies preaching the Gospel as one of the main tasks of bishops and priests. St Pius X went so far as saying that "for a priest there is no duty more grave or obligation more binding (to dispel ignorance)" (*Acerbo nimis*). In this connexion Vatican II states: "The people of God is formed into one in the first place by the Word of the living God (cf 1 Pet 1:23; Acts 6:7; 12:24), which is quite rightly sought from the mouths of priests (cf. 2 Cor 11:7).

The curing of a leper

Mt 8:2-4
Lk 5:12-16

⁴⁰And a leper came to him, beseeching him, and kneeling said to him, "If you will, you can make me clean." ⁴¹Moved with pity, he stretched out his hand and touched him, and said to him, "I will; be clean." ⁴²And immediately the leprosy left him, and he was made clean. ⁴³And he sternly charged him, and sent him away at once, ⁴⁴and said to him, "See that you say nothing to any one; but go, show yourself to the priest, and offer for your cleansing what Moses

Lev 13:49
14:2-32

---

daemonia eiciens. ⁴⁰Et venit ad eum leprosus deprecans eum et genu flectens et dicens ei: "Si vis, potes me mundare." ⁴¹Et misertus extendens manum suam tetigit eum et ait illi: "Volo, mundare!"; ⁴²et statim discessit ab eo lepra, et mundatus est. ⁴³Et infremuit in eum statimque eiecit illum ⁴⁴et dicit ei: "Vide, nemini quidquam dixeris; sed vade, ostende te sacerdoti et offer pro

---

For since nobody can be saved who has not first believed (Mk 16:16), it is the first task of priests as co-workers of the bishops to preach the Gospel of God to all men (cf. 2 Cor 11:7). In this way they carry out the Lord's command 'Go into all the world and preach the Gospel to every creature' (Mk 16:15) (cf. Mal 2:7; 1 Tim 4:11-13; etc.) and thus set up and increase the people of God" (*Presbyterorum ordinis*, 4).

Jesus' preaching is not just limited to words: he backs up his teaching with his authority and with deeds. The Church also has been sent to preach salvation *and* to effect the work of salvation which it proclaims—a work done through the sacraments and especially through the renewal of the sacrifice of Calvary in the Mass (cf. Vatican II, *Sacrosanctum Concilium*, 6).

In the Church of God all of us should listen devoutly to the preaching of the Gospel and we all should feel a responsibility to spread the Gospel by our words and actions. It is the responsibility of the hierarchy of the Church to teach the Gospel authentically—on the authority of Christ.

40-44. Leprosy was seen as a punishment from God (cf. Num 12:10-15). The disappearance of the disease was regarded as one of the blessings of the messianic times (Is 35:8; cf. Mt 11:5; Lk 7:22). Because leprosy was contagious the Law declared that lepers were impure and that they transmitted impurity to those who touched them and to places they entered. Therefore, they had to live apart (Num 5:2; 12:14ff) and to show that they were lepers by certain external signs. On the rite of purification, see the note on Mt 8:4.

The passage shows us the faithful and confident prayer of a man needing Jesus' help and begging him for it, confident that, if our Lord wishes, he can free him from the disease (cf Mt 8:2). "This man prostrated himself on the ground, as a sign of humility and shame, to teach each of us to be ashamed of the stains of his life. But shame should not prevent us from confessing: the leper showed his wound and begged for healing. If you will, he says, you can make

commanded, for a proof to the people."[f] 45But he went out and began to talk freely about it, and spread the news, so that Jesus[g] could no longer openly enter a town, but was out in the country; and people came to him from every quarter.

2

The curing of a paralytic

1And when he returned to Capernaum after some days, it was reported that he was at home. 2And many were gathered together, so that there was no longer room for them, not even about the door; and he was preaching the word to them. 3And they came, bringing to him a paralytic carried by four men. 4And when they could not get near him because of the crowd, they removed the roof above him; and when they had made an opening, they let down the pallet on which the paralytic lay. 5And when Jesus saw their

Mt 9:1-8
Lk 5:17-26

Mk 3:20

---

emundatione tua, quae praecepit Moyses, in testimonium illis." 45At ille egressus coepit praedicare multum et diffamare sermonem, ita ut iam non posset manifesto in civitatem introire, sed foris in desertis locis erat; et conveniebant ad eum undique.

1Et iterum intravit Capharnaum post dies, et auditum est quod in domo esset. 2Et convenerunt multi, ita ut non amplius caperentur neque ad ianuam, et loquebatur eis verbum. 3Et veniunt ferentes ad eum paralyticum, qui a quattuor portabatur. 4Et cum non possent offerre eum illi prae turba, nudaverunt tectum, ubi erat, et perfodientes summittunt grabatum, in quo paralyticus iacebat. 5Cum vidisset autem Iesus fidem illorum, ait paralytico: "Fili, dimittuntur peccata

---

me clean: that is, he recognized that the Lord had the power to cure him" (St Bede, *In Marci Evangelium expositio, in loc.*).

On the discretion and prudence Jesus required regarding his person, see the note on Mk 1:34 and Mt 9:30.

4. Many Jewish houses had a terraced roof accessible by steps at the back. The same structure can be found even today.

5. Here Jesus emphasizes the connexion between faith and the forgiveness of sins. The boldness of the people who brought in the paralytic shows their faith in Christ, and this faith moves Jesus to forgive the man's sins. We should

[f]Greek *to them*
[g]Greek *he*

Is 43:25
Lk 6:8; 9:47
Jn 16:19

Jn 5:8

faith, he said to the paralytic, "My son, your sins are forgiven." [6]Now some of the scribes were sitting there, questioning in their hearts, [7]"Why does this man speak thus? It is blasphemy! Who can forgive sins but God alone?" [8]And immediately Jesus, perceiving in his spirit that they thus questioned within themselves, said to them, "Why do you question thus in your hearts? [9]Which is easier, to say to the paralytic, 'Your sins are forgiven,' or to say, 'Rise, take up your pallet and walk'? [10]But that you may know that the Son of man has authority on earth to forgive sins"—he said to the paralytic—[11]"I say to you, rise, take up your pallet and go home." [12]And he rose, and immediately took up the pallet and went out before them all; so

---

tua." [6]Erant autem illic quidam de scribis sedentes et cogitantes in cordibus suis: [7]"Quid hic sic loquitur? Blasphemat! Quis potest dimittere peccata nisi solus Deus?" [8]Quo statim cognito Iesus spiritu suo quia sic cogitarent intra se, dicit illis: "Quid ista cogitatis in cordibus vestris? [9]Quid est facilius dicere paralytico: 'Dimittuntur peccata tua' an dicere: 'Surge et tolle grabatum tuum et ambula'? [10]Ut autem sciatis quia potestatem habet Filius hominis in terra dimittendi peccata—ait paralytico—: [11]Tibi dico: Surge, tolle grabatum tuum et vade in domum tuam." [12]Et surrexit et protinus sublato grabato abiit coram

---

question how God views our faith : the faith of these people leads to the instantaneous physical and spiritual curing of this man; we should notice also that one person's need can be helped by the merits of another.

In this man's physical paralysis St Jerome sees a type or figure of spiritual paralysis : the cripple was unable to return to God by his own efforts. Jesus, God and man, cured him of both kinds of paralysis (cf. *Comm. in Marcum, in loc.*). Cf. notes on Mt 9:2-7.

Jesus' words to the paralytic—"Your sins are forgiven"— reflect the fact that his pardon involves a personal encounter with Christ; the same happens in the sacrament of Penance : "In faithfully observing the centuries-old practice of the sacrament of Penance—the practice of individual confession with a personal act of sorrow and an intention to amend and make satisfaction—the Church is defending the human soul's individual right: man's right to a more personal encounter with the crucified forgiving Christ, with Christ saying, through the minister of the sacrament of Reconciliation: 'Your sins are forgiven'; 'Go, and do not sin again' (Jn 8:11). As is evident, this is also a right on Christ's part with regard to every human being redeemed by him: his right to meet each one of us in that key moment in the soul's life constituted by the moment of conversion and forgiveness" (John Paul II, *Redemptor hominis*, 20).

7-12. Here we find a number of indicators of Jesus' divinity : he forgives sins, he can read the human heart and has the power to instantly cure physical

that they were all amazed and glorified God, saying, "We never saw anything like this!"

The calling of Matthew

¹³He went out again beside the sea; and all the crowd gathered about him, and he taught them. ¹⁴And as he passed on, he saw Levi the son of Alphaeus sitting at the tax office, and he said to him, "Follow me." And he rose and followed him.

Mt 9:9-13
Lk 5:27-32
Jn 1:43

---

omnibus, ita ut admirarentur omnes et glorificarent Deum dicentes: "Numquam sic vidimus!" ¹³Et egressus est rursus ad mare; omnisque turba veniebat ad eum, et docebat eos. ¹⁴Et cum praeteriret, vidit Levin Alphaei sedentem ad teloneum

---

illnesses. The scribes know that only God can forgive sins; this is why they take issue with our Lord's statement and call it blasphemous. They require a sign to prove the truth of what he says. And Jesus offers them a sign : thus just as no one can deny that the paralytic has been cured, so no one can reasonably deny that he has been forgiven his sins. Christ, God and man, exercised power to forgive sins and, in his infinite mercy, he chose to extend this power to his Church. Cf. note on Mt 9:3-7.

14. St Mark and St Luke (5:27-32) both call him "Levi"; the First Gospel, on the other hand, calls him "Matthew" (Mt 9:9-13); but they are all referring to the same person. All three accounts describe the same event. Later on, St Mark and St Luke, when giving the list of Apostles (Mk 3:13-19; Lk 6:12-16), include Matthew, not Levi. The Fathers identify Matthew with Levi. Besides it was quite common for Jews to have two names : Jacob-Israel, Simon-Peter, Saul-Paul; Joseph- Caiaphas; John-Mark . . . Frequently, the name and surname were connected with some significant change in the life and mission of the person concerned. Did Jesus' saving intervention in this Apostle's life lead to a change of name? The Gospel does not tell us.

Levi-Matthew, as a publican or tax collector (Mt 9:9-13), was sitting at the 'tax office', a special place where one went to pay tribute. Publicans were tax-collectors appointed by the Romans. It was, therefore, an occupation hated and despised by the people; but it was also a much-coveted position because it was an easy way to become prosperous. Matthew leaves everything behind when Jesus calls him. He immediately responds to his vocation, because Jesus gives him the grace to accept his calling.

Jesus is the basis of our confidence in being able to change, provided we cooperate with his grace, no matter how unworthy our previous conduct may have been. And he is also the source of the confidence we need in order to be apostolic—helping others to be converted and to seek holiness of life. Because he is the Son of God he is able to raise up children of God even from stones (cf. Mt 3:9). Cf. note on Mt 9:9.

¹⁵And as he sat at table in his house, many tax collectors and sinners were sitting with Jesus and his disciples; for there were many who followed him. ¹⁶And the scribes of[h] the Pharisees, when they saw that he was eating with sinners and tax collectors, said to his disciples, "Why does he eat[i] with tax collectors and sinners?" ¹⁷And when Jesus heard it, he said to them, "Those who are well have no need of a physician, but those who are sick; I came not to call the righteous, but sinners."

---

et ait illi: "Sequere me." Et surgens secutus est eum. ¹⁵Et factum est cum accumberet in domo illius, et multi publicani et peccatores simul discumbebant cum Iesu et discipulis eius; erant enim multi et sequebantur eum. ¹⁶Et scribae pharisaeorum, videntes quia manducaret cum peccatoribus et publicanis, dicebant discipulis eius: "Quare cum publicanis et peccatoribus manducat?" ¹⁷Et Iesus hoc audito ait illis: "Non necesse habent sani medicum, sed qui male

---

17. The scribes and Pharisees reproach the disciples, and Jesus replies with a popular proverb: 'Those who are well have no need of a physician, but those who are sick.' He is the doctor of souls, come to cure sinners of their spiritual ailments.

Our Lord calls everyone, his redemptive mission extends to everyone; he affirms this on other occasions, using parables such as that of the marriage feast (Mt 22:1-14; Lk 14:16-24). How, then, can we explain the restriction he seems to place here by saying that he has not come to call the righteous? It is not really a restriction. Jesus uses the opportunity to reproach the scribes and Pharisees for their pride : they consider themselves just, and their reliance on their apparent virtue prevents them from hearing the call to conversion; they think they can be saved by their own efforts (cf. Jn 9:41). This explains the proverb Jesus quotes; certainly his preaching makes it quite clear that 'no one is good but God alone' (Mk 10:18) and that everyone must have recourse to the mercy and forgiveness of God in order to be saved. In other words, mankind is not divided into two—the just and the unjust. We are all sinners, as St Paul confirms: 'all have sinned and fall short of the glory of God' (Rom 3:23). Precisely because of this, Christ came to call all of us; he justifies those who respond to his call.

Our Lord's words should also move us to pray humbly and confidently for people who seem to want to continue living in sin. As St Teresa beseeched God: "Ah, how hard a thing am I asking of thee, my true God! I ask thee to love one who loves thee not, to open to one who has not called upon thee, to give health to one who prefers to be sick and who even goes about in search of sickness. Thou sayest, my Lord, that thou comest to seek sinners; these, Lord, are the true sinners. Look not upon our blindness, my God, but upon all the blood that

[h]Other ancient authorities read *and*
[i]Other ancient authorities add *and drink*

A discussion on fasting

¹⁸Now John's disciples and the Pharisees were fasting; and people came and said to him, "Why do John's disciples and the disciples of the Pharisees fast, but your disciples do not fast?" ¹⁹And Jesus said to them, "Can the wedding guests fast while the bridegroom is with them? As long as they have the bridegroom with them, they cannot fast. ²⁰The days will come, when the bridegroom is taken away from them, and then they will fast in that day. ²¹No one sews a

Mt 9:14-17
Lk 5:33-38

Jn 3:29

Jn 16:20

habent; non veni vocare iustos sed peccatores." ¹⁸Et erant discipuli Ioannis et pharisaei ieiunantes. Et veniunt et dicunt illi: "Cur discipuli Ioannis et discipuli pharisaeorum ieiunant, tui autem discipuli non ieiunant?" ¹⁹Et ait illis Iesus: "Numquid possunt convivae nuptiarum, quamdiu sponsus cum illis est, ieiunare? Quanto tempore habent secum sponsum, non possunt ieiunare; ²⁰venient autem dies cum auferetur ab eis sponsus, et tunc ieiunabunt in illa die. ²¹Nemo assumentum panni rudis assuit vestimento veteri; alioquin

was shed for us by thy Son. Let thy mercy shine out amid such tremendous wickedness. Behold, Lord, we are the works of thy hands" (*Exclamations of the Soul to God*, n.8).

The Fathers of the Church see this calling by Jesus as an invitation to repentance and penance. St John Chrysostom (*Hom. on St Matthew*, 30:3), for example, explains the phrase by putting these words in Jesus' mouth: 'I am not come that they should continue sinners but that they should change and become better.'

18-22. Using a particular case, Christ's reply tells us about the connexion between the Old and New Testaments. In the Old Testament the Bridegroom has not yet arrived; in the New Testament he is present, in the person of Christ. With him began the messianic times, a new era distinct from the previous one. The Jewish fasts, therefore, together with their system of religious observances, must be seen as a way of preparing the people for the coming of the Messiah. Christ shows the difference between the spirit he has brought and that of the Judaism of his time. This new spirit will not be something extra, added on to the old; it will bring to life the perennial teachings contained in the older Revelation. The newness of the Gospel—just like new wine—cannot fit within the moulds of the Old Law.

But this passage says more : to receive Christ's new teaching people must inwardly renew themselves and throw off the straight-jacket of old routines. Cf. note on Mt 9:14-17.

19-20. Jesus describes himself as the Bridegroom (cf. also Lk 12:35-36; Mt 25:1-13; Jn 3:29), thereby fulfilling what the Prophets had said about the relationship between God and his people (cf. Hos 2:18-22; Is 54:5ff). The Apostles are the guests at the wedding, invited to share in the wedding feast

piece of unshrunk cloth on an old garment; if he does, the patch tears away from it, the new from the old, and a worse tear is made. [22]And no one puts new wine into old wineskins; if he does, the wine will burst the skins, and the wine is lost, and so are the skins; but new wine is for fresh skins."[j]

The law of the sabbath

Mt 12:1-8
Lk 6:1-5

[23]One sabbath he was going through the grainfields; and as they made their way his disciples began to pluck ears of grain. [24]And the Pharisees said to him, "Look, why are they doing what is not lawful on the sabbath?" [25]And he said to them, "Have you never read what David did, when he was in need and hungry, he and those who were with him: [26]how

1 Sam 21:7
Lev 24:5-9

he entered the house of God, when Abiathar was high priest, and ate the bread of the Presence, which it is not lawful for any but the priests to eat, and also gave it to those who were

Deut 5:14

with him?" [27]And he said to them, "The sabbath was made

---

supplementum aufert aliquid ab eo, novum a veteri, et peior scissura fit. [22]Et nemo mittit vinum novellum in utres veteres, alioquin dirumpet vinum utres et vinum perit et utres; sed vinum novum in utres novos." [23]Et factum est cum ipse sabbatis ambularet per sata, discipuli eius coeperunt praegredi vellentes spicas. [24]Pharisaei autem dicebant ei: "Ecce, quid faciunt sabbatis, quod non licet?" [25]Et ait illis: "Numquam legistis quid fecerit David, quando necessitatem habuit et esuriit ipse et qui cum eo erant? [26]Quomodo introivit in domum Dei sub Abiathar principe sacerdotum et panes propositionis manducavit, quos non licet manducare nisi sacerdotibus, et dedit etiam eis, qui cum eo erant?" [27]Et

---

with the Bridegroom, in the joy of the kingdom of heaven (cf. Mt 22:1-14).

In v. 20 Jesus announces that the Bridegroom will be taken away from them: this is the first reference he makes to his passion and death (cf. Mk 8:31; Jn 2:19; 3:14). The vision of joy and sorrow we see here epitomizes our human condition during our sojourn on earth.

24. Cf. note on Mt 12:2.

26-27. The bread of the Presence consisted of twelve loaves or cakes placed each morning on the table in the sanctuary, as homage to the Lord from the twelve tribes of Israel (cf. Lev 24:5-9). The loaves withdrawn to make room for the fresh ones were reserved to the priests.

Abiathar's action anticipates what Christ teaches here. Already in the Old Testament God had established a hierarchy in the precepts of the Law so that the lesser ones yielded to the main ones.

[j]Other ancient authorities omit *but new wine is for fresh skins*

for man, not man for the sabbath; ²⁸so the Son of man is
lord even of the sabbath."

---

dicebat eis: "Sabbatum propter hominem factum est, et non homo propter
sabbatum; ²⁸itaque dominus est Filius hominis etiam sabbati."

This explains why a ceremonial precept (such as the one we are discussing)
should yield before a precept of the natural law. Similarly, the commandment
to keep the sabbath does not come before the duty to seek basic subsistence.
Vatican II uses this passage of the Gospel to underline the value of the human
person over and above economic and social development: "The social order
and its development must constantly yield to the good of the person, since the
order of things must be subordinate to the order of persons and not the other
way around, as the Lord suggested when he said that the sabbath was made for
man and not man for the sabbath. The social order requires constant improve-
ment: it must be founded in truth, built on justice, and enlivened by love"
(*Gaudium et spes*, 26).

Finally in this passage Christ teaches God's purpose in instituting the
sabbath: God established it for man's good, to help him rest and devote himself
to divine worship in joy and peace. The Pharisees, through their interpretation
of the Law, had turned this day into a source of anguish and scruple due to all
the various prescriptions and prohibitions they introduced.

By proclaiming himself 'lord of the sabbath', Jesus affirms his divinity and
his universal authority. Because he is lord he has the power to establish other
laws, as Yahweh had in the Old Testament.

28. The sabbath had been established not only for man's rest but also to
allow him give glory to God : that is the correct meaning of the expression "the
sabbath was made for man." Jesus has every right to say he is lord of the sabbath,
because he is God. Christ restores to the weekly day of rest its full, religious
meaning : it is not just a matter of fulfilling a number of legal precepts or of
concern for physical well-being : the sabbath belongs to God; it is one way,
suited to human nature, of rendering glory and honour to the Almighty. The
Church, from the time of the Apostles onwards, transferred the observance of
this precept to the following day, Sunday—the Lord's day—in celebration of
the resurrection of Christ.

"Son of man" : the origin of the messianic meaning of this expression is to
be found particularly in the prophecy in Dan 7:13ff, where Daniel, in a prophetic
vision, contemplates 'one like a son of man' coming down on the clouds of
heaven, who even goes right up to God's throne and is given dominion and
glory and royal power over all peoples and nations. This expression appears 69
times in the Synoptic Gospels; Jesus prefers it to other ways of describing the
Messiah—such as Son of David, Messiah, etc.—thereby avoiding the nationalistic overtones those expressions had in Jewish minds at the time (cf. "Introduction to the Gospel according to St Mark", p. 62 above).

3

The curing of the man with a withered hand

Mt 12:9-14
Lk 6:6-11
[1]Again he entered the synagogue, and a man was there who had a withered hand. [2]And they watched him, to see whether he would heal him on the sabbath, so that they might accuse him. [3]And he said to the man who had the withered hand, "Come here." [4]And he said to them, "Is it lawful on the sabbath to do good or to do harm, to save life Lk 14:4 or to kill?" But they were silent. [5]And he looked around at them with anger, grieved at their hardness of heart, and said Mt 22:16
Mk 12:13 to the man, "Stretch out your hand." He stretched it out, and his hand was restored. [6]The Pharisees went out, and immediately held counsel with the Herodians against him, how to destroy him.

Cures beside the Sea of Galilee

Mt 12:15-16
Lk 6:17-19
[7]Jesus withdrew with his disciples to the sea, and a great

---

[1]Et introivit iterum in synagogam. Et erat ibi homo habens manum aridam; [2]et observabant eum, si sabbatis curaret illum, ut accusarent eum. [3]Et ait homini habenti manum aridam: "Surge in medium." [4]Et dicit eis: "Licet sabbatis bene facere an male? Animam salvam facere an perdere?" At illi tacebant. [5]Et circumspiciens eos cum ira, contristatus super caecitate cordis eorum, dicit homini: "Extende manum." Et extendit, et restituta est manus eius. [6]Et exeuntes pharisaei statim cum herodianis consilium faciebant adversus eum quomodo

5. The evangelists refer a number of times to the way Jesus looks at people (e.g. at the young man : Mk 10:21; at St Peter : Lk 22:61; etc). This is the only time we are told he showed indignation—provoked by the hypocrisy shown in v. 2.

6. The Pharisees were the spiritual leaders of Judaism; the Herodians were those who supported the regime of Herod, benefitting politically and financially thereby. The two were completely opposed to one another and avoided each other's company, yet they combined forces against Jesus. The Pharisees wanted to see the last of him because they considered him a dangerous innovator. The most recent occasion may have been when he pardoned sins (Mk 2:1ff) and interpreted with full authority the law of the sabbath (Mk 3:2); they also want to get rid of him because they consider that he lowered their own prestige in the eyes of the people by the way he cured the man with the withered hand. The Herodians, for their part, despised the supernatural and eschatological tone of Christ's message, since they looked forward to a purely political and temporal Messiah.

multitude from Galilee followed; also from Judea [8]and
Jerusalem and Idumea and from beyond the Jordan and
from about Tyre and Sidon a great multitude, hearing all
that he did, came to him. [9]And he told his disciples to have
a boat ready for him because of the crowd, lest they should
crush him; [10]for he had healed many, so that all who had
diseases pressed upon him to touch him. [11]And whenever
the unclean spirits beheld him, they fell down before him
and cried out, "You are the Son of God." [12]And he strictly
ordered them not to make him known.

Mk 4:25

Mt 15:30

Lk 4:41

Mk 1:31

Jesus chooses twelve Apostles

[13]And he went up into the hills, and called to him those

Mt 10:1-4
Lk 6:12-16

---

eum perderent. [7]Et Iesus cum discipulis suis secessit ad mare. Et multa turba a
Galilaea secuta est et a Iudaea [8]et ab Hierosolymis et ab Idumaea; et, qui trans
Iordanem et circa Tyrum et Sidonem, multitudo magna, audientes, quae faciebat, venerunt ad eum. [9]Et dixit dicipulis suis, ut navicula sibi praesto esset
propter turbam, ne comprimerent eum. [10]Multos enim sanavit, ita ut irruerent
in eum, ut illum tangerent, quotquot habebant plagas. [11]Et spiritus immundi,
cum illum videbant, procidebant ei et clamabant dicentes: "Tu es Filius Dei!"
[12]Et vehementer comminabatur eis, ne manifestarent illum. [13]Et ascendit in

---

10. During our Lord's public life people were constantly crowding round
him to be cured (cf. Lk 6:19; 8:45; etc). As in the case of many other cures, St
Mark gives us a graphic account of what Jesus did to these people (cf. Mk 1:31,
41; 7:31-37; 8:22-26; Jn 9:1-7, 11, 15). By working these cures our Lord shows
that he is both God and man : he cures by virtue of his divine power and using
his human nature. In other words, only in the Word of God become man is the
work of our Redemption effected, and the instrument God used to save us was
the human nature of Jesus—his body and soul—in the unity of the person of
the Word (cf. Vatican II, *Sacrosanctum Concilium*, 5).

This crowding round Jesus is repeated by Christians of all times : the holy
human nature of our Lord is our only route to salvation; it is the essential means
we must use to unite ourselves to God. Thus, we can today approach our Lord
by means of the sacraments, especially and pre-eminently the Eucharist. And
through the sacraments there flows to us, from God, through the human nature
of the Word, a strength which cures those who receive the sacraments with faith
(cf. St Thomas Aquinas, *Summa theologiae*, III, q. 62, a. 5).

13. "He called to him those whom he desired" : God wants to show us that
calling, vocation, is an initiative of God. This is particularly true in the case of
the Apostles, which is why Jesus could tell them, later on, that "you did not
choose me, but I chose you" (Jn 15:16). Those who will have power and

whom he desired; and they came to him. [14]And he
appointed twelve,[k] to be with him, and to be sent out to

montem et vocat ad se, quos voluit ipse, et venerunt ad eum. [14]Et fecit

authority in the Church will not obtain this because first they offer their services
and then Jesus accepts their offering : on the contrary, "not through their own
initiative and preparation, but rather by virtue of divine grace, would they be
called to the apostolate" (St Bede, *In Marci Evangelium expositio, in loc*.).

14-19. The Twelve chosen by Jesus (cf. 3:14) receive a specific vocation
to be "people sent out", which is what the word "apostles" means. Jesus chooses
them for a mission which he will give them later (6:6-13) and to enable them
perform this mission he gives them part of his power. The fact that he chooses
twelve is very significant. This is the same number as the twelve Patriarchs of
Israel, and the Apostles represent the new people of God, the Church founded
by Christ. Jesus sought in this way to emphasize the continuity that exists
between the Old and New Testaments. The Twelve are the pillars on which
Christ builds his Church (cf. Gal 2:9); their mission to make disciples of the
Lord (to teach) all nations, sanctifying and governing the believers (Mt
28:16-20; Mk 16:15; Lk 24:45-48; Jn 20:21-23).

The very designation of them as the Twelve shows that they form a
well-defined and complete group; therefore, after Judas' death Matthias is
elected to take his place (Acts 1:15-26).

14. The Second Vatican Council sees in this text the establishment of the
College of Apostles: "The Lord Jesus, having prayed at length to the Father,
called to himself those whom he willed and appointed twelve to be with him,
whom he might send to preach the Kingdom of God (cf. Mk 3:13-19; Mt
10:1-42). These apostles (cf. Lk 6:13) he constituted in the form of a college
or permanent assembly, at the head of which he placed Peter, chosen from
amongst them" (cf. Jn 21:15-17) [. . .]. "That divine mission, which was
committed by Christ to the apostles, is destined to last until the end of the world
(cf. Mt 28:20), since the Gospel, which they were charged to hand on, is, for
the Church, the principle of all its life for all time. For that very reason the
apostles were careful to appoint successors in this hierarchically constituted
society." (*Lumen gentium*, 19-20). Therefore, the Pope and the bishops, who
succeed to the College of the Twelve, are also called by our Lord to be always
with Jesus and to preach the Gospel, aided by priests.

Life in union with Christ and apostolic zeal must be very closely linked
together; in other words, effectiveness in apostolate always depends on union
with our Lord, on continuous prayer and on sacramental life : "Apostolic zeal
is a divine craziness I want you to have. Its symptoms are: hunger to know the
Master; constant concern for souls; preseverance that nothing can shake" (J.
Escrivá, *The Way*, 934).

[k]Other ancient authorities add *whom also he named apostles*

preach ¹⁵and have authority to cast out demons: ¹⁶Simon whom he surnamed Peter; ¹⁷James the son of Zebedee and John the brother of James, whom he surnamed Boanerges, that is, sons of thunder; ¹⁸Andrew, and Philip, and Bartholomew, and Matthew, and Thomas, and James the son of Alphaeus, and Thaddaeus, and Simon the Cananaean, ¹⁹and Judas Iscariot, who betrayed him.

Jn 1:42
Lk 9:54

His relatives are concerned about Jesus

Then he went home; ²⁰and the crowd came together again, so that they could not even eat. ²¹And when his friends heard it, they went out to seize him, for they said, "He is beside himself."

Mk 6:31
Jn 7:20;
8:48, 52;
10:20

Allegations of the scribes

²²And the scribes who came down from Jerusalem said,

Mt 12:24-32
Lk 11:15-22;
12:10

Duodecim, ut essent cum illo, et ut mitteret eos praedicare ¹⁵habentes potestatem eiciendi daemonia: ¹⁶et imposuit Simoni nomen Petrum; ¹⁷et Iacobum Zebedaei et Ioannem fratrem Iacobi, et imposuit eis nomina Boanerges, quod est Filii tonitrui; ¹⁸et Andream et Philippum et Bartholomaeum et Matthaeum et Thomam et Iacobum Alphaei et Thaddaeum et Simonem Cananaeum ¹⁹et Iudam Iscarioth, qui et tradidit illum. ²⁰Et venit ad domum; et convenit iterum turba, ita ut non possent neque panem manducare. ²¹Et cum audissent sui, exierunt tenere eum; dicebant enim: "In furorem versus est." ²²Et scribae, qui

16. At this point, before the word "Simon" the sentence "He formed the group of the twelve" occurs in many manuscripts (it is similar to the phrase "he appointed twelve" in v. 14) but it is not included in the New Vulgate. The repetition of the same expression and the article in *"the* twelve" show the importance of the establishment of the Apostolic College.

20-21. Some of his relatives, whose outlook was too human, regarded Jesus' total commitment to apostolate as excessive : the only explanation, they thought, was that he was out of his mind. On reading these words of the Gospel, we cannot help being moved, realizing what Jesus did for love of us : people even thought him mad. Many saints, following Christ's example, have been taken for madmen—but they were mad with love, mad with love for Jesus Christ.

22-23. Even Jesus' miracles were misunderstood by these scribes, who accuse him of being a tool of the prince of devils, Beelzebul. This name may be connected with Beelzebub (which spelling is given in some codexes), the name of a god of the Philistine city of Eqron (Accaron), which means "god of the flies." But it is more likely that the prince of devils is called Beelzebul,

"He is possessed by Beelzebul, and by the prince of demons he casts out the demons." [23]And he called them to him, and said to them in parables, "How can Satan cast out Satan? [24]If a kingdom is divided against itself, that kingdom cannot stand. [25]And if a house is divided against itself, that house will not be able to stand. [26]And if Satan has risen up against himself and is divided, he cannot stand, but is coming to an end. [27]But no one can enter a strong man's house and plunder his goods, unless he first binds the strong man; then indeed he may plunder his house.

Sin against the Holy Spirit

Lk 12:10
1 Jn 5:16

[28]Truly, I say to you, all sins will be forgiven the sons of

---

ab Hierosolymis descenderant, dicebant: "Beelzebul habet" et: "In principe daemonum eicit daemonia." [23]Et convocatis eis, in parabolis dicebat illis: "Quomodo potest Satanas Satanam eicere? [24]Et si regnum in se dividatur, non potest stare regnum illud; [25]et si domus in semetipsam dispertiatur, non poterit domus illa stare. [26]Et si Satanas consurrexit in semetipsum et dispertitus est, non potest stare, sed finem habet. [27]Nemo autem potest in domum fortis ingressus vasa eius diripere, nisi prius fortem alliget; et tunc domum eius diripiet. [28]Amen dico vobis: Omnia dimittentur filiis hominum peccata et

---

which means "god of excrement" : "excrement" is the word the Jews used to describe pagan sacrifices. Whether Beelzebub or Beelzebul, in the last analysis it refers to him to whom these sacrifices were offered, the devil (1 Cor 10:20). He is the same mysterious but real person whom Jesus calls Satan, which means "the enemy", whose dominion over the world Christ has come to wrest from him (1 Cor 15:24-28; Col 1:13f) in an unceasing struggle (Mt 4:1-10; Jn 16:11). These names show us that the devil really exists : he is a real person who has at his beck and call others of his kind (Mk 5:9).

24-27. Our Lord invites the Pharisees, who are blind and obstinate, to think along these lines : if someone expels the devil this means that he is stronger than the devil : once more we are exhorted to recognize in Jesus the God of strength, the God who uses his power to free man from enslavement to the devil. Satan's dominion has come to an end : the prince of this world is about to be cast out. Jesus' victory over the power of darkness, which is completed by his death and resurrection, shows that the light has already entered the world, as our Lord himself told us: "Now is the judgment of this world, now shall the ruler of this world be cast out; and I, when I am lifted up from the earth, will draw all men to myself" (Jn 12:31-32).

28-30. Jesus has just worked a miracle but the scribes refuse to recognize it "for they had said 'He has an unclean spirit'" (v. 30). They do not want to

men, and whatever blasphemies they utter; [29]but whoever blasphemes against the Holy Spirit never has forgiveness, but is guilty of an eternal sin"—[30]for they had said, "He has an unclean spirit."

Mk 3:22

The true kinsmen of Jesus

[31]And his mother and his brethren came; and standing outside they went to him and called him. [32]And a crowd was sitting about him: and they said to him, "Your mother and your brethren[1] are outside, asking for you." [33]And he replied, "Who are my mother and my brethren?" [34]And

Mt 12:46-50
Lk 8:19-21

---

blasphemiae, quibus blasphemaverint; [29]qui autem blasphemaverit in Spiritum Sanctum non habet remissionem in aeternum, sed reus est aeterni delicti." [30]Quoniam dicebant: "Spiritum immundum habet." [31]Et venit mater eius et fratres eius et foris stantes miserunt ad eum vocantes eum. [32]Et sedebat circa eum turba, et dicunt ei: "Ecce mater tua et fratres tui et sorores tuae foris quaerunt te." [33]Et respondens eis ait: "Quae est mater mea et fratres mei?" [34]Et circumspiciens eos, qui in circuitu eius sedebant, ait: "Ecce mater mea et fratres

---

admit that God is the author of the miracle. In this attitude lies the special gravity of blasphemy against the Holy Spirit—attributing to the prince of evil, to Satan, the good works performed by God himself. Anyone acting in this way will become like the sick person who has so lost confidence in the doctor that he rejects him as if an enemy and regards as poison the medicine that can save his life. That is why our Lord says that he who blasphemes against the Holy Spirit will not be forgiven : not because God cannot forgive all sins, but because that person, in his blindness towards God, rejects Jesus Christ, his teaching and his miracles, and despises the graces of the Holy Spirit as if they were designed to trap him (cf. *St Pius V Catechism*, II, 5, 19; St Thomas Aquinas, *Summa theologiae*, II-II, q. 14, a. 3). Cf. note on Mt 12:31-32.

31-35. In Aramaic, the language used by the Jews, the word "brethren" is a broad term indicating kinship : nephews, first cousins and relatives in general are called 'brethren' (for further explanation cf. note on Mk 6:1-3). "Jesus did not say this to disown his mother, but to show that she is worthy of honour not only on account of having given birth to Jesus, but also because she has all the virtues" (Theophylact, *Enarratio in Evangelium Marci, in loc.*).

Therefore, the Church reminds us that the Blessed Virgin "in the course of her Son's preaching received the words whereby, in extolling a kingdom beyond the concerns and ties of flesh and blood, he declared blessed those who heard and kept the word of God as she was faithfully doing" (Vatican II, *Lumen gentium*, 58).

Our Lord, then, is also telling us that if we follow him we will share his life more intimately than if we were a member of his family. St Thomas explains

looking around on those who sat about him, he said, "Here are my mother and my brethren! [35]Whoever does the will of God is my brother, and sister, and mother."

4

PARABLES OF THE KINGDOM OF GOD

Parable of the sower. The meaning of the parables

Mt 13:1-23
Lk 8:4-15

[1]Again he began to teach beside the sea. And a very large

---

mei. [35]Qui enim fecerit voluntatem Dei, hic frater meus et soror mea et mater est."

[1]Et iterum coepit docere ad mare. Et congregatur ad eum turba plurima, ita ut in navem ascendens sederet in mari, et omnis turba circa mare super terram

---

this by saying that Christ "had an eternal generation and a generation in time, and gave preference to the former. Those who do the will of the Father reach him by heavenly generation [. . .]. Everyone who does the will of the Father, that is to say, who obeys him, is a brother or sister of Christ, because he is like him who fulfilled the will of his Father. But he who not only obeys but converts others, begets Christ in them, and thus becomes like the Mother of Christ" (*Commentary on St Matthew*, 12, 49-50).

1-34. Parables are a special method of preaching used by Jesus. By means of them he gradually unfolds before his listeners the mysteries of the Kingdom of God. Cf. note on Mt 13:3. Chapter 4 of St Mark, although much shorter, is the equivalent of chapter 13 of St Matthew and chapter 8:4-18 of St Luke, which is the shortest synoptic account of the Kingdom parables.

1-9. The ordinary Christian, who seeks holiness in his ordinary work, must be moved to find how often our Lord uses in his parables examples taken from work situations : "In his parables on the Kingdom of God, Jesus Christ constantly refers to human work: that of the shepherd (e.g. Jn 10:1-6), the farmer (cf. Mk 12:1-12), the doctor (cf. Lk 4:32), the sower (cf. Mk 4:1-9), the householder (cf. Mt 13:52), the servant (cf. Mt 24:25; Lk 12:42-48), the steward (cf. Lk 16:1-8), the fisherman (cf. Mt 13:47-50), the merchant (cf. Mt 13:45-46), the labourer (cf. Mt 20:1-16). He also speaks of the various forms of women's work (cf. Mt 13:33; Lk 15:8-9). He compares the apostolate to the manual work of harvesters (cf. Mt 9:37; Jn 4:35-38) or fishermen (cf. Mt 4:19). He refers to the work of scholars too (cf. Mt 13:52)" (John Paul II, *Laborem exercens*, 26).

---

[1]Other ancient authorities add *and your sisters*

crowd gathered about him, so that he got into a boat and sat in it on the sea; and the whole crowd was beside the sea on the land. 2And he taught them many things in parables, and in his teachings he said to them: 3"Listen! A sower went out to sow. 4And as he sowed, some seed fell along the path, and the birds came and devoured it. 5Other seed fell on rocky ground, where it had not much soil, and immediately it sprang up, since it had no depth of soil; 6and when the sun rose it was scorched, and since it had no root it withered away. 7Other seed fell among thorns and the thorns grew up and choked it, and it yielded no grain. 8And other seeds fell into good soil and brought forth grain, growing up and increasing and yielding thirtyfold and sixtyfold and a hundredfold." 9And he said, "He who has ears to hear, let him hear."

---

erant. 2Et docebat eos in parabolis multa et dicebat illis in doctrina sua. 3"Audite. Ecce exiit seminans ad seminandum. 4Et factum est dum seminat, aliud cecidit circa viam, et venerunt volucres et comederunt illud. 5Aliud cecidit super petrosa, ubi non habebat terram multam, et statim exortum est, quoniam non habebat altitudinem terrae; 6et quando exortus est sol, exaestuavit et, eo quod non haberet radicem, exaruit. 7Et aliud cecidit in spinas, et ascenderunt spinae et suffocaverunt illud, et fructum non dedit. 8Et alia ceciderunt in terram bonam et dabant fructum: ascendebant et crescebant et afferebant unum triginta et unum sexaginta et unum centum." 9Et dicebat: "Qui habet aures audiendi,

---

3-9. With the parable of the sower Jesus wants to move his listeners to open their hearts generously to the word of God and put it into practice (cf. Lk 11:28). God expects the same docility also from each of us : "It is a vivid scene. The divine sower is also sowing his seed today. The work of salvation is still going on, and our Lord wants us to share that work. He wants Christians to open to his love all the paths of the earth. He invites us to spread the divine message, by both teaching and example, to the farthest corners of the earth [. . .]. If we look around, if we take a look at the world, which we love because it is God's handiwork, we will find that the parable holds true. The word of Jesus Christ is fruitful, it stirs many souls to dedication and fidelity. The life and conduct of those who serve God have changed history. Even many of those who do not know our Lord are motivated, perhaps unconsciously, by ideals which derive from Christianity.

"We can also see that some of the seed falls on barren ground or among thorns and thistles; some hearts close themselves to the light of faith. Ideals of peace, reconciliation and brotherhood are widely accepted and proclaimed, but all too often the facts belie them. Some people are futilely bent on smothering God's voice. To drown it out they use brute force or a method which is more

¹⁰And when he was alone, those who were about him with the twelve asked him concerning the parables. ¹¹And

1 Cor 5:12

he said to them, "To you has been given the secret of the

Is 6:9-10
Jn 12:40
Acts 28:26

kingdom of God, but for those outside everything is in parables; ¹²so that they may indeed see but not perceive,

---

audiat". ¹⁰Et cum esset singularis, interrogaverunt eum hi, qui circa eum erant cum Duodecim, parabolas. ¹¹Et dicebat eis: "Vobis datum est mysterium regni Dei; illis autem, qui foris sunt, in parabolis omnia fiunt, ¹²*ut videntes videant*

---

subtle but perhaps more cruel because it drugs the spirit—indifference" (J. Escrivá, *Christ is passing by*, 150).

The parable of the sower also shows us the wonderful economy of divine Providence, which distributes various graces among men but gives each person enough to reach salvation : "There was then in the eternal providence an incomparable privilege for the queen of queens, Mother of fair Love, and most singularly all perfect. There were also for certain others some special favours. But after this the sovereign goodness poured an abundance of graces and benedictions over the whole race of mankind and upon the angels; [. . .] every one received his portion as of seed which falls not only upon the good ground but upon the highway, amongst thorns, and upon rocks, that all might be inexcusable before the Redeemer, if they employ not this most abundant redemption for their salvation" (St Francis de Sales, *Treatise on the Love of God*, book 2, chap. 7).

11-12. The Kingdom of God is a mystery. If the Twelve know it, it is simply because the mercy of God has revealed it to them, not because they are better able, by themselves, to understand the meaning of the parables.

Jesus' use of parables had many advantages : firstly, because typically the human mind grasps concepts by first working on sense-information : in his teaching Christ often clothes spiritual things in corporal images. Secondly, Sacred Scripture is written for everyone, as St Paul says : "I am under obligation . . . both to the wise and to the foolish" (Rom 1:4) : this meant it made sense for him to put forward even the deepest truths by using comparisons—so that people could more easily grasp what he meant (cf. St Thomas Aquinas, *Summa theologiae* I, q.1, a.9).

The disciples are distinguished here from "those outside" (v. 11)—an expression which Jews applied to Gentiles, and which Jesus here applies to those Jews who do not want to understand the signs which he performs (cf. Lk 12:41).

Later on, our Lord does give his disciples even more exact instruction about the content of the parables. But, since the Jews do not want to accept the signs he performs, in them are fulfilled the words of the prophet Isaiah (6:9-10). The parables, which were an expression of our Lord's mercy, were the occasion for his condemning incredulous Jews, whose sins he cannot forgive because they do not wish to see or listen or be converted.

and may indeed hear but not understand; lest they should turn again, and be forgiven." ¹³And he said to them, "Do you not understand this parable? How then will you understand all the parables? ¹⁴The sower sows the word. ¹⁵And these are the ones along the path, where the word is sown; when they hear, Satan immediately comes and takes away the word which is sown in them. ¹⁶And these in like manner are the ones sown upon rocky ground, who, when they hear the word, immediaitely receive it with joy; ¹⁷and they have no root in themselves, but endure for a while; then, when tribulation or persecution arises on account of the word, immediately they fall away.ᵐ ¹⁸And others are the ones sown among thorns; they are those who hear the word, ¹⁹but the cares of the world, and the delight in riches, and the desire for other things, enter in and choke the word, and it proves unfruitful. ²⁰But those that were sown upon the good soil are the ones who hear the word and accept it and bear fruit, thirtyfold and sixtyfold and a hundredfold."

Mk 10:23-24

---

et non videant, et audientes audiant et non intellegant, ne quando convertantur, et dimittatur eis." ¹³Et ait illis: "Nescitis parabolam hanc, et quomodo omnes parabolas cognoscetis? ¹⁴Qui seminat, verbum seminat. ¹⁵Hi autem sunt, qui circa viam, ubi seminatur verbum: et cum audierint, confestim venit Satanas et aufert verbum, quod seminatum est in eos. ¹⁶Et hi sunt, qui super petrosa seminantur: qui cum audierint verbum, statim cum gaudio accipiunt illud ¹⁷et non habent radicem in se, sed temporales sunt; deinde orta tribulatione vel persecutione propter verbum, confestim scandalizantur. ¹⁸Et alii sunt, qui in spinis seminantur: hi sunt, qui verbum audierunt, ¹⁹et aerumnae saeculi et deceptio divitiarum et circa reliqua concupiscentiae introeuntes suffocant verbum, et sine fructu efficitur. ²⁰Et hi sunt, qui super terram bonam seminati

---

17. "They fall away" : they are "scandalized" : the word "scandal" originally refers to a stone or obstacle which could easily cause one to trip. Here, in the language of morality, it is used to refer to anything which leads others to commit sin (cf. note on Mt 18:1-7). The word is also applied in a broader sense to anything which could be an occasion of sin—e.g. sorrow and tribulation. In this passage, falling away or being scandalized means being demoralized, stumbling, giving in and falling. If a person maliciously professes to be shocked by a good action, he is guilty of "pharisaical" scandal : that is what St Paul means when he says that the cross of Christ was a stumbling-block to Jews, who refused to grasp that the saving plans of God were to be effected through pain and sacrifice (cf. 1 Cor. 1:23; cf. also Mk 14:27; Mt 16:23).

ᵐOr *stumble*

Parables of the lamp and the measure

^{Lk 8:16-18}
^{Mt 5:15}

^{Mt 10:26}
^{Lk 8:17}
^{Mt 7:2}
^{Lk 6:38}

^{Mt 13:12}
^{Lk 8:18}

²¹And he said to them, "Is a lamp brought in to be put under a bushel, or under a bed, and not on a stand? ²²For there is nothing hid, except to be made manifest; nor is anything secret, except to come to light. ²³If any man has ears to hear, let him hear." ²⁴And he said to them, "Take heed what you hear; the measure you give will be the measure you get, and still more will be given you. ²⁵For to him who has will more be given; and from him who has not, even what he has will be taken away."

sunt: qui audiunt verbum et suscipiunt et fructificant unum triginta et unum sexaginta et unum centum." ²¹Et dicebat illis: "Numquid venit lucerna, ut sub modio ponatur aut sub lecto? Nonne ut super candelabrum ponatur? ²²Non enim est aliquid absconditum, nisi ut manifestetur, nec factum est occultum, nisi ut in palam veniat. ²³Si quis habet aures audiendi, audiat." ²⁴Et dicebat illis: "Videte quid audiatis. In qua mensura mensi fueritis, remetietur vobis et adicietur vobis. ²⁵Qui enim habet, dabitur illi; et qui non habet, etiam quod

21. A "bushel" was a container used for measuring cereals and vegetables. It held a little over eight litres (two gallons).

22. This parable contains a double teaching. Firstly, it says that Christ's doctrine should not be kept hidden; rather, it must be preached throughout the whole world. We find the same idea elsewhere in the Gospels : "what you hear whispered, proclaim it upon the house-tops" (Mt 10:27); "Go into all the world and preach the Gospel to the whole of creation . . ." (Mk 16:15). The other teaching is that the Kingdom which Christ proclaims has such ability to penetrate all hearts that, at the end of time, when Jesus comes again, not a single human action, in favour or against Christ, will not become public and manifest. Cf. Mt 25:31-46.

24-25. Our Lord never gets tired of asking the Apostles, the seed which will produce the Church, to listen carefully to the teaching he is giving : they are receiving a treasure for which they will be held to account. "To him who has will more be given . . ." : he who responds to grace will be given more grace and will yield more and more fruit; but he who does not will become more and more impoverished (cf. Mt 25:14-30). Therefore, there is no limit to the development of the theological virtues : "If you say 'Enough,' you are already dead" (St Augustine, *Sermon* 51). A soul who wants to make progress in the interior life will pray along these lines : "Lord, may I have due measure in everything, except in Love" (J. Escrivá, *The Way*, 427).

26-29. Farmers spare no effort to prepare the ground for the sowing; but

Parables of the seed and of the mustard seed

²⁶And he said, "The kingdom of God is as if a man should scatter seed upon the ground, ²⁷and should sleep and rise night and day, and the seed should sprout and grow, he knows not how. ²⁸The earth produces of itself, first the blade, then the ear, then the full grain in the ear. ²⁹But when the grain is ripe, at once he puts in the sickle, because the harvest has come."

³⁰And he said, "With what can we compare the kingdom

Jas 5:7

Joel 3:13
Rev 14:15

Mt 13:31-32, 34
Lk 13:18-19

---

habet, auferetur ab illo." ²⁶Et dicebat: "Sic est regnum Dei, quemadmodum si homo iaciat sementem in terram ²⁷et dormiat et exsurgat nocte ac die, et semen germinet et increscat, dum nescit ille. ²⁸Ultro terra fructificat primum herbam, deinde spicam, deinde plenum frumentum in spica. ²⁹Et cum se produxerit fructus, statim mittit falcem, quoniam adest messis." ³⁰Et dicebat: "Quomodo

---

once the grain is sown there is nothing more they can do until the harvest; the grain develops by itself. Our Lord uses this comparison to describe the inner strength that causes the Kingdom of God on earth to grow up to the day of harvest (cf. Joel 3:13 and Rev. 14:15), that is, the day of the Last Judgment.

Jesus is telling his disciples about the Church : the preaching of the Gospel, the generously sown seed, will unfailingly yield its fruit, independently of who sows or who reaps : it is God who gives the growth (cf. 1 Cor 3:5-9). It will all happen "he knows not how", without men being fully aware of it.

The Kingdom of God also refers to the action of grace in each soul : God silently works a transformation in us, whether we sleep or watch, causing resolutions to take shape in our soul— resolutions to be faithful, to surrender ourselves, to respond to grace—until we reach "mature manhood" (cf. Eph 4:13). Even though it is necessary for man to make this effort the real initiative lies with God, "because it is the Holy Spirit who, with his inspirations, gives a supernatural tone to our thoughts, desires and actions. It is he who leads us to receive Christ's teaching and to assimilate it in a profound way. It is he who gives us the light by which we perceive our personal calling and the strength to carry out all that God expects of us. If we are docile to the Holy Spirit, the image of Christ will be found more and more fully in us, and we will be brought closer every day to God the Father. 'For whoever are led by the Spirit of God, they are the children of God' (Rom 8:14)" (J. Escrivá, *Christ is passing by*, 135).

30-32. The main meaning of this parable has to do with the contrast between the great and the small. The seed of the Kingdom of God on earth is something very tiny to begin with (Lk 12:32; Acts 1:15); but it will grow to be a big tree. Thus we see how the small initial group of disciples grows in the early years of the Church (cf Acts 2:47; 6:7; 12:24), and spreads down the centuries and becomes a great multitude "which no man could number" (Rev 7:9).

of God, or what parable shall we use for it? [31]It is like a grain of mustard seed, which, when sown upon the ground,

Dan 4:9, 18
Ezek 17:23; 31:6

is the smallest of all the seeds on earth; [32]yet when it is sown it grows up and becomes the greatest of all shrubs, and puts forth large branches, so that the birds of the air can make nests in its shade."

The end of the parables discourse

[33]With many such parables he spoke the word to them, as they were able to hear it; [34]he did not speak to them without a parable, but privately to his own disciples he explained everything.

MIRACLES AND ACTIVITY IN GALILEE

The calming of the storm

Mt 8:18, 23-27
Lk 8:22-25

[35]On that day, when evening had come, he said to them, "Let us go across to the other side." [36]And leaving the crowd, they took him with them just as he was, in the boat.

---

assimilabimus regnum Dei aut in qua parabola ponemus illud? [31]Sicut granum sinapis, quod cum seminatum fuerit in terra, minus est omnibus seminibus, quae sunt in terra; [32]et cum seminatum fuerit, ascendit et fit maius omnibus holeribus et facit ramos magnos, ita ut possint sub umbra eius aves caeli habitare." [33]Et talibus multis parabolis loquebatur eis verbum, prout poterant audire; [34]sine parabola autem non loquebatur eis. Seorsum autem discipulis suis disserebat omnia. [35]Et ait illis illa die, cum sero esset factum: "Transeamus contra." [36]Et dimittentes turbam, assumunt eum, ut erat in navi; et aliae naves erant cum illo.

This mysterious growth which our Lord refers to also occurs in each soul: "the Kingdom of God is in the midst of you" (Lk 17:21); we can see a prediction of this in the words of Psalm 92:12 : "The righteous grow like a cedar in Lebanon." To allow the mercy of God to exalt us, to make us grow, we must make ourselves small, humble (Ezek 17:22-24; Lk 18:9-14).

35-41. The episode of the calming of the storm, the memory of which must often have helped the Apostles regain their serenity in the midst of struggles and difficulties, also helps us never lose the supernatural way of looking at things : a Christian's life is like a ship: "As a vessel on the sea is exposed to a thousand dangers—pirates, quicksands, hidden rocks, tempests—so man in this life, is encompassed with perils, arising from the temptations of hell, from the

And other boats were with him. [37]And a great storm of wind
arose, and the waves beat into the boat, so that the boat was
already filling. [38]But he was in the stern, asleep on the
cushion; and they woke him and said to him, "Teacher, do
you not care if we perish?" [39]And he awoke and rebuked
the wind, and said to the sea, "Peace! Be still!" And the
wind ceased, and there was a great calm. [40]He said to them,
"Why are you afraid? Have you no faith?" [41]And they were
filled with awe, and said to one another, "Who then is this,
that even wind and sea obey him?"

Jn 1:3ff

Ps 89:10;
107:23-32

Mk 1:27

---

[37]Et exoritur procella magna venti, et fluctus se mittebant in navem, ita ut iam
impleretur navis. [38]Et erat ipse in puppi supra cervical dormiens; et excitant
eum et dicunt ei: "Magister, non ad te pertinet quia perimus?" [39]Et exsurgens
comminatus est vento et dixit mari: "Tace, obmutesce." Et cessavit ventus, et
facta est tranquillitas magna. [40]Et ait illis: "Quid timidi estis? Necdum habetis
fidem?" [41]Et timuerunt magno timore et dicebant ad alterutrum: "Quis putas
est iste, quia et ventus et mare oboediunt ei?"

---

occasions of sin, from the scandals or bad counsels of men, from human respect,
and, above all from the passions of corrupt nature [. . .]. This should not cause
him to lose confidence. Rather [. . .] when you find yourself assaulted by a
violent passion [. . .] take whatever steps you can to avoid the occasions [of sin]
and place your reliance on God [. . .]: when the tempest is violent, the pilot
never takes his eyes from the light which guides him to port. In like manner,
we should keep our eyes always turned to God, who alone can deliver us from
the many dangers to which we are exposed" (St Augustine, *Sermon* 51; for the
fourth Sunday after Epiphany).

5

The Gerasene demoniac

Mt 8:28-34
Lk 8:26-40

[1]They came to the other side of the sea, to the country of the Gerasenes.[n] [2]And when he had come out of the boat, there met him out of the tombs a man with an unclean spirit, [3]who lived among the tombs; and no one could bind him any more, even with a chain; [4]for he had often been bound with fetters and chains, but the chains he wrenched apart, and the fetters he broke in pieces; and no one had the strength to subdue him. [5]Night and day among the tombs and on the mountains he was always crying out, and bruising himself with stones. [6]And when he saw Jesus from afar, he ran and worshipped him; [7]and crying out with a loud voice, he said, "What have you to do with me, Jesus, Son of the Most High God? I adjure you by God, do not torment me." [8]For he had said to him, "Come out of the man, you unclean spirit!" [9]And Jesus[o] asked him, "What is your name?" He replied, "My name is Legion; for we are many." [10]And he begged him eagerly not to send them out

Mk 1:24
Jas 2:19

[1]Et venerunt trans fretum maris in regionem Gerasenorum. [2]Et exeunte eo de navi, statim occurrit ei de monumentis homo in spiritu immundo, [3]qui domicilium habebat in monumentis; et neque catenis iam quisquam eum poterat ligare, [4]quoniam saepe compedibus et catenis vinctus dirupisset catenas et compedes comminuisset, et nemo poterat eum domare; [5]et semper nocte ac die in monumentis et in montibus erat clamans et concidens se lapidibus. [6]Et videns Iesum a longe cucurrit et adoravit eum [7]et clamans voce magna dicit: "Quid mihi et tibi, Iesu fili Dei Altissimi? Adiuro te per Deum, ne me torqueas." [8]Dicebat enim illi: "Exi, spiritus immunde, ab homine." [9]Et interrogabat eum: "Quod tibi nomen est?" Et dicit ei: "Legio nomen mihi est, quia multi sumus." [10]Et deprecabatur eum multum, ne se expelleret extra regionem. [11]Erat autem

1-20. The inhabitants of Gerasa were mostly pagans, as one can gather from the fact that there was such a huge herd of swine there (which must have belonged to a number of different people). Jews were forbidden to raise pigs or eat pork (Lev 11:7).

This miracle emphasizes, once more, the existence of the devil and his influence over men's lives : if God permits it, the devil can harm not only humans but also animals. When Christ allows the demons to enter the swine, the malice of the demons becomes obvious : they are tormented at not being

[n]Other ancient authorities read *Gergesenes*, some, *Gadarenes*
[o]Greek *he*

of the country. ¹¹Now a great herd of swine was feeding there on the hillside; ¹²and they begged him, "Send us to the swine, let us enter them." ¹³So he gave them leave. And the unclean spirits came out, and entered the swine; and the herd, numbering about two thousand, rushed down the steep bank into the sea, and were drowned in the sea.

¹⁴The herdsmen fled, and told it in the city and the country. And people came to see what it was that had happened. ¹⁵And they came to Jesus, and saw the demoniac sitting there, clothed and in his right mind, the man who had had the legion; and they were afraid. ¹⁶And those who had seen it told what had happened to the demoniac and to the swine. ¹⁷And they began to beg Jesusᴾ to depart from their neighbourhood. ¹⁸And as he was getting into the boat,

---

ibi circa montem grex porcorum magnus pascens; ¹²et deprecati sunt eum dicentes: "Mitte nos in porcos, ut in eos introeamus." ¹³Et concessit eis. Et exeuntes spiritus immundi introierunt in porcos. Et magno impetu grex ruit per praecipitium in mare, ad duo milia, et suffocabantur in mari. ¹⁴Qui autem pascebant eos, fugerunt et nuntiaverunt in civitatem et in agros; et egressi sunt videre quid esset facti. ¹⁵Et veniunt ad Iesum; et vident illum, qui a daemonio vexabatur, sedentem, vestitum et sanae mentis, eum qui legionem habuerat, et timuerunt. ¹⁶Et qui viderant, narraverunt illis qualiter factum esset ei, qui daemonium habuerat, et de porcis. ¹⁷Et rogare eum coeperunt, ut discederet a finibus eorum. ¹⁸Cumque ascenderet navem, qui daemonio vexatus fuerat,

---

able to do men harm and therefore they ask Christ to let them, at least, inflict themselves on animals. This he does, in order to show that they would have the same effect on men as they have on these swine, if God did not prevent them.

Clearly it was not Jesus' intention to punish the owners of the swine by the loss of the herd : since they were pagans they were not subject to the precepts of the Jewish law. Rather, the death of the swine is visible proof that the demon has gone out of the possessed man.

Jesus permitted the loss of some material goods because these were of infinitely less value than the spiritual good involved in the cure of the possessed man. Cf. note on Mt 8:28-34.

15-20. Notice the different attitudes to Jesus Christ : the Gerasenes beg him to go away; the man freed from the devil wants to stay with him and follow him. The inhabitants of Gerasa have had our Lord near them, they have seen his divine powers, but they are very self-centred : all they can think about is the material damage they have suffered through the loss of the herd; they do not realize the marvel Jesus has worked. Christ has invited them and offered

ᴾGreek *him*

the man who had been possessed with demons begged him that he might be with him. ¹⁹But he refused, and said to him, "Go home to your friends, and tell them how much the Lord has done for you, and how he has had mercy on you." ²⁰And he went away and began to proclaim in the Decapolis how much Jesus had done for him; and all men marvelled.

Mk 7:31

Jairus' daughter is restored to life. The curing of the woman with a hemorrhage

Mt 9:18-26
Lk 8:41-56

²¹And when Jesus had crossed again in the boat to the other side, a great crowd gathered about him; and he was

---

deprecabatur eum, ut esset cum illo. ¹⁹Et non admisit eum, sed ait illi: "Vade in domum tuam ad tuos, et annuntia illis quanta tibi Dominus fecerit et misertus sit tui." ²⁰Et abiit et coepit praedicare in Decapoli quanta sibi fecisset Iesus, et omnes mirabantur. ²¹Et cum transcendisset Iesus in navi rursus trans fretum,

---

them his grace but they do not respond : they reject him. The man who has been cured wants to follow Jesus with the rest of his disciples but our Lord refuses; instead he gives him a task which shows Christ's unlimited compassion for all men, even for those who reject him : the man is to stay in Gerasa and proclaim to the whole neighbourhood what the Lord has done for him. Perhaps they will think again and realize who he is who has visited them, and escape from the sins their greed has led them to commit. These two attitudes are to be found whenever Christ passes by—as are Jesus' mercy and continuous offer of grace: our Lord does not want the death of the sinner but rather that he should turn from his way and live (cf. Ezek 18:23).

20. The "Decapolis" or "country of the ten cities", among the more famous of which are Damascus, Philadelphia, Scythopolis, Gadara, Pella and Gerasa. The region was located to the east of the lake of Gennesaret and was inhabited mainly by pagans of Greek and Syrian origin. This territory came under the Roman governor of Syria.

21-43. Both Jairus and the woman with the flow of blood give us an example of faith in Christ's omnipotence, for only a miracle can cure Jairus' daughter, who is on her death-bed, and heal this lady, who has done everything humanly possible to get better. Similarly, the Christian should always expect God to help him overcome the obstacles in the way of his sanctification. Normally, God's help comes to us in an unspectacular way, but we should not doubt that, if it is necessary for our salvation, God will again work miracles. However, we should bear in mind that what the Lord expects of us is that we should every day fulfil his will.

22. At the head of each synagogue was the archisynagogist, whose function it was to organize the meetings of the synagogue on sabbaths and holy days, to

beside the sea. ²²Then came one of the rulers of the synagogue, Jairus by name, and seeing him, he fell at his feet,
²³and besought him, saying, "My little daughter is at the
point of death. Come and lay your hands on her, so that she
may be made well, and live." ²⁴And he went with him.

And a great crowd followed him and thronged about him.
²⁵And there was a woman who had a flow of blood for
twelve years, ²⁶and who had suffered much under many
physicians, and had spent all that she had, and was no better
but rather grew worse. ²⁷She had heard the reports about
Jesus, and came up behind him in the crowd and touched
his garment. ²⁸For she said, "If I touch even his garments,
I shall be made well." ²⁹And immediately the hemorrhage
ceased; and she felt in her body that she was healed of her
disease. ³⁰And Jesus, perceiving in himself that power had

Mk 7:32

Mk 6:56

Lk 6:19

---

convenit turba multa ad illum, et erat circa mare. ²²Et venit quidam de archi-
synagogis nomine Iairus et videns eum procidit ad pedes eius ²³et deprecatur
eum multum dicens: "Filiola mea in extremis est; veni, impone manus super
eam, ut salva sit et vivat." ²⁴Et abiit cum illo. Et sequebatur eum turba multa et
comprimebant illum. ²⁵Et mulier, quae erat in profluvio sanguinis annis duodecim ²⁶et fuerat multa perpessa a compluribus medicis et erogaverat omnia
sua nec quidquam profecerat sed magis deterius habebat, ²⁷cum audisset de
Iesu, venit in turba retro et tetigit vestimentum eius; ²⁸dicebat enim: "Si vel
vestimenta eius tetigero, salva ero." ²⁹Et confestim siccatus est fons sanguinis
eius, et sensit corpore quod sanata esset a plaga. ³⁰Et statim Iesus cognoscens

---

lead the prayers and hymns and to indicate who should explain the Sacred
Scripture. He was assisted in his task by a council and also had an aide who
looked after the material side of things.

25. This woman suffered from an illness which implied legal impurity (Lev
15:25ff). Medical attention had failed to cure her; on the contrary, as the Gospel
puts it so realistically, she was worse than ever. In addition to her physical
suffering—which had gone on for twelve years—she suffered the shame of
feeling unclean according to the Law. The Jews not only regarded a woman in
this position as being impure : everything she touched became unclean as well.
Therefore, in order not to be noticed by the people, the woman came up to Jesus
from behind and, out of delicacy, touched only his garment. Her faith is
enriched by her expression of humility : she is conscious of being unworthy to
touch our Lord. "She touched the hem of his garment, she approached him in
a spirit of faith, she believed, and she realized that she was cured [. . .]. So we
too, if we wish to be saved, should reach out in faith to touch the garment of
Christ" (St Ambrose, *Expositio Evangelii sec. Lucam*, VI, 56 and 58).

gone forth from him, immediately turned about in the crowd, and said, "Who touched my garments?" [31]And his disciples said to him, "You see the crowd pressing around you, and yet you say, 'Who touched me?'" [32]And he looked around to see who had done it. [33]But the woman, knowing what had been done to her, came in fear and trembling and fell down before him, and told him the whole truth. [34]And he said to her, "Daughter, your faith has made you well; go in peace, and be healed of your disease."

[35]While he was speaking, there came from the ruler's house some who said, "Your daughter is dead. Why trouble the Teacher any further?" [36]But ignoring[q] what they said, Jesus said to the ruler of the synagogue, "Do not fear, only believe." [37]And he allowed no one to follow him except Peter and James and John the son of James. [38]When they

Lk 7:50

---

in semetipso virtutem, quae exierat de eo, conversus ad turbam aiebat: "Quis tetigit vestimenta mea?" [31]Et dicebant ei discipuli sui: "Vides turbam comprimentem te et dicis: 'Quis me tetigit?' " [32]Et circumspiciebat videre eam, quae hoc fecerat. [33]Mulier autem timens et tremens, sciens quod factum esset in se, venit et procidit ante eum et dixit ei omnem veritatem. [34]Ille autem dixit ei: "Filia, fides tua te salvam fecit. Vade in pace et esto sana a plaga tua." [35]Adhuc eo loquente, veniunt ab archisynagogo dicentes: "Filia tua mortua est; quid ultra vexas magistrum?" [36]Iesus autem, verbo, quod dicebatur, audito, ait archisynagogo: "Noli timere; tantummodo crede!" [37]Et non admisit quemquam sequi se nisi Petrum et Iacobum et Ioannem fratrem Iacobi. [38]Et veniunt ad

---

30. In all that crowd pressing around him only this woman actually touched Jesus—and she touched him not only with her hand but with the faith she bore in her heart. St Augustine comments : "She touches him, the people crowd him. Is her touching not a sign of her belief?" (*In Ioann. Evang.*, 26, 3). We need contact with Jesus. We have been given no other means under heaven by which to be saved (cf. Acts 4:12). When we receive Jesus in the Holy Eucharist, we obtain this physical contact through the sacramental species. We too need to enliven our faith if these encounters with our Lord are to redound to our salvation (cf. Mt 13:58).

37. Jesus did not want more than these three Apostles to be present : three was the number of witnesses laid down by the Law (Deut 19:15). "For Jesus, being humble, never acted in an ostentatious way" (Theophilactus, *Enarratio in Evangelium Marci, in loc.*). Besides these were the three disciples closest to Jesus : later, only they will be with him at the Transfiguration (cf. 9:2) and at his agony in the Garden of Gethsemane (cf. 14:33).

[q]Or *Overhearing*. Other ancient authorities read *hearing*

came to the house of the ruler of the synagogue, he saw a tumult, and people weeping and wailing loudly. ³⁹And when he had entered, he said to them, "Why do you make a tumult and weep? The child is not dead but sleeping." ⁴⁰And they laughed at him. But he put them all outside, and took the child's father and mother and those who were with him, and went in where the child was. ⁴¹Taking her by the hand he said to her, "Talitha cumi"; which means, "Little

Jn 11:11
Act 20:10

Acts 9:40

Lk 7:14

domum archisynagogi; et videt tumultum et flentes et eiulantes multum, ³⁹et ingressus ait eis: "Quid turbamini et ploratis? Puella non est mortua, sed dormit." ⁴⁰Et irridebant eum. Ipse vero, eiectis omnibus, assumit patrem puellae et matrem et, qui secum erant, et ingreditur, ubi erat puella; ⁴¹et tenens manum puellae ait illi: "Talitha qum!"—quod est interpretatum: "Puella, tibi dico, surge!"—⁴²Et confestim surrexit puella et ambulabat; erat enim annorum

39. Jesus' words are in contrast with those of the ruler's servants; they say: "Your daughter is dead"; whereas he says: "She is not dead but sleeping". "To men's eyes she was dead, she could not be awoken; in God's eyes she was sleeping, for her soul was alive and was subject to God's power, and her body was resting, awaiting the resurrection. Hence the custom which arose among Christians of referring to the dead, whom we know will rise again, as those who are asleep" (St Bede, *In Marci Evangelium expositio, in loc.*). What Jesus says shows us that, for God, death is only a kind of sleep, for he can awaken anyone from the dead whenever he wishes. The same happens with the death and resurrection of Lazarus. Jesus says : "Our friend Lazarus has fallen asleep, but I go to awaken him out of sleep." And, when the disciples think that it is ordinary sleep he is referring to, our Lord tells them plainly : "Lazarus is dead" (cf. Jn 11:11ff).

40-42. Like all the Gospel miracles the raising of the daughter of Jairus demonstrates Christ's divinity. Only God can work miracles; sometimes he does them in a direct way, sometimes by using created things as a medium. The exclusively divine character of miracles— expecially the miracle of raising the dead—is noticed in the Old Testament : "The Lord wills and brings to life; he brings down to Sheol and raises up" (1 Sam 2:6), because he has "power over life and death" (Wis 16:13). And also in the Old Testament God uses men to raise the dead to life : the prophet Elijah revives the son of the widow of Sarepta by "crying to the Lord" (cf. 1 Kings 17:21), and Elisha prevails on him to raise the son of the Shunammite (2 Kings 4:33).

In the same way, in the New Testament the Apostles do not act by their own power but by that of Jesus to whom they first offer fervent prayer : Peter restores to life a Christian woman of Joppa named Tabitha (Acts 9:36ff); and Paul, in Troas, brings Eutychus back to life after he falls from a high window (Acts 20:7ff). Jesus does not refer to any superior power; his authority is sovereign :

Mk 1:44

girl, I say to you arise." [42]And immediately the girl got up and walked; for she was twelve years old. And immediately they were overcome with amazement. [43]And he strictly charged them that no one should know this, and told them to give her something to eat.

6

No prophet is honoured in his own country

Mt 13:53-58
Lk 4:16-30
Jn 7:15

[1]He went away from there and came to his own country; and his disciples followed him. [2]And on the sabbath he began to teach in the synagogue; and many who heard him were astonished, saying, "Where did this man get all this? What is the wisdom given to him? What mighty works are

Lk 2:34f

wrought by his hands! [3]Is not this the carpenter, the son of

---

duodecim. Et obstupuerunt continuo stupore magno. [43]Et praecepit illis vehementer, ut nemo id sciret, et dixit dari illi manducare.

[1]Et egressus est inde et venit in patriam suam, et sequuntur illum discipuli sui. [2]Et facto sabbato, coepit in synagoga docere; et multi audientes admirabantur dicentes: "Unde huic haec, et quae est sapientia, quae data est illi, et virtutes tales, quae per manus eius efficiuntur? [3]Nonne iste est faber, filius Mariae et frater Iacobi et Iosetis et Iudae et Simonis? Et nonne sorores eius hic nobiscum

---

all he has to do is give the order and the daughter of Jairus is brought back to life; this shows that he is God.

1-3. Jesus is here described by his occupation and by the fact that he is the son of Mary. Does this indicate that St Joseph is dead already? We do not know, but it is likely. In any event, the description is worth underlining : in the Gospels of St Matthew and St Luke we are told of the virginal conception of Jesus. St Mark's Gospel does not deal with our Lord's infancy, but there may be an allusion here to his virginal conception and birth, in his being described as "the son of Mary."

"Joseph, caring for the child as he had been commanded, made Jesus a craftsman, transmitting his own professional skill to him. So the neighbours of Nazareth will call Jesus both *faber* and *fabri filius* : the craftsman and the son of the craftsman" (J. Escrivá, *Christ is passing by*, 55). This message of the Gospel reminds us that our vocation to work is not marginal to God's plans.

"The truth that by means of work man participates in the activity of God

Mary and brother of James and Joses and Judah and Simon, and are not his sisters here with us?" And they took offence[r] at him. [4]And Jesus said to them, "A prophet is not without honour, except in his own country, and among his own kin,

Jn 4:44

---

sunt?" Et scandalizabantur in illo. [4]Et dicebat eis Iesus: "Non est propheta sine honore nisi in patria sua et in cognatione sua et in domo sua." [5]Et non poterat

---

himself, his Creator, was *given particular prominence by Jesus Christ*—the Jesus at whom many of his first listeners in Nazareth 'were astonished, saying, "Where did this man get all this? What is the wisdom given to him? . . . Is not this the carpenter?"' (Mk 6:23). For Jesus not only proclaimed but first and foremost fulfilled by his deeds the 'gospel', the word of eternal Wisdom, that had been entrusted to him. Therefore this was also 'the gospel of work', because *he who proclaimed it was himself a man of work*, a craftsman like Joseph of Nazareth (cf. Mt 13:55). And if we do not find in his words a special command to work—but rather on one occasion a prohibition against too much anxiety about work and life (Mt 6:25-34)—at the same time the eloquence of the life of Christ is unequivocal: he belongs to the 'working world', he has appreciation and respect for human work. It can indeed be said that *he looks with love upon human work* and the different forms that it takes, seeing in each one of these forms a particular facet of man's likeness with God, the Creator and Father" (John Paul II, *Laborem exercens*, 26).

St Mark mentions by name a number of brothers of Jesus, and refers in general to his sisters. But the word "brother" does not necessarly mean son of the same parents. It can also indicate other degrees of relationship—cousins, nephews etc. Thus in Genesis 13:8 and 14:14 and 16 Lot is called the brother of Abraham (translated as "kinsman" in RSV), whereas we know that he was Abraham's nephew, the son of Abraham's brother Haran. The same is true of Laban, who is called the brother of Jacob (Genesis 29:15) although he was his mother's brother (Gen 29:15); there are other instances : cf. 1 Chronicles 23:21-22, etc. This confusion is due to the poverty of Hebrew and Aramaic language : in the absence of distinct terms, the same word, brother, is used to designate different degrees of relationship.

From other Gospel passages we know that James and Joses, who are mentioned here, were sons of Mary of Clophas (Jn 19:25). We know less about Judas and Simon : it seems that they are the apostles Simon the Cananaean (Mt 10:4) and Judas the son of James (Lk 6:16), the author of the Catholic Epistle, in which he describes himself as "brother" of James. In any event, although James, Simon and Judas are referred to as brothers of Jesus, it is nowhere said they were "sons of Mary"—which would have been the natural thing if they had been our Lord's brothers in the strict sense. Jesus always appears as an only son : to the people of Nazareth, he is "the son of Mary" (Mt 13:55). When he was dying Jesus entrusted his mother to St John (cf. Jn 19:26-27), which shows

---

[r]Or *stumbled*

and in his own house." [5]And he could do no mighty work there, except that he laid his hands upon a few sick people and healed them. [6]And he marvelled because of their unbelief.

JESUS JOURNEYS WITH HIS APOSTLES

And he went about among the villages teaching.

The mission of the Twelve

Mt 10:1, 9-15
Lk 9:1-6; 10:1

[7]And he called to him the twelve, and began to send them out two by two, and gave them authority over the unclean spirits. [8]He charged them to take nothing for their journey except a staff; no bread, no bag, no money in their belts; [9]but to wear sandals and not put on two tunics. [10]And he

---

ibi virtutem ullam facere, nisi paucos infirmos impositis manibus curavit; [6]et mirabatur propter incredulitatem eorum. Et circumibat castella in circuitu docens. [7]Et convocat Duodecim et coepit eos mittere binos et dabat illis potestatem in spiritus immundos; [8]et pracepit eis, ne quid tollerent in via nisi virgam tantum: non panem, non peram neque in zona aes, [9]sed ut calcearentur

---

that Mary had no other children. To this is added the constant belief of the Church, which regards Mary as the ever-virgin : "a perfect virgin before, while, and forever after she gave birth" (Paul IV, *Cum quorumdam*).

5-6. Jesus worked no miracles here : not because he was unable to do so, but as punishment for the unbelief of the townspeople. God wants man to use the grace offered him, so that, by cooperating with grace, he become disposed to receive further graces. As St Augustine neatly puts it, "He who made you without your own self, will not justify you without yourself" (*Sermon* 169).

7. Cf. note on Mk 1:27; 3:14-19.

8-9. Jesus requires them to be free of any form of attachment if they are to preach the Gospel. A disciple, who has the mission of bringing the Kingdom of God to souls through preaching, should not rely on human resources but on God's Providence. Whatever he does need in order to live with dignity as a herald of the Gospel, he must obtain from those who benefit from his preaching, for the labourer deserves his maintenance (cf. Mt 10:10).

"The preacher should so trust in God that he is convinced that he will have everything he needs to support life, even if he cannot himself obtain it; for he should not neglect eternal things through worrying about temporal things" (St

said to them, "Where you enter a house, stay there until you leave the place. [11]And if any place will not receive you and they refuse to hear you, when you leave, shake off the dust that is on your feet for a testimony against them." [12]So they went out and preached that men should repent. [13]And they cast out many demons, and anointed with oil many that were sick and healed them.

Jas 5:14-15

Opinions about Jesus

[14]King Herod heard of it; for Jesus's[s] name had become

Mt 14:1-12
Lk 9:7-9
3:19-20

---

sandaliis et ne induerentur duabus tunicis. [10]Et dicebat eis: "Quocumque introieritis in domum, illic manete, donec exeatis inde. [11]Et quicumque locus non receperit vos nec audierint vos, exeuntes inde excutite pulverem de pedibus vestris in testimonium illis." [12]Et exeuntes praedicaverunt, ut paenitentiam agerent; [13]et daemonia multa eiciebant et ungebant oleo multos aegrotos et sanabant. [14]Et audivit Herodes rex; manifestum enim factum est nomen eius. Et dicebant: "Ioannes Baptista resurrexit a mortuis, et propterea inoperantur virtutes in illo." [15]Alii autem dicebant: "Elias est." Alii vero dicebant: "Propheta

---

Bede, *In Marci Evangelium expositio, in loc.*). "By these instructions the Lord did not mean that the evangelists should not seek to live in any other way than by depending on what was offered them by those to whom they preached the Gospel; otherwise this very Apostle [St Paul] would have acted contrary to this precept when he earned his living by the labours of his own hands" (St Augustine, *De consensu Evangelistarum*, II, 30).

13. St Mark is the only evangelist who speaks of anointing the sick with oil. Oil was often used for treating wounds (cf. Is 1:6; Lk 10:34), and the Apostles also use it for the miraculous cure of physical illnesses by virtue of the power given them by Jesus. Hence the use of oil as the matter of the sacrament of the Anointing of the Sick, which cures wounds of the soul and even, if appropriate, bodily diseases. As the Council of Trent teaches—*Doctrina de sacramento extremae unctionis*, chap. 1—in this verse of St Mark there can be seen a "hint" of the sacrament of Anointing of the Sick, which our Lord will institute and which later on "is recommended and promulgated to the faithful by St James the Apostle" (cf. Jas 5:14ff).

14. Following popular custom, St Mark called Herod "king", but in strict legal terminology he was only tetrarch, which is the way St Matthew (14:1) and St Luke (9:7) describe him, that is, a governor of certain consequence. The Herod referred to here was Herod Antipas, the son of Herod the Great who was king of the Jews at the time of Jesus' birth. Cf. note on Mt 2:1.

[s]Greek *his*

known. Some[t] said, "John the baptizer has been raised from the dead; that is why these powers are at work with him." [15]But others said, "It is Elijah." And others said, "It is a prophet, like one of the prophets of old." [16]But when Herod heard of it, he said, "John, whom I beheaded, has been raised."

John the Baptist beheaded

[17]For Herod had sent and seized John, and bound him in prison for the sake of Herodias, his brother Philip's wife; because he had married her. [18]For John said to Herod, "It is not lawful for you to have your brother's wife." [19]And Herodias had a grudge against him, and wanted to kill him. But she could not, [20]For Herod feared John, knowing that he was a righteous and holy man, and kept him safe. When

Lev 18:16

Acts 24:24

---

est, quasi unus ex prophetis." [16]Quo audito, Herodes aiebat: 'Quem ego decollavi Ioannem, hic resurrexit!" [17]Ipse enim Herodes misit ac tenuit Ioannem et vinxit eum in carcere propter Herodiadem uxorem Philippi fratris sui, quia duxerat eam. [18]Dicebat enim Ioannes Herodi: "Non licet tibi habere uxorem fratris tui." [19]Herodias autem insidiabatur illi et volebat occidere eum nec poterat: [20]Herodes enim metuebat Ioannem, sciens eum virum iustum et sanctum, et custodiebat eum, et audito eo multum haesitabat et libenter eum audiebat. [21]Et cum dies opportunus accidisset, quo Herodes natali suo cenam

---

16-29. It is interesting that the extensive account of the death of John the Baptist is inserted here in the Gospel narrative. The reason is St John the Baptist's special relevance in the history of salvation : he is the Precursor, entrusted with the task of preparing the way for the Messiah. Besides, John the Baptist had a great reputation among the people : they believed him to be a prophet (Mk 11:32); some even thought he was the Messiah (Lk 3:15; Jn 1:20); and they flocked to him from many places (Mk 1:5). Jesus himself said: "Among those born of women there has risen no one greater than John the Baptist" (Mt 11:11). Later, the apostle St John will speak of him in the Gospel: "There was a man sent from God, whose name was John" (Jn 1:6); but the sacred text points out that, despite this, he was not the light, but rather the witness to the light (Jn 1:6-8). More correctly, he was the lamp carrying the light (Jn 5:35). We are told here that he was a righteous man and preached to everyone what had to be preached : he had a word for people at large, for publicans, for soldiers (Lk 3:10-14); for Pharisees and Sadducees (Mt 3:7-12); for King Herod himself (Mk 6:18-20). This humble, upright and austere man paid with his life for the witness he bore to Jesus the Messiah (Jn 1:29 and 36-37).

[t]Other ancient authorities read *he*

he heard him, he was much perplexed; and yet he heard him gladly. 21But an opportunity came when Herod on his birthday gave a banquet for his courtiers and officers and the leading men of Galilee. 22For when Herodias' daughter came in and danced, she pleased Herod and his guests; and the king said to the girl, "Ask me for whatever you wish, and I will grant it." 23And he said to her, "Whatever you ask me, I will give you, even half of my kingdom." 24And she went out, and said to her mother, "What shall I ask?" And she said, "The head of John the baptizer." 25And she came in immediately with haste to the king, and asked, saying, "I want you to give me at once the head of John the Baptizer on a platter." 26And the King was exceedingly sorry; but because of his oath and his guests he did not want to break his word to her. 27And immediately the king sent a soldier of the guard and gave orders to bring his head. He went and beheaded him in the prison, 28And brought his head on a platter, and gave it to the girl; and the girl gave it to her mother. 29When his disciples heard of it, they came and took his body, and laid it in a tomb.

Esther 5:3, 6

Lk 18:23

---

fecit principibus suis et tribunis et primis Galilaeae, 22cumque introisset filia ipsius Herodiadis et saltasset, placuit Herodi simulque recumbentibus. Rex ait puellae: "Pete a me, quod vis, et dabo tibi." 23Et iuravit illi multum: "Quidquid petieris a me, dabo tibi, usque ad dimidium regni mei." 24Quae cum exisset, dixit matri suae: "Quid petam?" At illa dixit: "Caput Ioannis Baptistae." 25Cumque introisset statim cum festinatione ad regem, petivit dicens: "Volo ut protinus des mihi in disco caput Ioannis Baptistae." 26Et contristatus rex propter iusiurandum et propter recumbentes noluit eam decipere 27et statim misso spiculatore rex praecepit afferri caput eius. Et abiens decollavit eum in carcere 28et attulit caput eius in disco et dedit illud puellae et puella dedit illud matri suae. 29Quo audito discipuli eius venerunt et tulerunt corpus eius et posuerunt

---

26. Oaths and promises immoral in content should never be made, and, if made, should never be kept. This is the teaching of the Church, which is summed up in the *St Pius X Catechism*, 383, in the following way : "Are we obliged to keep oaths we have sworn to do unjust and unlawful things? Not only are we not obliged : we sin by making such oaths, for they are prohibited by the Law of God or of the Church."

30-31. We can see here the intensity of Jesus' public ministry. Such was his dedication to souls that St Mark twice mentions that the disciples did not even have time to eat (cf. Mk 3:20). A Christian should be ready to sacrifice his time and even his rest in the service of the Gospel. This attitude of

The Apostles return

Lk 9:10; 10:17
Mk 2:2

Mt 14:13-21
Lk 9:11-17
Jn 6:1-13

³⁰The apostles returned to Jesus, and told him all that they had done and taught. ³¹And he said to them, "Come away by yourselves to a lonely place, and rest a while." For many were coming and going, and they had no leisure even to eat. ³²And they went away in the boat to a lonely place by themselves.

First miracle of the loaves

Num 27:17
Ezek 34:5
Mt 9:36

Mk 8:1-9

³³Now many saw them going, and knew them, and they ran there on foot from the towns, and got there ahead of them. ³⁴As he landed he saw a great throng, and he had compassion on them, because they were like sheep without a shepherd; and he began to teach them many things. ³⁵And when it grew late, his disciples came to him and said, "This is a lonely place, and the hour is now late; ³⁶send them

---

illud in monumento. ³⁰Et convenientes apostoli ad Iesum renuntiaverunt illi omnia, quae egerant et docuerant. ³¹Et ait illis: "Venite vos ipsi seorsum in desertum locum et requiescite pusillum." Erant enim, qui veniebant et redibant multi, et nec manducandi spatium habebant. ³²Et abierunt in navi in desertum locum seorsum. ³³Et viderunt eos abeuntes et cognoverunt multi, et pedestre de omnibus civitatibus concurrerunt illuc et praevenerunt eos. ³⁴Et exiens vidit multam turbam et misertus est super eos, quia erant sicut oves non habentes pastorem, et coepit docere illos multa. ³⁵Et cum iam hora multa facta esset, accesserunt discipuli eius dicentes: "Desertus est locus hic, et hora iam est

---

availability will lead us to change our plans whenever the good of souls so requires.

But Jesus also teaches us here to have common sense and not to go to such extremes that we physically cannot cope: "The Lord makes his disciples rest, to show those in charge that people who work or preach cannot do so without breaks" (St Bede, *In Marci Evangelium expositio, in loc.*). "He who pledges himself to work for Christ should never have a free moment, because to rest is not to do nothing: it is to relax in activities which demand less effort" (J. Escrivá, *The Way*, 357).

34. Our Lord had planned a period of rest, for himself and his disciples, from the pressures of the apostolate (Mk 6:31-32). And he has to change his plans because so many people come, eager to hear him speak. Not only is he not annoyed with them : he feels compassion on seeing their spiritual need. "My people are destroyed for lack of knowledge" (Hos 4:6). They need instruction and our Lord wants to meet this need by preaching to them. "Jesus is moved by hunger and sorrow, but what moves him most is ignorance" (J. Escrivá *Christ is passing by*, 109).

away, to go into the country and villages round about and buy themselves something to eat." ³⁷But he answered them, "You give them something to eat." And they said to him, "Shall we go and buy two hundred denarii[u] worth of bread, and give it to them to eat?" ³⁸And he said to them, "How many loaves have you? Go and see." And when they had found out, they said, "Five, and two fish." ³⁹Then he commanded them all to sit down by companies upon the green grass. ⁴⁰So they sat down in groups, by hundreds and by fifties. ⁴¹And taking the five loaves and the two fish he looked up to heaven, and blessed, and broke the loaves, and gave them to the disciples to set before the people; and he

Mk 7:34

---

multa; ³⁶dimitte illos, ut euntes in villas et vicos in circuitu emant sibi, quod manducent." ³⁷Respondens autem ait illis: "Date illis vos manducare." Et dicunt ei: "Euntes emamus denariis ducentis panes et dabimus eis manducare?" ³⁸Et dicit eis: "Quot panes habetis? Ite, videte." Et cum cognovissent, dicunt: "Quinque et duos pisces." ³⁹Et praecepit illis, ut accumbere facerent omnes secundum contubernia super viride fenum. ⁴⁰Et discubuerunt secundum areas per centenos et per quinquagenos. ⁴¹Et acceptis quinque panibus et duobus piscibus, intuens in caelum benedixit et fregit panes et dabat discipulis suis, ut ponerent ante eos; et duos pisces divisit omnibus. ⁴²Et manducaverunt omnes

---

37. A denarius was what an artisan earned for a normal day's work. The disciples must, therefore, have thought it little less than impossible to fulfil the Master's command, because they would not have had this much money.

41. This miracle is a figure of the Holy Eucharist: Christ performed it shortly before promising that sacrament (cf. Jn 6:1ff), and the Fathers have always so interpreted it. In this miracle Jesus shows his supernatural power and his love for men—the same power and love as make it possible for Christ's one and only body to be present in the eucharistic species to nourish the faithful down the centuries. In the words of the sequence composed by St Thomas Aquinas for the Mass of Corpus Christi : "Sumit unus, sumunt mille, quantum isti, tantum ille, nec sumptus consumitur" (Be one or be a thousand fed, they eat alike that living bread which, still received, ne'er wastes away).

This gesture of our Lord—looking up to heaven—is recalled in the Roman canon of the Mass : "Et elevatis oculis in caelum, ad Te Deum Patrem suum omnipotentem" (and looking up to heaven, to you, his almighty Father). At this point in the Mass we are preparing to be present at a miracle greater than that of the multiplication of the loaves—the changing of bread into his own body, offered as food for all men.

[u]The denarius was a day's wage for a labourer

divided the two fish among them all. [42]And they all ate and were satisfied. [43]And they took up twelve baskets full of broken pieces and of the fish. [44]And those who ate the loaves were five thousand men.

Jesus walks on water

Mt 14:22-36
Jn 6:15-21

[45]Immediately he made his disciples get into the boat and go before him to the other side, to Bethsaida, while he dismissed the crowd. [46]And after he had taken leave of them, he went into the hills to pray. [47]And when evening came the boat was out on the sea, and he was alone on the land. [48]And he saw that they were distressed in rowing, for

Ps 77:20
Job 9:8
Is 43:16

---

et saturati sunt; [43]et sustulerunt fragmenta duodecim cophinos plenos, et de piscibus. [44]Et erant, qui manducaverunt panes, quinque milia virorum. [45]Et statim coegit discipulos suos ascendere navem, ut praecederent trans fretum ad Bethsaidam, dum ipse dimitteret populum. [46]Et cum dimisisset eos, abiit in montem orare. [47]Et cum sero factum esset, erat navis in medio mari, et ipse solus in terra. [48]Et videns eos laborantes in remigando, erat enim ventus contrarius eis, circa quartam vigiliam noctis venit ad eos ambulans super mare

---

42. Christ wanted the left-overs to be collected (cf. Jn 6:12) to teach us not to waste things God gives us, and also to have them as a tangible proof of the miracle.

The collecting of the left-overs is a way of showing us the value of little things done out of love for God—orderliness, cleanliness, finishing things completely. It also reminds the sensitive believer of the extreme care that must be taken of the eucharistic species. Also, the generous scale of the miracle is an expression of the largesse of the messianic times. The Fathers recall that Moses distributed the manna for each to eat as much as he needed but some left part of it for the next day and it bred worms (Ex 16:16-20). Elijah gave the widow just enough to meet her needs (1 Kings 17:13-16). Jesus, on the other hand, gives generously and abundantly.

48. The Romans divided the night into four parts or watches, whose length varied depending on the season. St Mark (13:35) gives the popular names for these watches: evening, midnight, cockcrow, morning. Therefore, it is towards dawn that Jesus comes to the disciples.

He wishes to teach us that even when we are in very pressurised and difficult situations, he is nearby, ready to help us; but he expects us to make an effort, to strengthen our hope and temper our resolve (cf. note on Mt 14:24-33); as an early Greek commentator puts it : "The Lord allowed his disciples to enter danger to make them suffer, and he did not immediately come to their aid: he left them in peril for the whole night, to teach them to be patient and not to be

the wind was against them. And about the fourth watch of the night he came to them, walking on the sea. He meant to pass by them, [49]but when they saw him walking on the sea they thought it was a ghost, and cried out; [50]for they all saw him, and were terrified. But immediately he spoke to them and said, "Take heart, it is I; have no fear." [51]And he got into the boat with them and the wind ceased. And they were utterly astounded, [52]for they did not understand about the loaves, but their hearts were hardened.

Mk 4:39

Mk 8:17

Cures at Gennesaret

[53]And when they had crossed over, they came to land at Gennesaret, and moored to the shore. [54]And when they got

---

et volebat praeterire eos. [49]At illi, ut viderunt eum ambulantem super mare, putaverunt phantasma esse et exclamaverunt; [50]omnes enim eum viderunt et conturbati sunt. Statim autem locutus est cum eis et dicit illis: "Confidite, ego sum; nolite timere!" [51]Et ascendit ad illos in navem, et cessavit ventus. Et valde nimis intra se stupebant: [52]non enim intellexerant de panibus, sed erat cor illorum obcaecatum. [53]Et cum transfretassent in terram, pervenerunt Gennesaret et applicuerunt. [54]Cumque egressi essent de navi, continuo cognoverunt

---

accustomed to receiving immediate succour in tribulation" (Theophylact, *Enarratio in Evangelium Marci, in loc.*).

52. The disciples do not yet see Jesus' miracles as signs of his divinity. They witness the multiplication of the loaves and the fish (Mk 6:33-44) and the second multiplication of the loaves (Mk 8:17), but their hearts and minds are still hardened; they fail to grasp the full import of what Jesus is teaching them through his actions—that he is the Son of God. Jesus is patient and understanding with their defects, even when they fail to grasp what he says when he speaks about his own passion (Lk 18:34). Our Lord will give them further miracles and further teaching to enlighten their minds, and, later, he will send the Holy Spirit to teach them all things and remind them of everything he said (cf. Jn 14:26).

St Bede the Venerable comments on this whole episode (Mk 6:45-52) in this way : "In a mystical sense, the disciples' efforts to row against the wind point to the efforts the Holy Church must make against the waves of the enemy world and the outpourings of evil spirits in order to reach the haven of its heavenly home. It is rightly said that the boat was out on the sea and He alone on the land, because the Church has never been so intensely persecuted by the Gentiles that it seemed as if the Redeemer had abandoned it completely. But the Lord sees his disciples struggling, and to sustain them he looks at them compassionately and sometimes frees them from peril by clearly coming to their aid" (*In Marci Evangelium expositio, in loc.*).

out of the boat, immediately the people recognized him, [55]and ran about the whole neighbourhood and began to bring sick people on their pallets to any place where they heard he was. [56]And wherever he came in, in villages, cities, or country, they laid the sick in the market places, and besought him that they might touch even the fringe of his garment; and as many as touched it were made well.

Mk 5:27-28
Acts 5:15
19:11f

7

The traditions of the elders

Mt 15:1-20

Lk 11:38

[1]Now when the Pharisees gathered together to him, with some of the scribes, who had come from Jerusalem, [2]they saw that some of his disciples ate with hands defiled, that is, unwashed. [3](For the Pharisees, and all the Jews, do not

---

eum [55]et percurrentes universam regionem illam coeperunt in grabatis eos, qui se male habebant, circumferre, ubi audiebant eum esse. [56]Et quocumque introibat in vicos aut in civitates vel in villas, in plateis ponebant infirmos, et deprecabantur eum ut vel fimbriam vestimenti eius tangerent; et, quotquot tangebant eum, salvi fiebant.
[1]Et conveniunt ad eum pharisaei et quidam de scribis venientes ab Hierosolymis; [2]et cum vidissent quosdam ex discipulis eius communibus manibus, id est non lotis, manducare panes [3]—pharisaei enim et omnes Iudaei, nisi

---

1-2. Hands were washed not for reasons of hygiene or good manners but because the custom had religious significance : it was a rite of purification. In Exodus 30:17ff the Law of God laid down how priests should wash before offering sacrifice. Jewish tradition had extended this to all Jews before every meal, in an effort to give meals a religious significance, which was reflected in the blessings which marked the start of meals. Ritual purification was a symbol of the moral purity a person should have when approaching God (Ps 24:3ff; 51:4 and 9); but the Pharisees had focussed on the mere external rite. Therefore Jesus restores the genuine meaning of these precepts of the Law, whose purpose is to teach the right way to render homage to God (cf. Jn 4:24).

3-5. We can see clearly from this text that very many of those to whom St Mark's Gospel was first addressed were Christians who had been pagans and were unfamiliar with Jewish customs. The Evangelist explains these customs in some detail, to help them realize the significance of the events and teachings reported in the Gospel story.

eat unless they wash their hands,[v] observing the tradition
of the elders; [4]and when they come from the market place,
they do not eat unless they purify[w] themselves; and there
are many other traditions which they observe, the washing
of cups and pots and vessels of bronze.[x]) [5]And the Pharisees
and the scribes asked him, "Why do your disciples not live[y]
according to the tradition of the elders, but eat with hands
defiled?" [6]And he said to them, "Well did Isaiah prophesy
of you hypocrites, as it is written,

> 'This people honours me with their lips,
> but their heart is far from me;
> [7]in vain do they worship me,
> teaching as doctrines the precepts of men.'

[8]You leave the commandment of God, and hold fast the
tradition of men."

[9]And he said to them, "You have a fine way of rejecting
the commandment of God, in order to keep your tradition!
[10]For Moses said, 'Honour your father and your mother';
and 'He who speaks evil of father or mother, let him surely

Is 29:13

---

pugillo lavent manus, non manducant, tenentes traditionem seniorum; [4]et a foro
nisi baptizentur, non comedunt; et alia multa sunt, quae acceperunt servanda:
baptismata calicum et urceorum et aeramentorum et lectorum —[5]et interrogant
eum pharisaei et scribae: "Quare discipuli tui non ambulant iuxta traditionem
seniorum, sed communibus manibus manducant panem?" [6]At ille dixit eis:
"bene prophetavit Isaias de vobis hypocritis, sicut scriptum est: *'Populus hic
labiis me honorat, cor autem eorum longe est a me; [7]in vanum autem me colunt;
docentes doctrinas praecepta hominum.*" [8]Relinquentes mandatum Dei tenetis
traditionem hominum." [9]Et dicebat illis: "Bene irritum facitis praeceptum Dei,
ut traditionem vestram servetis. [10]Moyses enim dixit: *'Honora patrem tuum et
matrem tuam'* et: *'Qui maledixerit patri aut matri, morte moriatur'*; [11]vos autem

---

Similarly, Sacred Scripture needs to be preached and taught in a way which
puts it within reach of its hearers. This is why Vatican II teaches that "it is for
the bishops suitably to instruct the faithful [. . .] by giving them translations of
the sacred texts which are equipped with necessary and really adequate explanations. Thus the children of the Church can familiarize themselves safely and
profitably with the Sacred Scriptures, and become steeped in their spirit" (*Dei
Verbum*, 25).

---

[v]One Greek work is of uncertain meaning and is not translated
[w]Other ancient authorities read *baptize*
[x]Other ancient authorities add *and beds*
[y]Greek *walk*

Ex 20:12; 21:17
Deut 5:16
Lev 20:9

die'; ¹¹but you say, 'If a man tells his father or his mother, What you would have gained from me is Corban' (that is, given to God)ᶻ—¹²then you no longer permit him to do anything for his father or mother, ¹³thus making void the word of God through your tradition which you hand on. And many such things you do."

What defiles a man

Acts 10:14-15

¹⁴And he called the people to meet him, and said to them, "Hear me, all of you, and understand: ¹⁵there is nothing outside a man which by going into him can defile him; but the things that come out of a man are what defile him."ᵃ ¹⁷And when he had entered the house, and left the people, his disciples asked him about the parable. ¹⁸And he said to them, "Then are you also without understanding? Do you not see that whatever goes into a man from outside cannot

Col 2:16, 21-22

defile him, ¹⁹since it enters, not his heart but his stomach,

dicitis: 'Si dixerit homo patri aut matri: Corban, quod est donum, quodcumque ex me tibi profuerit', ¹²ultra non permittitis ei facere quidquam patri aut matri ¹³rescindentes verbum Dei per traditionem vestram, quam tradidistis; et similia huiusmodi multa facitis." ¹⁴Et advocata iterum turba, dicebat illis: "Audite me omnes et intellegite: ¹⁵Nihil est extra hominem introiens in eum, quod possit eum coinquinare; sed quae de homine procedunt, illa sunt, quae coinquinant hominem."⁽¹⁶⁾ ¹⁷Et cum introisset in domum a turba, interrogabant eum discipuli eius parabolam. ¹⁸Et ait illis: "Sic et vos imprudentes estis? Non intellegitis quia omne extrinsecus introiens in hominem non potest eum coinquinare, ¹⁹quia non introit in cor eius sed in ventrem et in secessum exit?", purgans omnes

11-13. For an explanation of this text cf. note on Mt 15:5-6. Jesus Christ, who is the authentic interpreter of the Law, because as God he is its author, explains the scope of the fourth commandment and points out the mistakes made by Jewish casuistry. There were many other occasions when he corrected mistaken interpretations offered by the Jewish teachers : for example, when he recalls that phrase of the Old Testament, "Go and learn what this means, I desire mercy, and not sacrifice" (Hos 6:6; 1 Sam 15:22; Sir 35:4) in Mt 9:13.

15. Some important codexes add here : "If any man has ears to hear, let him hear," which would form v.16.

18-19. We know from Tradition that St Mark was the interpreter of St Peter and that, in writing his Gospel under the inspiration of the Holy Spirit, he gathered up the Roman catechesis of the head of the Apostles.

ᶻOr an offering
ᵃOther ancient authorities add verse 16, If any man has ears to hear, let him hear

and so passes on?"[b] (Thus he declared all foods clean.)
[20]And he said, "What comes out of a man is what defiles a
man. [21]For from within, out of the heart of man, come evil
thoughts, fornication, theft, murder, adultery, [22]coveting,   Mt 6:23; 20:15
wickedness, deceit, licentiousness, envy, slander, pride,
foolishness. [23]All these evil things come from within, and
they defile a man.

The curing of the Syrophoenician woman

[24]And from there he arose and went away to the region   Mt 15:21-28
of Tyre and Sidon.[c] And he entered a house, and would not

---

escas. [20]Dicebat autem: "Quod de homine exit, illud coinquinat hominem; [21]ab
intus enim de corde hominum cogitationes malae procedunt, fornicationes,
furta, homicidia, [22]adulteria, avaritiae, nequitiae, dolus, impudicitia, oculus
malus, blasphemia, superbia, stultitia: [23]omnia haec mala ab intus procedunt et
coinquinant hominem." [24]Inde autem surgens abiit in fines Tyri et Sidonis. Et

---

The vision which St Peter had in Joppa (Acts 10:10-16) showed him the full
depth of what Jesus teaches here about food. When he returns to Jerusalem, St
Peter himself tells us this in his report on the conversion of Cornelius : "I
remembered the word of the Lord" (Acts 11:16). The now non-obligatory
character of such prescriptions laid down by God in the Old Testament (cf. Lev
11) would have been something St Peter included in his preaching. For
interpretation of this text cf. also note on Mt 15:10-20.

20-23. "In order to help us understand divine things, Scripture uses the
expression 'heart' in its full human meaning, as the summary and source,
expression and ultimate basis, of one's thoughts, words and actions" (J. Escrivá
Christ is passing by, 164).

The goodness or malice, the moral quality, of our actions does not depend
on their spontaneous, instinctive character. The Lord himself tells us that sinful
actions can come from the human heart.

We can understand how this can happen if we realize that, after original sin,
man "was changed for the worse" in both body and soul and was, therefore,
prone to evil (cf. Council of Trent, *De peccato originali*). Our Lord here restores
morality in all its purity and intensity.

24. The region of Tyre and Sidon is nowadays the southern part of Lebanon
—Phoenicia in ancient times. The distance from the lake of Gennesaret to the
frontier of Tyre and Sidon is not more than 50 kms (30 miles). Jesus withdrew
from Palestine to avoid persecution by the Jewish authorities and to give the
Apostles more intensive training.

[b]Or *is evacuated*
[c]Other ancient authorities omit *and Sidon*

have any one know it; yet he could not be hid. ^{25}But immediately a woman, whose little daughter was possessed by an unclean spirit, heard of him, and came and fell down at his feet. ^{26}Now the woman was a Greek, a Syrophoenician by birth. And she begged him to cast the demon out of her daughter. ^{27}And he said to her, "Let the children first be fed, for it is not right to take the children's bread and throw it to the dogs." ^{28}But she answered him, "Yes, Lord; yet even the dogs under the table eat the children's crumbs." ^{29}And he said to her, "For this saying you may go your way; the demon has left your daughter." ^{30}And she went home, and found the child lying in bed, and the demon gone.

Mt 15:29-31

The curing of a deaf man

Mk 5:23

Mk 8:23

^{31}Then he returned from the region of Tyre, and went through Sidon to the Sea of Galilee, through the region of the Decapolis. ^{32}And they brought him a man who was deaf and had an impediment in his speech; and they besought him to lay his hand upon him. ^{33}And taking him aside from

---

ingressus domum neminem voluit scire et non potuit latere. ^{25}Sed statim ut audivit de eo mulier, cuius habebat filia spiritum immundum, veniens procidit ad pedes eius. ^{26}Erat autem mulier Graeca, Syrophoenissa genere. Et rogabat eum, ut daemonium eiceret de filia eius. ^{27}Et dicebat illi: "Sine prius saturari filios; non est enim bonum sumere panem filiorum et mittere catellis." ^{28}At illa respondit et dicit ei: "Domine, etiam catelli sub mensa comedunt de micis puerorum." ^{29}Et ait illi: "Propter hunc sermonem vade; exiit daemonium de filia tua." ^{30}Et cum abisset domum suam, invenit puellam iacentem supra lectum et daemonium exisse. ^{31}Et iterum exiens de finibus Tyri venit per Sidonem ad mare Galilaeae inter medios fines Decapoleos. ^{32}Et adducunt ei surdum et mutum et deprecantur eum, ut imponat illi manum. ^{33}Et apprehendens eum de

---

27. Our Lord actually uses the diminutive—"little dogs" to refer to the Gentiles—thereby softening a scornful expression which Jews used. On the episode of the Canaanite woman cf. notes on parallel passages, Mt 15:21-28.

32-33. Sacred Scripture quite often shows the laying on of hands as a gesture indicating the transfer of power or blessing (cf. Gen 48:14ff; 2 Kings 5:11; Lk 13:13). Everyone knows that saliva can help heal minor cuts. In the language of Revelation fingers symbolized powerful divine action (cf. Ex 8:19; Ps 8:4; Lk 11:20). So Jesus uses signs which suit in some way the effect he wants to achieve, though we can see from the text that the effect—the instantaneous cure of the deaf and dumb man—far exceeds the sign used.

the multitude privately, he put his fingers into his ears, and
he spat and touched his tongue; [34]and looking up to heaven,
he sighed, and said to him, "Ephphatha," that is, "Be
opened." [35]And his ears were opened, his tongue was
released, and he spoke plainly. [36]And he charged them to
tell no one; but the more he charged them, the more
zealously they proclaimed it. [37]And they were astonished
beyond measure, saying, "He has done all things well; he
even makes the deaf hear and the dumb speak."

Jn 11:41

Mk 1:43-45

Is 35:5

8

Second miracle of the loaves

[1]In those days, when again a great crowd had gathered, and
they had nothing to eat, he called his disciples to him, and

Mt 15:32-39

---

turba seorsum misit digitos suos in auriculas eius et expuens tetiget linguam
eius [34]et suspiciens in caelum ingemuit et ait illi: "Effetha", quod est:
"Adaperire." [35]Et statim apertae sunt aures eius, et solutum est vinculum
linguae eius, et loquebatur recte. [36]Et praecepit illis, ne cui dicerent; quanto
autem eis praecipiebat, tanta magis plus praedicabant. [37]Et eo amplius admirabantur dicentes: "Bene omnia fecit, et surdos facit audire et mutos loqui!"
[1]In illis diebus iterum cum turba multa esset, nec haberent, quod manducarent,

In the miracle of the deaf and dumb man we can see a symbol of the way
God acts on souls : for us to believe, God must first open our heart so we can
listen to his word. Then, like the Apostles, we too can proclaim the *magnalia
Dei*, the mighty works of God (cf. Acts 2:11). In the Church's liturgy (cf. the
hymn *Veni Creator*) the Holy Spirit is compared to the finger of the right hand
of God the Father (*Digitus paternae dexterae*). The Consoler produces in our
souls, in the supernatural order, effects comparable to those which Christ
produces in the body of the deaf and dumb man.

1-9. Jesus repeats the miracle of the multiplication of the loaves and the
fish: the first time (Mk 6:33-44) he acted because he saw a huge crowd like
"sheep without a shepherd"; now he takes pity on them because they have been
with him for three days and have nothing to eat.

This miracle shows how Christ rewards people who persevere in following
him : the crowd had been hanging on his words, forgetful of everything else.
We should be like them, attentive and ready to do what he commands, without
any vain concern about the future, for that would amount to distrusting divine
providence.

said to them, [2]"I have compassion on the crowd, because they have been with me now three days, and have nothing to eat; [3]and if I send them away hungry to their homes, they will faint on the way; and some of them have come a long way." [4]And his disciples answered him, "How can one feed these men with bread here in the desert?" [5]And he asked them, "How many loaves have you?" They said, "Seven." [6]And he commanded the crowd to sit down on the ground; and he took the seven loaves, and having given thanks he broke them and gave them to his disciples to set before the people; and they set them before the crowd. [7]And they had a few small fish; and having blessed them, he commanded that these also should be set before them. [8]And they ate, and were satisfied; and they took up the broken pieces left over, seven baskets full. [9]And there were about four thousand people. [10]And he sent them away; and immediately he got into the boat with his disciples, and went to the district of Dalmanutha.[d]

The leaven of the Pharisees

[11]The Pharisees came and began to argue with him,

convocatis discipulis, ait illis: [2]"Misereor super turbam, quia iam triduo sustinent me, nec habent, quod manducent; [3]et si dimisero eos ieiunos in domum suam, deficient in via; et quidam ex eis de longe venerunt." [4]Et responderunt ei discipuli sui: "Unde istos poterit quis hic saturare panibus in solitudine?" [5]Et interrogabat eos: "Quot panes habetis?" Qui dixerunt: "Septem." [6]Et praecipit turbae discumbere supra terram; et accipiens septem panes, gratias agens fregit et dabat discipulis suis, ut apponerent; et apposuerunt turbae, [7]Et habebant pisciculos paucos; et benedicens eos, iussit hos quoque apponi. [8]Et manducaverunt et saturati sunt, et sustulerunt quod superaverat de fragmentis, septem sportas. [9]Erant autem quasi quattuor milia. Et dimisit eos. [10]Et statim ascendens navem cum discipulis suis venit in partes Dalmanutha. [11]Et exierunt pharisaei

10. "Dalmanutha" : this must have been somewhere near the lake of Gennesaret, but it is difficult to localize it more exactly. This is the only time it is mentioned in Sacred Scripture. In the parallel passage in St Matthew (15:39) Magadan (sometimes Magdala) is mentioned.

11-12. Jesus expresses the deep sadness he feels at the hard-heartedness of the Pharisees : they remain blind and unbelieving despite the light shining around them and the wonderful things Christ is doing. If someone rejects the

[d]Other ancient authorities read *Magadan* or *Magdala*

seeking from him a sign from heaven, to test him. [12]And he sighed deeply in his spirit, and said, "Why does this generation seek a sign? Truly, I say to you, no sign shall be given to this generation." [13]And he left them, and getting into the boat again he departed to the other side.

[14]Now they had forgotten to bring bread; and they had only one loaf with them in the boat. [15]And he cautioned

Lk 12:1

---

et coeperunt conquirere cum eo quaerentes ab illo signum de caelo, tentantes eum. [12]Et ingemiscens spiritu suo ait: "Quid generatio ista quaerit signum? Amen dico vobis: Non dabitur generationi isti signum." [13]Et dimittens eos, iterum ascendens, abiit trans fretum. [14]Et obliti sunt sumere panes et nisi unum panem non habebant secum in navi. [15]Et praecipiebat eis dicens: "Videte, cavete

---

miracles God has offered him, it is useless for him to demand new signs, because he asks for them not because he is sincerely seeking the truth but out of ill will : he is trying to tempt God (cf. Lk 16:27-31). Requiring new miracles before one will believe, not accepting those already performed in the history of salvation, amounts to asking God to account for himself before a human tribunal (cf. Rom 2:1-11). Unfortunately, many people do act like this. But God can only be found if we have an open and humble attitude to him. "I have no need of miracles : there are more than enough for me in the Gospel. But I do need to see you fulfilling your duty and responding to grace" (J. Escrivá, *The Way*, 362).

12. The generation to which Jesus refers does not include all the people of his time, but only the Pharisees and their followers (cf. Mk 8:38; 9:19; Mt 11:16), who do not want to see in Jesus' miracles the sign and guarantee of his messianic mission and dignity : they even attribute his miracles to Satan (Mt 12:28).

If they do not accept the signs offered to them, they will be given no other sign of the spectacular kind they seek, for the Kingdom of God does not come noisily (Lk 17:20-21) and even if it did they in their twisted way would manage to misinterpret the event (Lk 16:31). According to Mt 12:38-42 and Lk 11:29-32, they are offered yet another sign—the miracle of Jonah, the sign of the death and resurrection of Christ; but not even this remarkable proof will lead the Pharisees to shed their pride.

15-16. In another Gospel passage—Lk 13:20-21 and Mt 31:33—Jesus uses the simile of the leaven to show the vitality of his teaching. Here "leaven" is used in the sense of bad disposition. In the making of bread, leaven is what causes the dough to rise; the Pharisees' hypocrisy and Herod's dissolute life, stemming from their personal ambition, were the "leaven" which was poisoning from within the "dough" of Israel and which would eventually corrupt it. Jesus seeks to warn his disciples about these dangers, and to have them understand them, saying, "Take heed, beware of the leaven of the Pharisees and the leaven of Herod."e [16]And they discussed

Mk 6:52

it with one another, saying, "We have no bread." [17]And being aware of it, Jesus said to them, "Why do you discuss the fact that you have no bread? Do you not yet perceive or

Jer 5:21
Ezek 12:2

understand? Are your hearts hardened? [18]Having eyes do you not see, and having ears do you not hear? And do you

Mk 6:41-44

not remember? [19]When I broke the five loaves for the five thousand, how many baskets full of broken pieces did you

Mk 8:6-9

take up?" They said to him, "Twelve." [20]"And the seven for the four thousand, how many baskets full of broken pieces did you take up?" And they said to him, "Seven." [21]And he said to them, "Do you not yet understand?"

The curing of a blind man at Bethsaida

Mk 6:56
Mk 7:32-33
Jn 9:6

[22]And they came to Bethsaida. And some people brought to him a blind man, and begged him to touch him. [23]And,

---

a fermento pharisaeorum et fermento Herodis!" [16]Et disputabant ad inviciem, quia panes non haberent. [17]Quo cognito ait illis: "Quid disputatis, quia panes non habetis? Nondum cognoscitis nec intellegitis? Caecatum habetis cor vestrum? [18]*Oculos habentes non videtis, et aures habentes non auditis?* Nec recordamini, [19]quando quinque panes fregi in quinque milia, quot cophinos fragmentorum plenos sustulistis?". Dicunt ei: "Duodecim." [20]"Quando illos septem in quattuor milia, quot sportas plenas fragmentorum tulistis?" Et dicunt ei: "Septem." [21]Et dicebat eis: "Nondum intellegitis?" [22]Et veniunt Bethsaida.

---

that if they are to take in his doctrine they need a pure and simple heart.

But the disciples fail to understand : "They weren't educated; they weren't very bright, if we judge from their reaction to supernatural things. Finding even the most elementary examples and comparisons beyond their reach, they would turn to the Master and ask: 'Explain the parable to us.' When Jesus uses the image of the 'leaven' of the Pharisees, they think that he's reproaching them for not having purchased bread.... These were the disciples called by our Lord. Such stuff is what Christ chose. And they remain just like that until they are filled with the Holy Spirit and thus become pillars of the Church. They are ordinary people, full of defects and shortcomings, more eager to say than to do. Nevertheless, Jesus calls them to be fishers of men, co-redeemers, dispensers of the grace of God" (J. Escrivá, *Christ is passing by*, 2). The same thing can happen to us. Although we may not be very gifted, the Lord calls us, and love of God and docility to his words will cause to grow in our souls unsuspected fruit of holiness and supernatural effectiveness.

23. Cf. note on Mk 7:32-33.

eOther ancient authorities read *the Herodians*

he took the blind man by the hand, and led him out of the
village. And when he had spit on his eyes and laid his hands
upon him, he asked him, "Do you see anything?" 24And he
looked up and said, "I see men; but they look like trees,
walking." 25Then again he laid his hands upon his eyes; and
he looked intently and was restored, and saw everything
clearly. 26And he sent him away to his home, saying, "Do
not even enter the village."

Mk 7:36

Peter's profession of faith

27And Jesus went on with his disciples, to the villages of
Caesarea Philippi; and on the way he asked his disciples,
"Who do men say that I am?" 28And they told him, "John
the Baptist; and others say, Elijah; and others one of the
prophets." 29And he asked them, "But who do you say I

Mt 16:13-28
Lk 9:18-27

Mk 6:15

Jn 6:67-69

Et adducunt ei caecum et rogabant eum, ut illum tangat. 23Et apprehendens
manum caeci eduxit eum extra vicum et exspuens in oculos eius, impositis
manibus ei, interrogabat eum: "Vides aliquid?" 24Et aspiciens dicebat: "Video
homines, quia velut arbores video ambulantes." 25Deinde iterum imposuit
manus super oculos eius; et coepit videre et restitutus est et videbat clare omnia.
26Et misit illum in domum suam dicens: "Nec in vicum introieris." 27Et egressus
est Iesus et discipuli eius in castella Caesareae Philippi; et in via interrogabat
discipulos suos dicens eis: "Quem me dicunt esse homines?" 28Qui responderunt illi dicentes: "Ioannem Baptistam, alii Eliam, alii vero unum de
prophetis." 29Et ipse interrogabat eos: "Vos vero quem me dicitis esse?"

22-25. Normally the cures which Jesus worked were instantaneous; not so
in this case. Why? Because the blind man's faith was very weak, it would seem,
to begin with. Before curing the eyes of his body, Jesus wanted the man's faith
to grow; the more it grew and the more trusting the man became, the more sight
Jesus gave him. In this way Jesus acted in keeping with his usual pattern: not
working miracles unless there was a right predisposition, yet encouraging a
good disposition in the person and giving more grace as he responds to the
grace already given.

God's grace is essential even for desiring holy things : "Give us light, Lord.
Behold, we need it more than the man who was blind from his birth, for he
wished to see the light and could not, whereas nowadays, Lord, no one wishes
to see it. Oh, what a hopeless ill is this! Here, my God, must be manifested thy
power and thy mercy" (St Teresa, *Exclamations of the Soul to God*, 8).

29. Peter's profession of faith is reported here in a shorter form than in Mt
16:18-19. Peter seems to go no further than say that Jesus is the Christ, the
Messiah. Eusebius of Caesarea, in the fourth century, explains the Evangelist's
reserve by the fact that he was the interpreter of St Peter, who omitted from his

Mk 9:9

am?" Peter answered him, "You are the Christ." [30]And he charged them to tell no one about him.

Mk 9:31
10:32-34

Jesus foretells his passion and resurrection. Christian renunciation

[31]And he began to teach them that the Son of man must suffer many things, and be rejected by the elders and the chief priests and the scribes, and be killed, and after three days rise again. [32]And he said this plainly. And Peter took him, and began to rebuke him. [33]But turning and seeing his disciples, he rebuked Peter, and said, "Get behind me, Satan! For you are not on the side of God, but of men."

[34]And he called to him the multitude with his disciples,

Respondens Petrus ait ei: "Tu es Christus." [30]Et comminatus est eis, ne cui dicerent de illo. [31]Et coepit docere illos: "Oportet Filium hominis multa pati et reprobari a senioribus et a summis sacerdotibus et scribis et occidi et post tres dies resurgere"; [32]et palam verbum loquebatur. Et apprehendens eum Petrus coepit increpare eum. [33]Qui conversus et videns discipulos suos comminatus est Petro et dicit: "Vade retro me, Satana, quoniam non sapis, quae Dei sunt, sed quae sunt hominum." [34]Et convocata turba cum discipulis suis, dixit eis:

---

preaching anything which might appear to be self-praise. The Holy Spirit, when inspiring St Mark, wanted the Gospel to reflect the preaching of the prince of the Apostles, leaving it to other evangelists to fill out certain important details to do with the episode of the confession of Peter.

The sketchiness of the narrative still shows Peter's role quite clearly : he is the first to come forward affirming the messiahship of Jesus. Our Lord's question, "But who do you say that I am?", shows what Jesus is asking the Apostles for—not an opinion, more or less favourable, but firm faith. It is St Peter who expresses this faith (cf. note on Mt 16:13-20).

31-33. This is the first occasion when Jesus tells his disciples about the sufferings and death he must undergo. He does it twice more, later on (cf. Mk 9:31 and 10:32). The Apostles are surprised, because they cannot and do not want to understand why the Master should have to suffer and die, much less that he should be so treated "by the elders and the chief priests and the scribes." But Peter, with his usual spontaneity, immediately begins to protest. And Jesus replies to him using the same words as he addressed to the devil when he tempted him (cf. Mt 4:10); he wants to affirm, once again, that his mission is spiritual, not earthly, and that therefore it cannot be understood by using mere human criteria : it is governed by God's designs, which were that Jesus should redeem us through his passion and death. So too, for a Christian, suffering, united with Christ, is also a means of salvation.

34. When Jesus said "If any man would come after me . . .", he was well

and said to them, "If any man would come after me, let him
deny himself and take up his cross and follow me. ³⁵For Mt 10:39

"Si quis vult post me sequi, deneget seipsum et tollat crucem suam et sequatur
me. ³⁵Qui enim voluerit animam suam salvam facere, perdet eam; qui autem

aware that in fulfilling his mission he would be brought to death on a cross; this
is why he speaks clearly about his passion (vv:31-32). The Christian life, lived
as it should be lived, with all its demands, is also a cross which one has to carry,
following Christ.

Jesus' words, which must have seemed extreme to his listeners, indicate the
standard he requires his followers to live up to. He does not ask for short-lived
enthusiasm or occasional dedication; he asks everyone to renounce himself, to
take up his cross and follow him. For the goal he sets men is eternal life. This
whole Gospel passage has to do with man's eternal destiny. The present life
should be evaluated in the light of this eternal life: life on earth is not definitive,
but transitory and relative; it is a means to be used to achieve definitive life in
heaven : "All that, which worries you for the moment, is of relative importance.
What is of absolute importance is that you be happy, that you be saved" (J.
Escrivá, *The Way*, 297).

"There is a kind of fear around, a fear of the Cross, of our Lord's Cross.
What has happened is that people have begun to regard as crosses all the
unpleasant things that crop up in life, and they do not know how to take them
as God's children should, with supernatural outlook. So much so, that they are
even removing the roadside crosses set up by our forefathers . . . !

"In the Passion, the Cross ceased to be a symbol of punishment and became
instead a sign of victory. The Cross is the emblem of the Redeemer: *in quo est
salus, vita et resurrectio nostra:* there lies our salvation, our life and our
resurrection" (J. Escrivá, *The Way of the Cross*, II, 5).

35. "Life" : in the original text and the New Vulgate the word literally means
"soul." But here, as in many other cases, "soul" and "life" are equivalent. The
word "life" is used, clearly, in a double sense: earthly life and eternal life, the
life of man here on earth and man's eternal happiness in heaven. Death can put
an end to earthly life, but it cannot destroy eternal life (cf. Mt 10:28), the life
which can only be given by Him who brings the dead back to life.

Understood in this way, we can grasp the paradoxical meaning of our Lord's
phrase : whoever wishes to save his (earthly) life will lose his (eternal) life. But
whoever loses his (earthly) life for me and the Gospel, will save his (eternal)
life. What, then, does saving one's (earthly) life mean? It means living this life
as if there were none other—letting oneself be controlled by the lust of the flesh
and the lust of the eyes and the pride of life (cf. 1 Jn 2:16). And losing one's
(earthly) life means mortifying, by continuous ascetical effort, this triple
concupisence—that is, taking up one's cross (v. 34)—and consequently seeking and savouring the things that are God's and not the things of the earth (cf.
Col 3:1-2).

whoever would save his life will lose it: and whoever loses his life for my sake and the gospel's will save it. [36]For what does it profit a man to gain the whole world and forfeit his life? [37]For what can a man give in return for his life? [38]For whoever is ashamed of me and of my words in this adulterous and sinful generation, of him will the Son of man also be ashamed, when he comes in the glory of his Father with the holy angels."

Mt 10:33

---

perdiderit animam suam propter me et evangelium, salvam eam faciet. [36]Quid enim prodest homini, si lucretur mundum totum et detrimentum faciat animae suae? [37]Quid enim dabit homo commutationem pro anima sua? [38]Qui enim me confusus fuerit et mea verba in generatione ista adultera et peccatrice, et Filius hominis confundetur eum, cum venerit in gloria Patris sui cum angelis sanctis."

36-37. Jesus promises eternal life to those who are willing to lose earthly life for his sake. He has given us example : he is the Good Shepherd who lays down his life for his sheep (Jn 10:15); and he fulfilled in his own case what he said to the Apostles on the night before he died : "Greater love has no man than this that a man lay down his life for his friends" (Jn 15:13).

38. Each person's eternal destiny will be decided by Christ. He is the Judge who will come to judge the living and the dead (Mt 16:27). The sentence will depend on how faithful each has been in keeping the Lord's commandments— to love God and to love one's neighbour, for God's sake. On that day Christ will not recognize as his disciple anyone who is ashamed to imitate Jesus' humility and example and follow the precepts of the Gospel for fear of displeasing the world or worldly people : he has failed to confess by his life the faith which he claims to hold. A Christian, then, should never be ashamed of the Gospel (Rom 1:16); he should never let himself be drawn away by the worldliness around him; rather he should exercise a decisive influence on his environment, counting on the help of God's grace. The first Christians changed the ancient pagan world. God's arm has not grown shorter since their time (cf. Is 59:1). Cf. Mt 10:32-33 and note on same.

and a voice came out of the cloud, "This is my beloved Son;[g] listen to him." [8]And suddenly looking around they no longer saw any one with them but Jesus only.

[9]And as they were coming down the mountain, he charged them to tell no one what they had seen, until the Son of man should have risen from the dead. [10]So they kept the matter to themselves, questioning what the rising from the dead meant. [11]And they asked him, "Why do the scribes say that first Elijah must come?" [12]And he said to them, "Elijah does come first to restore all things; and how is it written of the Son of man, that he should suffer many things and be treated with contempt? [13]But I tell you that Elijah

Mk 1:11
2 Pet 1:17
Deut 18:15
Acts 3:22

Mk 8:30

Mal 3:1f, 23
Is 53:3

Mt 11:14
1 Kings 19:2, 10

vox de nube: "Hic est Filius meus dilectus; audite illum." [8]Et statim circumspicientes neminem amplius viderunt nisi Iesum tantum secum. [9]Et descendentibus illis de monte, praecipit illis, ne cui, quae vidissent, narrarent, nisi cum Filius hominis a mortuis resurrexerit. [10]Et verbum continuerunt apud se conquirentes quid esset illud: "a mortuis resurgere." [11]Et interrogabant eum dicentes: "Quid ergo dicunt scribae quia Eliam oporteat venire primum?" [12]Qui ait illis: "Elias cum venerit primo, restituet omnia; et quomodo scriptum est super Filio hominis, ut multa patiatur et contemnatur? [13]Sed dico vobis: Et Elias

"Beloved" : this reveals that Christ is the only-begotten Son of the Father in whom are fulfilled the prophecies of the Old Testament. Fray Luis de Leon comments : "Christ is the Beloved, that is to say, he has always been, is now and ever shall be loved above all else [. . .] for no single creature or all created things taken together are as loved by God, and because only he is the object of true adoration" (*The Names of Christ*, book 3, The Beloved).

10. That the dead would rise was already revealed in the Old Testament (cf. Dan 12:2-3; 2 Mac 7:9; 12:43) and was believed by pious Jews (cf Jn 11:23-25). However, they were unable to understand the profound truth of the death and resurrection of the Lord : they expected a glorious and triumphant Messiah, despite the prophecy that he would suffer and die (cf. Is 53). Hence the Apostles' oblique approach; they too do not dare to directly question our Lord about his resurrection.

11-13. The scribes and Pharisees interpret the messianic prophecy in Malachi (3:1-2) as meaning that Elijah will appear in person, dramatically, to be followed by the all-triumphant Messiah, with no shadow of pain or humiliation. Jesus tells them that Elijah has indeed come, in the person of John the Baptist (Mt 17:13) and has prepared the way of the Messiah, a way of pain and suffering.

[g]Or *my Son, my* (or the) *Beloved*

has come, and they did to him whatever they pleased, as it is written of him."

The curing of an epileptic boy

Mt 17:14-21
Lk 9:37-42

¹⁴And when they came to the disciples, they saw a great crowd about them, and scribes arguing with them. ¹⁵And immediately all the crowd, when they saw him, were greatly amazed, and ran up to him and greeted him. ¹⁶And he asked them, "What are you discussing with them?" ¹⁷And one of the crowd answered him, "Teacher, I brought my son to you, for he has a dumb spirit; ¹⁸and wherever it seizes him, it dashes him down; and he foams and grinds his teeth and becomes rigid; and I asked your disiples to cast it out, and they were not able." ¹⁹And he answered them, "O faithless generation, how long am I to be with

venit; et fecerunt illi, quaecumque volebant, sicut scriptum est de eo." ¹⁴Et venientes ad discipulos viderunt turbam magnam circa eos et scribas conquirentes cum illis. ¹⁵Et confestim omnis populus videns eum stupefactus est, et accurrentes salutabant eum. ¹⁶Et interrogavit eos: "Quid inter vos conquiritis?" ¹⁷Et respondit ei unus de turba: "Magister, attuli filium meum ad te habentem spiritum mutum; ¹⁸et ubicumque eum apprehenderit, allidit eum, et spumat et stridet dentibus et arescit. Et dixi discipulis tuis, ut eicerent illum, et non potuerunt." ¹⁹Qui respondens eis dicit: "O generatio incredula, quamdiu

V.12 is a question which Jesus puts to his disciples, but they should really have asked it themselves, had they realized that Christ's resurrection presupposed the Messiah's suffering and death. Since they fail to ask it, Jesus does, to teach them that he like Elijah (that is, John the Baptist) must experience suffering before entering his glory.

17. The demon who possessed this boy is described as a "dumb spirit" because dumbness was the main feature of the possession. On diabolic possession cf. note on Mt 12:22-24.

19-24. As on other occasions, Jesus requires submission of faith before he works the miracle. The exclamation of Jesus refers to the request of the boy's father (v.22), which seemed to suggest some doubt about God's omnipotence. The Lord corrects this way of asking and requires him to have firm faith. In v. 24 we can see that the father has quite changed; then Jesus does the miracle. The man's strengthened faith made him all-powerful, for someone with faith relies not on himself but on Jesus Christ. Through faith, then, we become sharers in God's omnipotence. But faith is a gift of God, which man, especially at times when he is wavering, should ask for humbly and tenaciously, like the father of this boy : "I believe, help my unbelief," and like the Apostles : "Increase our faith!" (Lk 17:5).

you? How long am I to bear with you? Bring him to me."
20And they brought the boy to him; and when the spirit saw
him, immediately it convulsed the boy, and he fell on the
ground and rolled about, foaming at the mouth. 21And
Jesush asked his father, "How long has he had this?" And
he said, "From childhood. 22And it has often cast him into
the fire and into the water, to destroy him; but if you can do
anything, have pity on us and help us." 23And Jesus said to
him, "If you can! All things are possible to him who
believes." 24Immediately the father of the child cried outi
and said, "I believe; help my unbelief!" 25And when Jesus
saw that a crowd came running together, he rebuked the
unclean spirit, saying to it, "You dumb and deaf spirit, I
command you, come out of him, and never enter him
again." 26And after crying out and convulsing him terribly,
it came out, and the boy was like a corpse; so that most of
them said, "He is dead." 27But Jesus took him by the hand
and lifted him up, and he arose. 28And when he had entered
the house, his disciples asked him privately, "Why could
we not cast it out?" 29And he said to them, "This kind cannot
be driven out by anything but prayer and fasting."j

Mk 11:23
Lk 17:5

Mk 1:26

Mk 5:41

---

apud vos ero? Quamdiu vos patiar? Afferte illum ad me." 20Et attulerunt illum
ad eum. Et cum vidisset illum, spiritus statim conturbavit eum, et corruens in
terram volutabatur spumans. 21Et interrogavit patrem eius: "Quantum temporis
est, ex quo hoc ei accidit?" At ille ait: "Ab infantia; 22et frequenter eum etiam
in ignem et in aquas misit, ut eum perderet; sed si quid potes, adiuva nos,
misertus nostri." 23Iesus autem ait illi: "'Si potes!' Omnia possibilia credenti."
24Et continuo exclamans pater pueri aiebat: "Credo; adiuva incredulitatem
meam." 25Et cum videret Iesus concurrentem turbam, comminatus est spiritui
immundo dicens illi: "Mute et surde spiritus, ego tibi praecipio: Exi ab eo et
amplius ne introeas in eum." 26Et clamans et multum discerpens eum exiit; et
factus est sicut mortuus, ita ut multi dicerent: "Mortuus est!" 27Iesus autem
tenens manum eius elevavit illum, et surrexit. 28Et cum introisset in domum,

---

28-29. "In teaching the Apostles how to expel a spirit as evil as this he is
teaching all of us how we should live, and telling us that prayer is the resource
we should use to overcome even the severest temptations, whether they come
from unclean spirits or from men. Prayer does not consist only in the words we
use to invoke God's clemency but also in everything we do, out of faith, as
homage to God. The Apostle bears witness to this when he says : 'Pray
constantly' (1 Thess 5:7)" (St Bede, *In Marci Evangelium expositio, in loc.*).

hGreek *he*   iOther ancient authorities add *with tears*   jOther ancient authorities omit *and fasting*

Second prophecy of the Passion

Mt 17:22-23
Lk 9:43-45
Jn 7:1
Mk 8:31
10:32-34

Lk 9:45; 18:34

³⁰They went on from there and passed through Galilee. And he would not have any one know it; ³¹for he was teaching his disciples, saying to them, "The Son of man will be delivered into the hands of men, and they will kill him; and when he is killed, after three days he will rise." ³²But they did not understand the saying, and they were afraid to ask him.

Being the servant of all. Scandal

Mt 18:1-9
Lk 9:46-50

Mk 10:44

³³And they came to Capernaum; and when he was in the house he asked them, "What were you discussing on the way?" ³⁴But they were silent; for on the way they had discussed with one another who was the greatest. ³⁵And he

---

discipuli eius secreto interrogabant eum: "Quare nos non potuimus eicere eum?" ²⁹Et dixit illis "Hoc genus in nullo potest exire nisi in oratione." ³⁰Et inde profecti peragrabant Galilaeam; nec volebat quemquam scire. ³¹Docebat enim discipulos suos et dicebat illis: "Filius Hominis tradetur in manus hominum, et occident eum, et occisus post tres dies resurget." ³²At illi ignorabant verbum et timebant eum interrogare. ³³Et venerunt Capharnaum. Qui cum domi esset, interrogabat eos: "Quid in via tractabatis?" ³⁴At illi tacebant. Siquidem inter se in via disputaverant, quis esset maior. ³⁵Et residens vocavit Duodecim

---

30-32. Although moved when he sees the crowds like sheep without a shepherd (Mt 9:36), Jesus leaves them, to devote time to careful instruction of the Apostles. He retires with them to out-of-the-way places, and there he explains points of his public preaching which they had not understood (Mt 13:36). Here, specifically, for a second time, he announces his death and resurrection.

In his relationships with souls Jesus acts in the same way : he calls man to be with him in the quiet of prayer and there he teaches him about his more intimate plans and about the more demanding side of the Christian life. Later, like the Apostles, Christians were to spread this teaching to the ends of the earth.

34-35. Jesus uses this argument going on behind his back to teach his disciples about how authority should be exercised in his Church—not by lording it over others, but by serving them. In fulfilling his own mission to found the Church whose head and supreme lawgiver he is, he came to serve and not to be served (Mt 20:28).

Anyone who does not strive to have this attitude of self- forgetful service, not only lacks one of the main pre-requisites for proper exercise of authority but also runs the risk of being motivated by ambition or pride. "To be in charge of an apostolic undertaking demands readiness to suffer everything, from everybody, with infinite charity" (J. Escrivá, *The Way*, 951).

sat down and called the twelve; and he said to them, "If any one would be first, he must be last of all and servant of all." [36]And he took a child, and put him in the midst of them; and taking him in his arms, he said to them, [37]"Whoever receives one such child in my name receives me; and whoever receives me, receives not me but him who sent me."

[38]John said to him, "Teacher, we saw a man casting out demons in your name,[k] and we forbade him, because he was not following us." [39]But Jesus said, "Do not forbid him; for no one who does a mighty work in my name will be able soon after to speak evil of me. [40]For he that is not against us is for us. [41]For truly, I say to you, whoever gives you a

Mk 10:16

Mt 10:40
Jn 13:20

Num 11:27-28

1 Cor 12:3

Mt 12:30

Mt 10:42

---

et ait illis: "Si quis vult primus esse, erit omnium novissimus et omnium minister." [36]Et accipiens puerum, statuit eum in medio eorum; quem ut complexus esset, ait illis: [37]"Quisquis unum ex huiusmodi pueris receperit in nomine meo, me recipit; et quicumque me susceperit, non me suscipit, sed eum qui me misit." [38]Dixit illi Ioannes: "Magister, vidimus quemdam in nomine tuo eicientem daemonia, et prohibebamus eum, quia non sequebatur nos." [39]Iesus autem ait: "Nolite prohibere eum. Nemo est enim, qui faciat virtutem in nomine meo et possit cito male loqui de me; [40]qui enim non est adversum nos, pro nobis est. [41]Quisquis enim potum dederit vobis calicem aquae in nomine, quia Christi

36-37. To demonstrate to his Apostles the abnegation and humility needed in their ministry, he takes a child into his arms and explains the meaning of this gesture : if we receive for Christ's sake those who have little importance in the world's eyes, it is as if we are embracing Christ himself and the Father who sent him. This little child whom Jesus embraces represents every child in the world, and everyone who is needy, helpless, poor or sick—people who are not naturally attractive.

38-40. Our Lord warns the Apostles, and through them all Christians, against exclusivism in the apostolate—the notion that "good is not good unless I am the one who does it." We must assimilate this teaching of Christ's : good is good, even if it is not I who do it. Cf. note on Lk 9:49-50.

41. The value and merit of good works lies mainly in the love of God with which they are done : "A little act, done for love, is worth so much" (J. Escrivá, *The Way*, 814). God regards in a special way acts of service to others, however small : "Do you see that glass of water or that piece of bread which a holy soul gives to a poor person for God's sake; it is a small matter, God knows, and in

[k]Other ancient authorities add *who does not follow us*

cup of water to drink because you bear the name of Christ, will by no means lose his reward.

⁴²"Whoever causes one of these little ones who believe in me to sin,[1] it would be better for him if a great millstone were hung around his neck and he were thrown into the sea.

Mt 5:30 ⁴³And if your hand causes you to sin,[1] cut it off; it is better

---

estis, amen dico vobis: Non perdet mercedem suam. ⁴²Et quisquis scandalizaverit unum ex his pusillis credentibus in me, bonum est ei magis, ut circumdetur mola asinaria collo eius, et in mare mittatur. ⁴³Et si scandalizaverit te manus tua, abscide illam: bonum est tibi debilem introire in vitam, quam

---

human judgment hardly worthy of consideration : God, notwithstanding, recompenses it, and forthwith gives for it some increase of charity" (St Francis de Sales, *Treatise on the Love of God*, book 2, chap. 2).

42. "Scandal is anything said, done or omitted which leads another to commit sin" (*St Pius X Catechism*, 417). Scandal is called, and is, diabolical when the aim of the scandal-giver is to provoke his neighbour to sin, understanding sin as offence against God. Since sin is the greatest of all evils, it is easy to understand why scandal is so serious and, therefore, why Christ condemns it so roundly. Causing scandal to children is especially serious, because they are so less able to defend themselves against evil. What Christ says applies to everyone, but especially to parents and teachers, who are responsible before God for the souls of the young.

43. "Hell", literally "Gehenna" or *Ge-hinnom*, was a little valley south of Jerusalem, outside the walls and below the city. For centuries it was used as the city dump. Usually garbage was burned to avoid it being a focus of infection. Gehenna was, proverbially, an unclean and unhealthy place : our Lord used this to explain in a graphic way the unquenchable fire of hell.

43-48. After teaching the obligation everyone has to avoid giving scandal to others, Jesus now gives the basis of Christian moral teaching on the subject of "occasions of sin"—situations liable to lead to sin. He is very explicit : a person is obliged to avoid proximate occasions of sin, just as he is obliged to avoid sin itself; as God already put it in the Old Testament : "Whoever lives in danger will perish by it" (Sir 3:26-27). The eternal good of our soul is more important than any temporal good. Therefore, anything that places us in proximate danger of committing sin should be cut off and thrown away. By putting things in this way our Lord makes sure we recognize the seriousness of this obligation.

The Fathers see, in these references to hands and eyes and so forth, people who are persistent in evil and ever-ready to entice others to evil behaviour and

[1]Greek *stumble*

for you to enter life maimed than with two hands to go to hell,[m] to the unquenchable fire. [45]And if your foot causes you to sin, cut it off; it is better for you to enter life lame than with two feet to be thrown into hell.[m,n] [47]And if your eye causes you to sin,[l] pluck it out; it is better for you to enter the kingdom of God with one eye than with two eyes to be thrown into hell,[m] [48]where their worm does not die, and the fire is not quenched. [49]For every one will be salted with fire.[o] [50]Salt is good; but if the salt has lost its saltness, how will you season it? Have salt in yourselves, and be at peace with one another."

Mt 5:29

Lev 2:13
Mt 5:13
Lk 14:34
Col 4:6

---

duas manus habentem ire in gehennam, in ignem inexstinguibilem.[(44)] [45]Et si pes tuus te scandalizat, amputa illum: bonum est tibi claudum introire in vitam, quam duos pedes habentem mitti in gehennam.[(46)] [47]Et si oculus tuus scandalizat te, eice eum: bonum est tibi luscum introire in regnum Dei, quam duos oculos habentem mitti in gehennam, [48]ubi *vermis eorum non moritur et ignis non exstinguitur*; [49]omnis enim igne salietur. [50]Bonum est sal; quod si sal insulsum fuerit, in quo illud condietis? Habete in vobis sal et pacem habete inter vos."

---

erroneous beliefs. These are the people we should distance ourselves from, so as to enter life, rather than accompany them to hell (St Augustine, *De consensu Evangelistarum*, IV, 16; St John Chrysostom, *Hom. on St Matthew*, 60).

44. "Where their worm does not die, and the fire is not quenched" : these words constituting v. 44 are not in the better manuscripts. They are taken from Isaiah 66:24 and are repeated as a kind of refrain in vv. 46 (omitted for the same reason as v. 44) and 48. Our Lord uses them to refer to the torments of hell. Often "the worm that does not die" is explained as the eternal remorse felt by those in hell; and the "fire which is not quenched," as their physical pain. The Fathers also say that both things may possibly refer to physical torments. In any case, the punishment in question is terrible and unending.

49-50. "Every one will be salted with fire." St Bede comments on these words : "Everyone will be salted with fire, says Jesus, because spiritual wisdom must purify all the elect of any kind of corruption through carnal desire. Or he may be speaking of the fire of tribulation, which exercises the patience of the faithful to enable them to reach perfection" (St Bede, *In Marci Evangelium expositio, in loc.*).

Some codexes add : "and every sacrifice will be salted with salt". This phrase

[m]Greek *Gehenna*
[n]Verses 44 and 46 (which are identical with verse 48) are omitted by the best ancient authorities
[o]Other ancient authorities add *and every sacrifice will be salted with salt*

The indissolubility of marriage

Mt 19:1-9   ¹And he left there and went to the region of Judea and beyond the Jordan, and crowds gathered to him again; and again, as his custom was, he taught them.

²And Pharisees came up and in order to test him asked, "Is it lawful for a man to divorce his wife?" ³He answered

---

¹Et inde exsurgens venit in fines Iudaeae ultra Iordanem, et conveniunt iterum turbae ad eum, et, sicut consueverat, iterum docebat illos. ²Et accedentes

---

in Leviticus (2:12), prescribed that all sacrificial offerings should be seasoned with salt to prevent corruption. This prescription of the Old Testament is used here to teach Christians to offer themselves as pleasing victims, impregnated with the spirit of the Gospel, symbolised by salt. Our Lord's address, which arises out of a dispute over who is the greatest, ends with a lesson about fraternal peace and charity. On salt which has lost its taste cf. note on Mt 5:13.

1-12. This kind of scene occurs often in the Gospel. The malice of the Pharisees contrasts with the simplicity of the crowd, who listen attentively to Jesus' teaching. The Pharisees' questions aimed at tricking Jesus into going against the Law of Moses. But Jesus Christ, Messiah and Son of God, has perfect understanding of that Law. Moses had permitted divorce because of the hardness of that ancient people : women had an ignominious position in those primitive tribes (they were regarded almost as animals or slaves); Moses, therefore, protected women's dignity against these abuses by devising the certificate of divorce; this was a real social advance. It was a document by which the husband repudiated his wife and she obtained freedom. Jesus restores to its original purity the dignity of man and woman in marriage, as instituted by God at the beginning of creation. "A man leaves his father and his mother and cleaves to his wife, and they become one flesh" (Gen 2:24): in this way God established from the very beginning the unity and indissolubility of marriage. The Church's Magisterium, the only authorized interpreter of the Gospel and of the natural law, has constantly guarded and defended this teaching and has proclaimed it solemnly in countless documents (Council of Florence, *Pro Armeniis;* Council of Trent, *De Sacram. matr.;* Pius XI, *Casti connubii;* Vatican II, *Gaudium et spes,* 48; etc.).

Here is a good summary of this doctrine : "The indissolubility of marriage is not a caprice of the Chuch nor is it merely a positive ecclesiastical law. It is a precept of natural law, of divine law, and responds perfectly to our nature and to the supernatural order of grace" (J. Escrivá, *Conversations,* 97). Cf. note on Mt 5:31-32.

them, "What did Moses command you?" [4]They said, Deut 24:1
Mt 5:31-32
"Moses allowed a man to write a certificate of divorce, and
to put her away." [5]But Jesus said to them, "For your Gen 1:27
hardness of heart he wrote this commandment. [6]But from
the beginning of creation, 'God made them male and
female.' [7]'For this reason a man shall leave his father and Gen 2:24
mother and be joined to his wife,[p] [8]and the two shall become
one.'[q] So they are no longer two but one.[q] [9]What therefore
God has joined together, let not man put asunder."

---

pharisaei interrogabant eum, si licet viro uxorem dimittere, tentantes eum. [3]At
ille respondens dixit eis: "Quid vobis praecepit Moyses?" [4]Qui dixerunt:
"Moyses permisit *libellum repudii scribere et dimittere*." [5]Iesus autem ait eis:
"Ad duritiam cordis vestri scripsit vobis praeceptum istud. [6]Ab initio autem
creaturae *masculum et feminam fecit eos*. [7]*Propter hoc relinquet homo patrem
suum et matrem et adhaerebit ad uxorem suam*, [8]*et erunt duo in carne una*;
itaque iam non sunt duo sed una caro. [9]Quod ergo Deus coniunxit, homo non

---

5-9. When a Christian realizes that this teaching applies to everyone at all
times, he should not be afraid about people reacting against it : "It is a
fundamental duty of the Church to reaffirm strongly [. . .] the doctrine of the
indissolubility of marriage. To all those who, in our times, consider it too
difficult, or indeed impossible, to be bound to one person for the whole of life,
and to those caught up in a culture that rejects the indissolubility of marriage
and openly mocks the commitment of spouses to fidelity, it is necessary to
reaffirm the good news of the definitive nature of that conjugal love that has in
Christ its foundation and strength (cf. Eph 5:25).

"Being rooted in the personal and total self-giving of the couple, and being
required by the good of the children, the indissolubility of marriage finds its
ultimate truth in the plan that God has manifested in his revelation: he wills and
he communicates the indissolubility of marriage as a fruit, a sign and a
requirement of the absolutely faithful love that God has for man and that the
Lord Jesus has for the Church.

"Christ renews the first plan that the Creator inscribed in the hearts of man
and woman, and in the celebration of the sacrament of matrimony offers 'a new
heart' : thus the couples are not only able to overcome 'hardness of heart' (Mt
19:8), but also and above all they are able to share the full and definitive love
of Christ, the new and eternal Covenant made flesh. Just as the Lord Jesus is
the 'faithful witness' (Rev 3:14), the 'yes' of the promises of God (cf. 2 Cor
1:20) and thus the supreme realization of the unconditional faithfulness with
which God loves his people, so Christian couples are called to participate truly
in the irrevocable indissolubility that binds Christ to the Church, his bride, loved
by him to the end (cf. Jn 13:1).

[p]Other ancient authorities omit *and be joined to his wife*   [q]Greek *one flesh*

¹⁰And in the house the disciples asked him about this
Lk 16:18   matter. ¹¹And he said to them, "Whoever divorces his wife
and marries another, commits adultery against her; ¹²and if
she divorces her husband and marries another, she commits
adultery."

Jesus and the children

Mt 19:13-15   ¹³And they were bringing children to him, that he might
Lk 18:15-17   touch them; and the disciples rebuked them. ¹⁴But when
Jesus saw it he was indignant, and said to them, "Let the
children come to me, do not hinder them; for to such
Mt 18:3   belongs the kingdom of God. ¹⁵Truly, I say to you, whoever
does not receive the kingdom of God like a child shall not
Mk 9:36   enter it." ¹⁶And he took them in his arms and blessed them,
laying his hands upon them.

---

separet." ¹⁰Et domo iterum discipuli de hoc interrogabant eum. ¹¹Et dicit illis:
"Quicumque dimiserit uxorem suam et aliam duxerit, adulterium committit in
eam; ¹²et si ipsa dimiserit virum suum et alii nupserit, moechatur." ¹³Et
offerebant illi parvulos, ut tangeret illos; discipuli autem comminabantur eis.
¹⁴At videns Iesus, indigne tulit et ait illis: "Sinite parvulos venire ad me. Ne
prohibueritis eos; talium est enim regnum Dei. ¹⁵Amen dico vobis: Quisquis
non receperit regnum Dei velut parvulus, non intrabit in illud." ¹⁶Et complexans

---

"To bear witness to the inestimable value of the indissolubility and fidelity
of marriage is one of the most precious and most urgent tasks of Christian
couples in our time" (John Paul II, *Familiaris consortio*, 20).

13-16. This Gospel account has an attractive freshness and vividness about
it which may be connected with St Peter, from whom St Mark would have taken
the story. It is one of the few occasions when the Gospels tell us that Christ
became angry. What provoked his anger was the disciples' intolerance: they
felt that these people bringing children to Jesus were a nuisance : it meant a
waste of his time; Christ had more serious things to do than be involved with
little children. The disciples were well-intentioned; it was just that they were
applying the wrong criteria. What Jesus had told them quite recently had not
registered : "Whoever receives one such child in my name receives me; and
whoever receives me, receives not me but him who sent me" (Mk 9:37).

Our Lord also stresses that a Christian has to become like a child to enter
the Kingdom of heaven. "To be little you have to believe as children believe,
to love as children love, to abandon yourself as children do . . ., to pray as
children pray" (J. Escrivá, *Holy Rosary*, Prologue).

Our Lord's words express simply and graphically the key doctrine of man's
divine sonship : God is our Father and we are his sons and daughters, his

The rich young man

¹⁷And as he was setting out on his journey, a man ran up and knelt before him, and asked him, "Good Teacher, what must I do to inherit eternal life?" ¹⁸And Jesus said to him, "Why do you call me good? No one is good but God alone. ¹⁹You know the commandments: 'Do not kill, Do not commit adultery, Do not steal, Do not bear false witness, Do not defraud, Honour your father and mother.'" ²⁰And

Mt 19:16-30
Lk 18:18-30

Ex 20:12-17
Deut 5:16-20
24:14

eos benedicebat imponens manus super illos. ¹⁷Et cum egrederetur in viam, accurrens quidam et, genu flexo ante eum, rogabat eum: "Magister bone, quid faciam ut vitam aeternam percipiam?" ¹⁸Iesus autem dixit ei: "Quid me dicis bonum? Nemo bonus nisi unus Deus. ¹⁹Praecepta nosti: *ne occidas, ne adulteres, ne fureris, ne falsum testimonium dixeris, ne fraudem feceris, honora patrem tuum et matrem.*" ²⁰Ille autem dixit ei: "Magister, haec omnia

children; the whole of religion is summed up in the relationship of a son with his good Father. This awareness of God as Father involves a sense of dependence on our Father in heaven and trusting abandonment to his loving providence—in the way a child trusts its father or mother; the humility of recognizing that we can do nothing by ourselves; simplicity and sincerity, which make us straightforward and honest in our dealings with God and man.

17-18. As Matthew 19:16 makes clear, the young man approaches Jesus as an acknowledged teacher of the spiritual life, in the hope that he will guide him towards eternal life. It is not that Christ rejects the praise he is offered : he wants to show the depth of the young man's words : he is good, not because he is a good man but because he is God, who is goodness itself. So, the young man has spoken the truth, but he has not gone far enough. Hence the enigmatic nature of Jesus' reply and its profundity. The young man's approach is upright but too human; Jesus tries to get him to see things from an entirely supernatural point of view. If this man is to really attain eternal life he must see in Christ not just a good master but the divine Saviour, the only Master, the only one who, because he is God, is goodness itself. Cf. note on Mt 19:16-22.

19. Our Lord has not come to abolish the Law but to fulfil it (Mt 5:17). The commandments are the very core of the Law and keeping them is necessary for attaining eternal life. Christ brings these commandments to fulfilment in a double sense. First, because he helps us discover their full implications for our lives. The light of Revelation makes it easy for us to grasp the correct meaning of the precepts of the Decalogue—something that human reason, on its own, can only achieve with difficulty. Second, his grace gives us strength to counter our evil inclinations, which stem from original sin. The commandments, therefore, still apply in the Christian life : they are like signposts indicating the way that leads to heaven.

he said to him, "Teacher, all these I have observed from my youth." ²¹And Jesus looking upon him loved him, and said to him, "You lack one thing; go, sell what you have, and give to the poor, and you will have treasure in heaven; and

---

conservavi a iuventute mea." ²¹Iesus autem intuitus eum dilexit eum et dixit illi: "Unum tibi deest: vade, quaecumque habes, vende et da pauperibus et

---

21-22. Our Lord knows that this young man has a generous heart. This is why he treats him so affectionately and invites him to greater intimacy with God. But he explains that this means renunciation—leaving his wealth behind so as to give his heart whole and entire to Jesus. God calls everyone to holiness, but holiness is reached by many different routes. It is up to every individual to take the necessary steps to discover which route God wants him to follow. The Lord sows the seed of vocation in everyone's soul, to show him the way to go to reach the goal of holiness, which is common to all.

In other words, if a person does not put obstacles in the way, if he responds generously to God, he feels a desire to be better, to give himself more generously. As fruit of this desire he seeks to know God's will; he prays to God to help him, and asks people to advise him. In responding to this sincere search, God uses a great variety of instruments. Later, when a person thinks he sees the way God wants him to follow, he may still not take the decision to go that way : he is afraid of the renunciation it involves : at this point he should pray and deny himself if the light—God's invitation—is to win out against human calculation. For, although God is calling, man is always free, and therefore he can respond generously or be a coward, like the young man we are told about in this passage. Failure to respond generously to one's vocation always produces sadness.

21. "In its precise eloquence", John Paul II points out, commenting on this passage, "this deeply penetrating event expresses a great lesson in a few words: it touches upon substantial problems and basic questions that have in no way lost their relevance. Everywhere young people are asking important questions—questions on the meaning of life, on the right way to live, on the scale of values: 'What must I do . . .?' 'What must I do to share in everlasting life?' . . . To each one of you I say therefore: heed the call of Christ when you hear him saying to you: 'Follow me!' Walk in my path! Stand by my side! Remain in my love! There is a choice to be made: a choice for Christ and his way of life, and his commandment of love.

"The message of love that Christ brought is always important, always relevant. It is not difficult to see how today's world, despite its beauty and grandeur, despite the conquests of science and technology, despite the refined and abundant material goods that it offers, is yearning for more truth, for more love, for more joy. And all of this is found in Christ and in his way of life. . . . Faced with problems and disappointments, many people will try to escape from

come, follow me." ²²At that saying his countenance fell, and he went away sorrowful; for he had great possessions.

Poverty and renunciation

²³And Jesus looked around and said to his disciples, Mk 4:19

---

habebis thesaurum in caelo et veni, sequere me." ²²Qui contristatus in hoc verbo, abiit maerens: erat enim habens possessiones multas. ²³Et circum-

---

their responsibility: escape in selfishness, escape in sexual pleasure, escape in drugs, escape in violence, escape in indifference and cynical attitudes. But today, I propose to you the option of love, which is the opposite of escape. If you really accept that love from Christ, it will lead you to God. Perhaps in the priesthood or religious life; perhaps in some special service to your brothers and sisters: especially to the needy, the poor, the lonely, the abandoned, those whose rights have been trampled upon, or those whose basic needs have not been provided for. Whatever you make of your life, let it be something that reflects the love of Christ" (*Homily on Boston Common*).

22. "The sadness of the young man makes us reflect. We could be tempted to think that many possessions, many of the goods of this world, can bring happiness. We see instead in the case of the young man in the Gospel that his many possessions had become an obstacle to accepting the call of Jesus to follow him. He was not ready to say *yes* to Jesus and *no* to self, to say *yes* to love and *no* to escape. Real love is demanding. I would fail in my mission if I did not clearly tell you so. For it was Jesus— Jesus himself—who said: 'You are my friends if you do what I command you' (Jn 15:14). Love demands effort and a personal commitment to the will of God. It means discipline and sacrifice, but it also means joy and human fulfilment.

"Dear young people: do not be afraid of honest effort and honest work; do not be afraid of the truth. With Christ's help, and through prayer, you can answer his call, resisting temptations and fads, and every form of mass manipulation. Open your hearts to the Christ of the Gospels—to his love and his truth and his joy. Do not go away sad! . . .

"Follow Christ! You who are married: share your love and your burdens with each other; respect the human dignity of your spouses; accept joyfully the life that God gives through you; make your marriage stable and secure for your children's sake.

"Follow Christ! You who are single or who are preparing for marriage. Follow Christ! You who are young or old. Follow Christ! You who are sick or ageing; who are suffering or in pain. You who feel the need for healing, the need for love, the need for a friend—follow Christ!

"To all of you I extend—in the name of Christ—the call, the invitation, the plea: 'Come and follow Me'" (John Paul II, *Homily on Boston Common*).

23-27. The reaction of the rich young man gives our Lord another oppor-

141

Ps 62:11
2 Tim 6:17

"How hard it will be for those who have riches to enter the kingdom of God!" [24]And the disciples were amazed at his words. But Jesus said to them again, "Children, how hard it is for those who trust in riches[r] to enter the kingdom of God! [25]It is easier for a camel to go through the eye of a needle than for a rich man to enter the kingdom of God." [26]And they were exceedingly astonished, and said to him,[s]

Gen 18:14

"Then who can be saved?" [27]Jesus looked at them and said, "With men it is impossible, but not with God; for all things

---

spiciens Iesus ait discipulis suis: "Quam difficile, qui pecunias habent, in regnum Dei introibunt." [24]Discipuli autem obstupescebant in verbis eius. At Iesus rursus respondens ait illis: "Filii, quam difficile est in regnum Dei introire. [25]Facilius est camelum per foramen acus transire quam divitem intrare in regnum Dei." [26]Qui magis admirabantur dicentes ad semetipsos: "Et quis potest salvus fieri?" [27]Intuens illos Iesus ait: "Apud homines impossibile est sed non apud Deum: omnia enim possibilia sunt apud Deum." [28]Coepit Petrus ei dicere:

---

tunity to say something about the way to use material things. In themselves they are good : they are resources God has made available to people for their development in society. But excessive attachment to things is what makes them an occasion of sin. The sin lies in "trusting" in them, as if they solve all life's problems, and turning one's back on God. St Paul calls covetousness idolatry (Col 3:5). Christ excludes from the Kingdom of God anyone who becomes so attached to riches that his life is centered around them. Or, more accurately, that person excludes himself.

Possessions can seduce both those who already have them and those who are bent on acquiring them. Therefore, there are— paradoxically—poor people who are really rich, and rich people who are really poor. Since absolutely everyone has an inclination to be attached to material things, the disciples see salvation as an impossible goal : "Then who can be saved?" No one, if we rely on human resources. But God's grace makes everything possible. Cf. note on Mt 6:11.

Also, not putting our trust in riches means that anyone who does have wealth should use it to help the needy. This "demands great generosity, much sacrifice and unceasing effort on the part of the rich man. Let each one examine his conscience, a conscience that conveys a new message for our times. Is he prepared to support out of his own pocket works and undertakings organised in favour of the most destitute? Is he ready to pay higher taxes so that the public authorities can intensify their efforts in favour of development?" (Paul VI, *Populorum progressio*, 47).

---

[r]Other ancient authorities omit *for those who trust in riches*
[s]Other ancient authorities read *to one another*

are possible with God." [28]Peter began to say to him, "Lo, we have left everything and followed you." [29]Jesus said, "Truly, I say to you, there is no one who has left house or brothers or sisters or mother or father or children or lands,

---

"Ecce nos dimisimus omnia et secuti sumus te." [29]Ait Iesus: "Amen dico vobis: Nemo est, qui reliquerit domum aut fratres aut sorores aut matrem aut patrem aut filios aut agros propter me et propter evangelium, [30]qui non accipiat centies

---

28-30. Jesus Christ requires every Christian to practise the virtue of poverty: he also requires us to practise real and effective austerity in the possession and use of material things. But of those who have received a specific call to apostolate—as in the case, here, of the Twelve—he requires absolute detachment from property, time, family etc. so that they can be fully available, imitating Jesus himself who, despite being Lord of the universe, became so poor that he had nowhere to lay his head (cf. Mt 8:20). Giving up all these things for the sake of the Kingdom of heaven also relieves us of the burden they involve : like a soldier shedding some encumbrance before going into action, to be able to move with more agility. This gives one a certain lordship over all things: no longer the slave of things, one experiences that feeling St Paul referred to : "As having nothing, and yet possessing everything" (2 Cor 6:10). A Christian who sheds his selfishness in this way has acquired charity and, having charity, he has everything : "All are yours; you are Christ's; and Christ is God's" (1 Cor 3:22-23).

The reward for investing completely in Christ will be fully obtained in eternal life : but we will also get it in this life. Jesus says that anyone who generously leaves behind his possessions will be rewarded a hundred times over in this life.

He adds "with persecutions" (v. 30) because opposition is part of the reward for giving things up out of love for Jesus Christ : a Christian's glory lies in becoming like the Son of God, sharing in his cross so as later to share in his glory : "provided we suffer with him in order that we may also be glorified with him" (Rom 8:17); "all who desire to live a godly life in Christ Jesus will be persecuted' (2 Tim 3:12).

29. These words of our Lord particularly apply to those who by divine vocation embrace celibacy, giving up their right to form a family on earth. By saying "for my sake and for the Gospel" Jesus indicates that his example and the demands of his teaching give full meaning to this way of life : "This, then, is the mystery of the newness of Christ, of all that he is and stands for; it is the sum of the highest ideals of the Gospel and of the kingdom; it is a particular manifestation of grace, which springs from the paschal mystery of the Saviour and renders the choice of celibacy desirable and worthwhile on the part of those called by our Lord Jesus. Thus, they intend not only to participate in Christ's priestly office, but also to share with him his very condition of living" (Paul VI, *Sacerdotalis coelibatus*, 23).

for my sake and for the gospel, ³⁰who will not receive a hundredfold now in this time, houses and brothers and sisters and mothers and children and lands, with persecutions, and in the age to come eternal life. ³¹But many that are first will be last, and the last first."

Third prophecy of the Passion

Mt 20:17-19
Lk 18:31-34
Jn 11:16, 55
Mt 9:31

³²And they were on the road, going up to Jerusalem, and Jesus was walking ahead of them; and they were amazed, and those who followed were afraid. And taking the twelve again, he began to tell them what was to happen to him, ³³saying, "Behold, we are going up to Jerusalem; and the Son of man will be delivered to the chief priests and the scribes, and they will condemn him to death, and deliver him to the Gentiles; ³⁴and they will mock him, and spit upon him, and scourge him, and kill him; and after three days he will rise."

The sons of Zebedee make their request

Mt 20:20-28

³⁵And James and John, the sons of Zebedee, came forward to him, and said to him, "Teacher, we want you to

---

tantum nunc in tempore hoc, domos et fratres et sorores et matres et filios et agros cum persecutionibus, et in saeculo futuro vitam aeternam. ³¹Multi autem erunt primi novissimi et novissimi primi." ³²Erant autem in via ascendentes in Hierosolymam, et praecedebat illos Iesus, et stupebant; illi autem sequentes timebant. Et assumens iterum Duodecim coepit illis dicere, quae essent ei aventura: ³³"Ecce ascendimus in Hierosolymam; et Filius hominis tradetur principibus sacerdotum et scribis, et damnabunt eum morte et tradent eum gentibus ³⁴et illudent ei et conspuent eum et flagellabunt eum et interficient eum, et post tres dies resurget." ³⁵Et accedunt ad eum Iacobus et Ioannes filii

---

32. Jesus was making his way to Jerusalem with a burning desire to see fulfilled everything that he had foretold about his passion and death. He had already told his disciples that he would suffer there, which is why they cannot understand his eagerness. By his own example he is teaching us to carry the cross gladly, not to try to avoid it.

35-44. We can admire the Apostles' humility : they do not disguise their earlier weakness and shortcomings from the first Christians. God also has wanted the Holy Gospel to record the earlier weaknesses of those who will become the unshakeable pillars of the Church. The grace of God works wonders in people's souls: so we should never be pessimistic in the face of our own wretchedness : "I can do all things in him who strengthens me" (Phil 4:13).

do for us whatever we ask of you." ³⁶And he said to them, "What do you want me to do for you?" ³⁷And they said to him, "Grant us to sit, one at your right hand and one at your left, in your glory." ³⁸But Jesus said to them, "You do not know what you are asking. Are you able to drink the cup that I drink, or to be baptized with the baptism with which I am baptized?" ³⁹And they said to him, "We are able." And Jesus said to them, "The cup that I drink you will drink; and with the baptism with which I am baptized, you will be baptized; ⁴⁰but to sit at my right hand or at my left is not mine to grant, but it is for those for whom it has been prepared." ⁴¹And when the ten heard it, they began to be indignant at James and John. ⁴²And Jesus called them to him and said to them, "You know that those who are supposed to rule over the Gentiles lord it over them, and their great men exercise authority over them. ⁴³But it shall not be so among you; but whoever would be great among

Mk 14:36
Lk 12:50
Rom 6:3

Acts 12:2
Rev 1:9

Lk 22:25-27

Mk 9:35

Zebedaei dicentes ei: "Magister, volumus, ut quodcumque petierimus a te, facias nobis." ³⁶At ille dixit eis: "Quid vultis, ut faciam vobis?" ³⁷Illi autem dixerunt ei: "Da nobis, ut unus ad dexteram tuam et alius ad sinistram sedeamus in gloria tua." ³⁸Iesus autem ait eis: "Nescitis quid petatis. Potestis bibere calicem, quem ego bibo, aut baptismum, quo ego baptizor, baptizari?" ³⁹At illi dixerunt ei: "Possumus." Iesus autem ait eis: "Calicem quidem, quem ego bibo, bibetis et baptismum, quo ego baptizor, baptizabimini; ⁴⁰sedere autem ad dexteram meam vel ad sinistram non est meum dare, sed quibus paratum est." ⁴¹Et audientes decem coeperunt indignari de Iacobo et Ioanne. ⁴²Et vocans eos Iesus ait illis: "Scitis quia hi, qui videntur principari gentibus, dominantur eis, et principes eorum potestatem habent ipsorum. ⁴³Non ita est autem in vobis,

---

38. When we ask for anything in prayer, we should be ready, always, to accept God's will, even if it does not coincide with our own : "His Majesty knows best what is suitable for us; it is not for us to advise him what to give us, for he can rightly reply that we know not what we ask" (St Teresa, *Mansions*, II,8).

43-45. Our Lord's word and example encourage in us a genuine spirit of Christian service. Only the Son of God who came down from heaven and freely submitted to humiliation (at Bethlehem, Nazareth, Calvary, and in the Sacred Host) can ask a person to make himself last, if he wishes to be first.

The Church, right through history, continues Christ's mission of service to mankind : "Experienced in human affairs, the Church, without attempting to interfere in any way in the politics of States, 'seeks but a solitary goal: to carry forward the work of Christ himself under the lead of the befriending Spirit. And

you must be your servant, [44]and whoever would be first among you must be slave of all. [45]For the Son of man also came not to be served but to serve, and to give his life as a ransom of many."

The blind man of Jericho

Mt 20:29-34
Lk 18:35-43

[46]And they came to Jericho; and as he was leaving Jericho with his disciples and a great multitude, Bartimaeus, a blind beggar, the son of Timaeus, was sitting by the roadside. [47]And when he heard that it was Jesus of

---

sed quicumque voluerit fieri maior inter vos, erit vester minister, [44]et quicumque voluerit in vobis primus esse, erit omnium servus; [45]nam et Filius hominis non venit, ut ministraretur ei, sed ut ministraret et daret animam suam redemptionem pro multis." [46]Et veniunt Ierichum. Et proficiscente eo de Iericho et discipulis eius et plurima multitudine, filius Timaei Bartimaeus caecus sedebat iuxta viam mendicans. [47]Qui, cum audisset quia Iesus Nazarenus est,

---

Christ entered this world to give witness to the truth, to rescue and not to sit in judgment, to serve and not to be served' (Vatican II, *Gaudium et spes*, 3). Sharing the noblest aspirations of men and suffering when she sees them not satisfied, she wishes to help them attain their full flowering, and that is why she offers men what she possesses as her characteristic attribute: a global vision of man and of the human race" (Paul VI, *Populorum progressio*, 13).

Our attitude should be that of our Lord : we should seek to serve God and men with a truly supernatural outlook, not expecting any return; we should serve even those who do not appreciate the service we do them. This undoubtedly does not make sense, judged by human standards. However, the Christian identified with Christ takes "pride" precisely in serving others; by so doing he shares in Christ's mission and thereby attains his true dignity : "This dignity is expressed in readiness to serve, in keeping with the example of Christ, who 'came not to be served but to serve.' If, in the light of this attitude of Christ's, 'being a king' is truly possible only by 'being a servant', then 'being a servant' also demands so much spiritual maturity that it must really be described as 'being a king.' In order to be able to serve others worthily and effectively we must be able to master ourselves, possess the virtues that make this mastery possible" (John Paul II, *Redemptor hominis*, 21). Cf. note on Mt 20:27-28.

46-52. "Hearing the commotion the crowd was making, the blind man asks, 'What is happening?' They told him, 'It is Jesus of Nazareth.' At this his soul was so fired with faith in Christ that he cried out, 'Jesus, Son of David, have mercy on me!'

"Don't you feel the same urge to cry out? You who also are waiting at the side of the way, of this highway of life that is so very short? You who need more light, you who need more grace to make up your mind to seek holiness? Don't you feel an urgent need to cry out, 'Jesus, Son of David, have mercy on

Nazareth, he began to cry out and say, "Jesus, son of David, have mercy on me!" ⁴⁸And many rebuked him, telling him to be silent; but he cried out all the more, "Son of David, have mercy on me!" ⁴⁹And Jesus stopped and said, "Call him." And they called the blind man, saying to him, "Take heart; rise, he is calling you." ⁵⁰And throwing off his mantle he sprang up and came to Jesus. ⁵¹And Jesus said to him, "What do you want me to do for you?" And the blind man

---

coepit clamare et dicere: "Fili David Iesu, miserere mei!" ⁴⁸Et comminabantur ei multi, ut taceret; at ille multo magis clamabat: "Fili David, miserere mei!" ⁴⁹Et stans Iesus dixit: "Vocate illum!" Et vocant caecum dicentes ei: "Animaequior esto. Surge, vocat te!" ⁵⁰Qui, proiecto vestimento suo, exsiliens venit ad Iesum. ⁵¹Et respondens ei Iesus dixit: "Quid vis tibi faciam?" Caecus

---

me'? What a beautiful aspiration for you to repeat again and again! . . .

"'Many rebuked him, telling him to be silent.' As people have done to you, when you sensed that Jesus was passing your way. Your heart beat faster and you too began to cry out, prompted by an intimate longing. Then your friends, the need to do the done thing, the easy life, your surroundings, all conspired to tell you: 'Keep quiet, don't cry out. Who are you to be calling Jesus? Don't bother him.'

"But poor Bartimaeus would not listen to them. He cried our all the more : 'Son of David, have mercy on me.' Our Lord, who had heard him right from the beginning, let him persevere in his prayer. He does the same with you. Jesus hears our cries from the very first, but he waits. He wants us to be convinced that we need him. He wants us to beseech him, to persist, like the blind man waiting by the road from Jericho. 'Let us imitate him. Even if God does not immediately give us what we ask, even if many people try to put us off our prayers, let us still go on praying' (St John Chrysostom, *Hom. on St Matthew*, 66).

"'And Jesus stopped, and told them to call him.' Some of the better people in the crowd turned to the blind man and said, 'Take heart; rise, he is calling you.' Here you have the Christian vocation! But God does not call only once. Bear in mind that our Lord is seeking us at every moment: get up, he tells us, put aside your indolence, your easy life, your petty selfishness, your silly little problems. Get up from the ground, where you are lying prostrate and shapeless. Acquire height, weight and volume, and a supernatural outlook.

"And throwing off his mantle the man sprang up and came to Jesus. He threw off his mantle! I don't know if you have ever lived through a war, but many years ago I had occasion to visit a battlefield shortly after an engagement. There, strewn all over the ground, were greatcoats, water bottles, haversacks stuffed with family souvenirs, letters, photographs of loved ones . . . which belonged, moreover, not to the vanquished but to the victors! All these items had become superfluous in the bid to race forward and leap over the enemy defences. Just as happened to Bartimaeus, as he raced towards Christ.

said to him, "Master,[t] let me receive my sight." [52]And Jesus said to him, "Go your way; your faith has made you well." And immediately he received his sight and followed him on the way.

---

autem dixit ei: "Rabboni, ut videam!" [52]Et Iesus ait illi: "Vade; fides tua te salvum fecit." Et confestim vidit et sequebatur eum in via.

"Never forget that Christ cannot be reached without sacrifice. We have to get rid of everything that gets in the way—greatcoat, haversack, water bottle. You have to do the same in this battle for the glory of God, in this struggle of love and peace by which we are trying to spread Christ's kingdom. In order to serve the Church, the Pope and all souls, you must be ready to give up everything superfluous. . . .

"And now begins a dialogue with God, a marvellous dialogue that moves us and sets our hearts on fire, for you and I are now Bartimaeus. Christ, who is God, begins to speak and asks, *Quid tibi vis faciam?* 'What do your want me to do for you?' The blind man answers. 'Lord, that I may see.' How utterly logical! How about yourself, can you really see? Haven't you too experienced at times what happened to the blind man of Jericho? I can never forget how, when meditating on this passage many years back, and realising that Jesus was expecting something of me, though I myself did not know what it was, I made up my own aspirations: 'Lord, what is it you want! What are you asking of me'? I had a feeling that he wanted me to take on something new and the cry, *Rabboni, ut videam*, 'Master, that I may see,' moved me to beseech Christ again and again, 'Lord, whatever it is that you wish, let it be done.'

"Pray with me now to our Lord: *doce me facere voluntatem tuam, quia Deus meus es tu* (Ps 142:10) ('teach me to do thy will, for you art my God'). In short, our lips should express a true desire on our part to correspond effectively to our Creator's promptings, striving to follow out his plans with unshakeable faith, being fully convinced that he cannot fail us. . . .

"But let us go back to the scene outside Jericho. It is now to you that Christ is speaking. He asks you, 'What do you want me to do for you?' 'Master, let me receive my sight.' Then Jesus answers, 'Go your way. Your faith has made you well.' And immediately he received his sight and followed him on his way." Following Jesus on his way. You have understood what our Lord was asking from you and you have decided to accompany him on his way. You are trying to walk in his footsteps, to clothe yourself in Christ's clothing, to be Christ himself: well, your faith, your faith in the light our Lord is giving you, must be both operative and full of sacrifice. Don't fool yourself. Don't think you are going to find new ways. The faith he demands of us is as I have said. We must keep in step with him, working generously and at the same time uprooting and getting rid of everything that gets in the way" (J. Escrivá, *Friends of God*, 195-198).

[t]Or *Rabbi*

11

The Messiah enters Jerusalem

¹And when they drew near to Jerusalem, to Bethphage and Bethany, at the Mount of Olives, he sent two of his disciples, ²and said to them, "Go into the village opposite you, and immediately as you enter it you will find a colt tied, on which no one has ever sat; untie it and bring it. ³If any one says to you, 'Why are you doing this?' say, 'The Lord has need of it and will send it back here immediately.'"

Mt 21:1-9
Lk 19:29-38
Jn 12:12-16
Lk 23:53

Mk 14:14

---

¹Et cum appropinquarent Hierosolymae, Bethphage et Bethaniae ad montem Olivarum, mittit duos ex discipulis suis ²et ait illis: "Ite in castellum, quod est contra vos, et statim introeuntes illud invenietis pullum ligatum, super quem nemo adhuc hominum sedit; solvite illum et adducite. ³Et si quis vobis dixerit: 'Quid facitis hoc?', dicite: 'Domino necessarius est, et continuo illum remittit

---

1-11. Jesus had visited Jerusalem various times before, but he never did so in this way. Previously he had not wanted to be recognized as the Messiah; he avoided the enthusiasm of the crowd; but now he accepts their acclaim and even implies that it is justified, by entering the city in the style of a pacific king. Jesus's public ministry is about to come to a close : he has completed his mission; he has preached and worked miracles; he has revealed himself as God wished he should; now in this triumphant entry into Jerusalem he shows that he is the Messiah. The people, by shouting "Blessed is he who comes in the name of the Lord! Blessed is the kingdom of our father David that is coming!", are proclaiming Jesus as the long-awaited Messiah. When the leaders of the people move against him some days later, they reject this recognition the people have given him. Cf. notes on Mt 21:1-5 and 21:9.

3. Although, absolutely speaking, our Lord has no need of man, in fact he does choose to use us to carry out his plans just as he made use of the donkey for his entry into Jerusalem. "Jesus makes do with a poor animal for a throne. I don't know about you; but I am not humiliated to acknowledge that in the Lord's eyes I am a beast of burden : 'I am like a donkey in your presence; nevertheless I am continually with you. You hold my right hand,' (Ps 72:23), you take me by the bridle.

"Try to remember what a donkey is like—now that so few of them are left. Not an old, stubborn, vicious one that would give you a kick when you least expected, but a young one with his ears up like antennae. He lives on a meagre diet, is hard-working and has a quick, cheerful trot. There are hundreds of animals more beautiful, more deft and strong. But it was a donkey Christ chose when he presented himself to the people as king in response to their acclamation. For Jesus has no time for calculations, for astuteness, for the

Ps 118:25-26

Lk 1:32

Mt 21:12-22
Lk 19:45-48

4And they went away, and found a colt tied at the door out in the open street; and they untied it. 5And those who stood there said to them, "What are you doing, untying the colt?" 6And they told them what Jesus had said; and they let them go. 7And they brought the colt to Jesus, and threw their garments on it; and he sat upon it. 8And many spread their garments on the road, and others spread leafy branches which they had cut from the fields. 9And those who went before and those who followed cried out, "Hosanna! Blessed is he who comes in the name of the Lord! 10Blessed is the kingdom of our father David that is coming! Hosanna in the highest!"

11And he entered Jerusalem, and went into the temple; and when he had looked around at everything, as it was already late, he went out to Bethany with the twelve.

The barren fig tree. The expulsion of the money-changers

12On the following day, when they came from Bethany,

---

iterum huc.' " 4Et abeuntes invenerunt pullum ligatum ante ianuam foris in bivio et solvunt eum. 5Et quidam de illic stantibus dicebant illis: "Quid facitis solventes pullum?" 6Qui dixerunt eis, sicut dixerat Iesus; et dimiserunt eis. 7Et ducunt pullum ad Iesum et imponunt illi vestimenta sua; et sedit super eum. 8Et multi vestimenta sua straverunt in via, alii autem frondes, quas exciderant in agris. 9Et qui praeibant et qui sequebantur, clamabant: *"Hosanna! Benedictus, qui venit in nomine Domini!* 10Benedictum, quod venit regnum patris nostri David! *Hosanna* in excelsis!" 11Et introivit Hierosolymam in templum; et circumspectis omnibus, cum iam vespera esset hora, exivit in Bethaniam cum Duodecim. 12Et altera die cum exirent a Bethania, esuriit. 13Cumque vidisset a

---

cruelty of cold hearts, for attractive but empty beauty. What he likes is the cheerfulness of a young heart, a simple step, a natural voice, clean eyes, attention to his affectionate word of advice. That is how he reigns in the soul" (J. Escrivá, *Christ is passing by*, 181).

12. Jesus' hunger is another sign of his being truly human. When we contemplate Jesus we should feel him very close to us; he is true God and true man. His experience of hunger shows that he understands us perfectly: he has shared our needs and limitations. "How generous our Lord is in humbling himself and fully accepting his human condition! He does not use his divine power to escape from difficulties or effort. Let's pray that he will teach us to be tough, to love work, to appreciate the human and divine nobility of savouring the consequences of self-giving" (J. Escrivá, *Christ is passing by*, 161).

he was hungry. [13]And seeing in the distance a fig tree in Lk 3:9; 13:6-9 leaf, he went to see if he could find anything on it. When he came to it, he found nothing but leaves, for it was not the season for figs. [14]And he said to it, "May no one ever eat fruit from you again." And his disciples heard it.

[15]And they came to Jerusalem. And he entered the Jn 2:14-16 temple and began to drive out those who sold and those who bought in the temple, and he overturned the tables of the money-changers and the seats of those who sold pigeons; [16]and he would not allow any one to carry anything through

---

longe ficum habentem folia, venit si quid forte inveniret in ea; et cum venisset ad eam, nihil invenit praeter folia: non enim erat tempus ficorum. [14]Et respondens dixit ei: "Iam non amplius in aeternum quisquam fructum ex te manducet." Et audiebant discipuli eius. [15]Et venient Hierosolymam. Et cum introisset in templum, coepit eicere vendentes et ementes in templo et mensas nummulariorum et cathedras vendentium columbas evertit, [16]et non sinebat, ut

13-14. Jesus, of course, knew that it was not the right time for figs; therefore, he was not looking for figs to eat. His action must have a deeper meaning. The Fathers of the Church, whose interpretation St Bede reflects in his commentary on this passage, tell us that the miracle has an allegorical purpose: Jesus had come among his own people, the Jews, hungry to find fruit of holiness and good works, but all he found were external practices—leaves without fruit. Similarly, when he enters the temple, he upbraids those present for turning the temple of God, which is a house of prayer (prayer is the fruit of piety), into a place of commerce (mere leaves). "So you", St Bede concludes, "if you do not want to be condemned by Christ, should guard against being a barren tree, by offering to Jesus, who made himself poor, the fruit of piety which he expects of you" (*In Marci Evangelium expositio, in loc.*).

God wants both fruit and foliage; when, because the right intention is missing, there are only leaves, only appearances, we must suspect that there is nothing but purely human action, with no supernatural depth—behaviour which results from ambition, pride and a desire to attract attention.

"We have to work a lot on this earth and we must do our work well, since it is our daily tasks that we have to sanctify. But let us never forget to do everything for God's sake. If we were to do it for ourselves, out of pride, we would produce nothing but leaves, and no matter how luxuriant they were, neither God nor our fellow man would find any good in them" (J. Escrivá, *Friends of God*, 202).

15-18. Our Lord does not abide lack of faith or piety in things to do with the worship of God. If he acts so vigorously to defend the temple of the Old Law, it indicates how we should conduct ourselves in the Christian temple, where he is really and truly present in the Blessed Eucharist. "Piety has its own

151

Is 56:7
Jer 7:11

the temple. [17]And he taught, and said to them, "Is it not written, 'My house shall be called a house of prayer for all the nations'? But you have made it a den of robbers." [18]And the chief priests and the scribes heard it and sought a way to destroy him; for they feared him, because all the multitude was astonished at his teaching. [19]And when evening came they[u] went out of the city.

Mk 11:14

[20]As they passed by in the morning, they saw the fig tree withered away to its roots. [21]And Peter remembered and said to him, "Master,[v] look! The fig tree which you cursed has withered." [22]And Jesus answered them, "Have faith in God. [23]Truly, I say to you, whoever says to this mountain,

Jn 14:1
Mt 17:20
Lk 17:6

---

quisquam vas transferret per templum. [17]Et docebat dicens eis: "Non scriptum est: *'Domus mea domus orationis vocabitur omnibus gentibus'*? Vos autem fecistis eam *speluncam latronum.*" [18]Quo audito, principes sacerdotum et scribae quaerebant quomodo eum perderent; timebant enim eum, quoniam universa turba admirabatur super doctrina eius. [19]Et cum vespera facta esset, egrediebantur de civitate. [20]Et cum mane transirent, viderunt ficum aridam factam a radicibus. [21]Et recordatus Petrus dicit ei: "Rabbi, ecce ficus, cui maledixisti, aruit." [22]Et respondens Iesus ait illis: "Habete fidem Dei! [23]Amen dico vobis: Quicumque dixerit huic monti: 'Tollere et mittere in mare', et non haesitaverit in corde suo, sed crediderit quia, quod dixerit, fiat, fiet ei.

---

good manners. Learn them. It's a shame to see those 'pious' people who don't know how to attend Mass—even though they go daily,—nor how to bless themselves (they throw their hands about in the weirdest fashion), nor how to bend the knee before the Tabernacle (their ridiculous genuflections seem a mockery), nor how to bow their heads reverently before a picture of our Lady" (J. Escrivá, *The Way*, 541). Cf. note on Mt 21:12-13.

20-25. Jesus speaks to us here about the power of prayer. For prayer to be effective, absolute faith and trust are required : "A keen and living faith. Like Peter's. When you have it—our Lord has said so—you will move mountains, the humanly insuperable obstacles that rise up against your apostolic undertakings" (J. Escrivá, *The Way*, 489).

For prayer to be effective, we also need to love our neighbour, forgiving him everything : if we do, then God our Father will also forgive us. Since we are all sinners we need to admit the fact before God and ask his pardon (cf. Lk 18:9-14). When Christ taught us to pray he required that we have these predispositions (cf. Mt 6:12; also Mt 5:23 and notes on same). Here is how Theophylact (*Enarratio in Evangelium Marci, in loc.*) puts it : "When you pray, if you have anything against anyone, forgive him, so that your Father who is

[u]Other ancient authorities read *he*   [v]Or *Rabbi*

'Be taken up and cast into the sea,' and does not doubt in his heart, but believes that what he says will come to pass, it will be done for him. [24]Therefore I tell you, whatever you ask in prayer, believe that you receive it, and you will. [25]And whenever you stand praying, forgive, if you have anything against any one; so that your Father also who is in heaven may forgive you your trespasses."[w]

Mt 17:7
Jn 14:13
16:23

Mt 5:23

Jesus' authority

[27]And they came again to Jerusalem. And as he was walking in the temple, the chief priests and the scribes and the elders came to him, [28]and they said to him, "By what

Mt 21:23-27
Lk 20:1-8

---

[24]Propterea dico vobis: Omnia, quaecumque orantes petitis, credite quia iam accepistis, et erunt vobis. [25]Et cum statis in oratione, dimittite, si quid habetis adversus aliquem, ut et Pater vester, qui in caelis est, dimittat vobis peccata vestra."[(26)] [27]Et veniunt rursus Hierosolymam. Et cum ambularet in templo, accedunt ad eum summi sacerdotes et scribae et seniores [28]et dicebant illi: "In

---

in heaven may forgive you [. . .]. He who believes with great affection raises his whole heart to God and, in David's words, opens his soul to God. If he expands his heart before God in this way, he becomes one with him, and his burning heart is surer of obtaining what he desires."

Even when he is in the state of sin, man should seek God out in prayer; Jesus places no limitations at all : "Whatever you ask . . .". Therefore, our personal unworthiness should not be an excuse for not praying confidently to God. Nor should the fact that God already knows our needs be an excuse for not turning to him. St Teresa explains this when she prays : "O my God, can it be better to keep silent about my necessities, hoping that Thou wilt relieve them? No, indeed, for Thou, my Lord and my Joy, knowing how many they must be and how it will alleviate them if we speak to Thee of them, dost bid us pray to Thee and say that Thou will not fail to give" (St Teresa, *Exclamations*, 5). Cf. notes on Mt 6:5-6 and Mt 7:7-11.

26. As the RSV note points out, many ancient manuscripts add a v.26 : but it is clearly an addition, taken straight from Mt 6:15. This addition was included by the editors of the Old Vulgate.

27-33. Those who put this question to Jesus are the same people as, some days earlier, sought to destroy him (cf. Mk 11:18). They represent the official Judaism of the period (cf. note on Mt 2:4). Jesus had already given proofs and signs of being the Messiah, in his miracles and preaching; and St John the Baptist had borne witness about who Jesus was. This is why, before replying,

[w]Other ancient authorities add verse 26, "*But if you do not forgive, neither will your Father who is in heaven forgive your trespass*"

authority are you doing these things, or who gave you this authority to do them?" [29]Jesus said to them, "I will ask you a question; answer me, and I will tell you by what authority I do these things. [30]Was the baptism of John from heaven or from men? Answer me." [31]And they argued with one another, "If we say, 'From heaven,' he will say, 'Why then did you not believe him?' [32]But shall we say, 'From men'?"—they were afraid of the people, for all held that John was a real prophet. [33]So they answered Jesus, "We do not know." And Jesus said to them, "Neither will I tell you by what authority I do these things."

12

Mt 21:33-46
Lk 20:9-19
Is 5:1-2
The parable of the wicked tenants

[1]And he began to speak to them in parables. "A man planted

---

qua potestate haec facis? Vel quis tibi dedit hanc potestatem, ut ista facias?" [29]Iesus autem ait illis: "Interrogabo vos unum verbum, et respondete mihi, et dicam vobis, in qua potestate haec faciam: [30]Baptismum Ioannis de caelo erat an ex hominibus? Respondete mihi." [31]At illi cogitabant secum dicentes: "Si dixerimus: De caelo, dicet: 'Quare ergo non credidistis ei?' [32]Si autem dixerimus: Ex hominibus?" Timebant populum: omnes enim habebant Ioannem quia vere propheta esset. [33]Et respondentes dicunt Iesu: "Nescimus." Et Iesus ait illis: "Neque ego dico vobis, in qua potestate haec faciam."

[1]Et coepit illis in parabolis loqui: *"Vineam pastinavit homo, et circumdedit*

---

our Lord asks them to recognize the truth proclaimed by the Precursor. But they do not want to accept this truth; nor do they want to reject it publicly, out of fear of the people. Since they are not ready to admit their mistake, any further explanation Jesus might offer would serve no purpose.

This episode has many parallels in everyday life : anyone who seeks to call God to account will be confounded.

1-12. This parable is a masterly summary of history of salvation. To explain the mystery of his redemptive death, Jesus makes use of one of the most beautiful allegories of the Old Testament: the so-called "song of the vineyard," in which Isaiah (5:1-7) prophesied Israel's ingratitude for God's favours. On the basis of this Isaiah text, Jesus reveals the patience of God, who sends one messenger after another—the prophets of the Old Testament—until at last, as the text says, he sends "his beloved son", Jesus, whom the tenants will kill. This

a vineyard, and set a hedge around it, and dug a pit for the wine press, and built a tower, and let it out to tenants, and went into another country. ²When the time came, he sent a servant to the tenants, to get from them some of the fruit of the vineyard. ³And they took him and beat him, and sent him away empty-handed. ⁴Again he sent to them another servant, and they wounded him in the head, and treated him shamefully. ⁵And he sent another, and him they killed; and so with many others, some they beat and some they killed. ⁶He had still one other, a beloved son; finally he sent him to them, saying, 'They will respect my son.' ⁷But those tenants said to one another, 'This is the heir; come, let us kill him, and the inheritance will be ours.' ⁸And they took Heb 13:12 him and killed him, and cast him out of the vineyard. ⁹What will the owner of the vineyard do? He will come and destroy the tenants, and give the vineyard to others. ¹⁰Have you not Ps 118:22-23 read the scripture:

'The very stone which the builders rejected
has become the head of the corner;
¹¹this was the Lord's doing,
and it is marvellous in our eyes'?"

¹²And they tried to arrest him, but feared the multitude, for they perceived that he had told the parable against them; so they left him and went away.

---

saepem et fodit lacum et aedificavit turrim, et locavit eam agricolis et peregre profectus est. ²Et misit ad agricolis in tempore servum, ut ab agricolis acciperet de fructu vineae; ³qui apprehensum eum caeciderunt et dimiserunt vacuum. ⁴Et iterum misit ad illos alium servum; et illum in capite vulneraverunt et contumeliis affecerunt. ⁵Et alium misit, et illum occiderunt, et plures alios, quosdam caedentes, alios vero occidentes. ⁶Adhuc unum habebat, filium dilectum. Misit illum ad eos novissimum dicens: 'Reverebuntur filium meum.' ⁷Coloni autem illi dixerunt ad invicem: 'Hic est heres! Venite, occidamus eum, et nostra erit hereditas.' ⁸Et apprehendentes eum occiderunt et eiecerunt extra vineam. ⁹Quid ergo faciet dominus vineae? Veniet et perdet colonos et dabit

---

expression, as also that which God himself uses to describe Christ at Baptism (1:11) and the Transfiguration (9:7), points to the divinity of Jesus, who is the cornerstone of salvation, rejected by the builders in their selfishness and pride. To the Jews listening to Jesus telling this parable, his meaning must have been crystal clear. The rulers "perceived that he had told the parable against them" (v.12) and that it was about the fulfilment of the Isaiah prophecy (cf. note on Mt 21:33-46).

Mt 22:15-22
Lk 20:20-26
Mk 3:6 **On tribute to Caesar**

¹³And they sent to him some of the Pharisees and some of the Herodians, to entrap him in his talk. ¹⁴And they came and said to him, "Teacher, we know that you are true, and care for no man; for you do not regard the position of men, but truly teach the way of God. Is it lawful to pay taxes to Caesar, or not? ¹⁵Should we pay them, or should we not?" But knowing their hypocrisy, he said to them, "Why put me to the test? Bring me a coin,^x and let me look at it." ¹⁶And they brought one. And he said to them, "Whose likeness and inscription is this?" They said to him, "Caesar's." Rom 13:7 ¹⁷Jesus said to them, "Render to Caesar the things that are Caesar's, and to God the things that are God's." And they were amazed at him.

---

vineam aliis. ¹⁰Nec Scripturam hanc legistis: '*Lapidem, quem reprobaverunt aedificantes, hic factus est in caput anguli; *¹¹*a Domino factum est istud, et est mirabile in oculis nostri*'?" ¹²Et quaerebant eum tenere et timuerunt turbam; cognoverunt enim quoniam ad eos parabolam hanc dixerit. Et relicto eo abierunt. ¹³Et mittunt ad eum quosdam ex pharisaeis et herodianis, ut eum caperent in verbo. ¹⁴Qui venientes dicunt ei: "Magister, scimus quia verax es et non curas quemquam, nec enim vides in faciem hominum, sed in veritate viam Dei doces. Licet dare tributum Caesari an non? Dabimus an non dabimus?" ¹⁵Qui sciens versutiam eorum ait illis: "Quid me tentatis? Afferte mihi denarium, ut videam." ¹⁶At illi attulerunt. Et ait illis: "Cuius est imago haec et inscriptio?" Illi autem dixerunt ei: "Caesaris." ¹⁷Iesus autem dixit illis:

13-17. Jesus uses this situation to teach that man belongs totally to his Creator: "You must perforce give Caesar the coin which bears his likeness, but let you give your whole being to God, because it is his likeness, not Caesar's, that you bear" (St Jerome, *Comm. in Marcum, in loc.*).

Our Lord here asserts a principle which should guide the action of Christians in public life. The Church recognizes the rightful autonomy of earthly realities, but this does not mean that she has not a responsibility to light them up with the light of the Gospel. When they work shoulder to shoulder with other citizens to develop society, Christian lay people should bring a Christian influence to bear: "If the role of the Hierarchy is to teach and to interpret authentically the norms of morality to be followed in this matter, it belongs to lay people, without waiting passively for orders and directives, to take the initiative freely and to infuse a Christian spirit into the mentality, customs, laws and structures of the community in which they live. Changes are necessary, basic reforms are indispensable; lay people should strive resolutely to permeate them with the spirit of the Gospel" (Paul VI, *Populorum progressio*, 81).

^xGreek *a denarius*

The resurrection of the dead

¹⁸And Sadducees came to him, who say that there is no resurrection; and they asked him a question, saying, ¹⁹"Teacher, Moses wrote for us that if a man's brother dies and leaves a wife, but leaves no child, the man[y] must take the wife, and raise up children for his brother. ²⁰There were seven brothers; the first took a wife, and when he died left no children; ²¹and the second took her, and died, leaving no children; and the third likewise; ²²and the seven left no children. Last of all the woman also died. ²³In the resurrection whose wife will she be? For the seven had her as wife."

²⁴Jesus said to them, "Is not this why you are wrong, that you know neither the scriptures nor the power of God? ²⁵For when they rise from the dead, they neither marry nor are given in marriage, but are like angels in heaven. ²⁶And

Mt 22:23-33
Lk 20:27-38

Deut 25:5-6
Gen 28:8

Ex 3:2, 6
Mt 8:11
Lk 16:22

"Quae sunt Caesaris, reddite Caesari et, quae sunt Dei, Deo." Et mirabantur super eo. ¹⁸Et veniunt ad eum sadducaei, qui dicunt resurrectionem non esse, et interrogabant eum dicentes: ¹⁹"Magister, Moyses nobis scripsit, ut *si cuius frater mortuus fuerit et reliquerit uxorem et filium non reliquerit, accipiat frater eius uxorem et resuscitet semen fratri suo.* ²⁰Septem fratres erant: et primus accepit uxorem et moriens non reliquit semen; ²¹et secundus accepit eam et mortuus est, non relicto semine; et tertius similiter; ²²et septem non reliquerunt semen. Novissima omnium defuncta est et mulier. ²³In resurrectione, cum resurrexerint, cuius de his erit uxor? Septem enim habuerunt eam uxorem." ²⁴Ait illis Iesus: "Non ideo erratis, quia non scitis Scripturas neque virtutem Dei? ²⁵Cum enim a mortuis resurrexerint, neque nubent neque nubentur, sed

---

18-27. Before answering the difficulty proposed by the Sadducees, Jesus wants to identify the source of the problem—man's tendency to confine the greatness of God inside a human framework through excessive reliance on reason, not giving due weight to divine Revelation and the power of God. A person can have difficulty with the truths of faith; this is not surprising, for these truths are above human reason. But it is ridiculous to try to find contradictions in the revealed word of God; this only leads away from any solution of difficulty and may make it impossible to find one's way back to God. We need to approach Sacred Scripture, and, in general, the things of God, with the humility which faith demands. In the passage about the burning bush, which Jesus quotes to the Sadducees, God says this to Moses : "Put off your shoes from your feet, for the place on which you are standing is holy ground" (Ex 3:5).

[y]Greek *his brother*

as for the dead being raised, have you not read in the book of Moses, in the passage about the bush, how God said to him, 'I am the God of Abraham, and the God of Isaac, and the God of Jacob'? [27]He is not God of the dead, but of the living; you are quite wrong."

The greatest commandment of all

Mt 22:34-40
Lk 20:39-40
10:25-28

[28]And one of the scribes came up and heard them disputing with one another, and seeing that he answered them well, asked him, "Which commandment is the first of all?" [29]Jesus answered, "The first is, 'Hear, O Israel: The Lord our God, the Lord is one; [30]and you shall love the Lord

Deut 6:4-5

---

sunt sicut angeli in caelis. [26]De mortuis autem quod resurgant, non legistis in libro Moysis super rubum, quomodo dixerit illi Deus inquiens: *'Ego sum Deus Abraham et Deus Isaac et Deus Iacob'*? [27]Non est Deus mortuorum sed vivorum! Multum erratis." [28]Et accessit unus de scribis, qui audierat illos conquirentes, videns quoniam bene illis responderit, interrogavit eum: "Quod est primum omnium mandatum?" [29]Iesus respondit: "Primum est: *'Audi, Israel:*

28-34. The doctor of the law who asks Jesus this question is obviously an upright man who is sincerely seeking the truth. He was impressed by Jesus' earlier reply (vv. 18-27) and he wants to learn more from him. His question is to the point and Jesus devotes time to instructing him, though he will soon castigate the scribes, of whom this man is one (cf. Mk 12:38ff).

Jesus sees in this man not just a scribe but a person who is looking for the truth. And his teaching finds its way into the man's heart. The scribe repeats what Jesus says, savouring it, and our Lord offers him an affectionate word which encourages his definitive conversion: "You are not far from the kingdom of God." This encounter reminds us of his meeting with Nicodemus (cf. Jn 3:1ff). On the doctrinal content of these two commandments cf. note on Mt 22:34-40.

30. This commandment of the Old Law, ratified by Jesus, shows, above all, God's great desire to engage in intimate conversation with man: "Would it not have sufficed to publish a permission giving us leave to love him? [. . .]. He makes a stronger declaration of his passionate love of us, and commands us to love him with all our power, lest the consideration of his majesty and our misery, which make so great a distance and inequality between us, or some other pretext, divert us from his love. In this he well shows that he did not leave in us for nothing the natural inclination to love him, for to the end that it may not be idle, he urges us by his general commandment to employ it, and that this commandment may be effected, there is no living man he has not furnished him abundantly with all means requisite thereto" (St Francis de Sales, *Treatise on the Love of God*, book 2, chap. 8).

158

your God with all your heart, and with all your soul, and
with all your mind, and with all your strength.' ³¹The
second is this, 'You shall love your neighbour as yourself.'
There is no other commandment greater than these." ³²And
the scribe said to him, "You are right, Teacher; you have
truly said that he is one, and there is no other than he; ³³and
to love him with all the heart, and with all the understanding, and with all the strength, and to love one's neighbour as oneself, is much more than all whole burnt offerings
and sacrifices." ³⁴And when Jesus saw that he answered
wisely, he said to him, "You are not far from the kingdom
of God." And after that no one dared to ask him any
question.

Lev 19:18

Jn 15:12
Deut 6:4; 4:35

1 Sam 15:22
Ps 40:7-9

Acts 26:27-29

Christ the son and Lord of David

³⁵And as Jesus taught in the temple, he said, "How can
the scribes say that the Christ is the son of David? ³⁶David
himself, inspired byᶻ the Holy Spirit, declared,

'The Lord said to my Lord,

Sit at my right hand,

till I put thy enemies under thy feet'.

³⁷David himself calls him Lord; so how is he his son?"
And the great throng heard him gladly.

Mt 22:41-46
Lk 20:41-44

Ps 10:1
2 Sam 23:2
Mt 9:27
Jn 7:42

Lk 19:48
21:38

---

*Dominus Deus noster Dominus unus est, ³⁰et diliges Dominum Deum tuum ex
toto corde tuo et ex tota anima tua et ex tota mente tua et ex tota virtute tua.'*
³¹Secundum est illud: *'Diliges proximum tuum tamquam teipsum.'* Maius
horum aliud mandatum non est". ³²Et ait illi scriba: "Bene, Magister, in veritate
dixisti: *'Unus est, et non est alius praeter eum;* ³³et diligere eum ex toto corde
et ex toto intellectu et ex toto fortitudine'* et: *'Diligere proximum tamquam
seipsum'* maius est omnibus holocautomatibus et sacrificiis." ³⁴Et Iesus videns
quod sapienter respondisset, dixit illi: "Non es longe a regno Dei." Et nemo

---

35-37. Jesus here bears witness, with his special authority, to the fact that
Scripture is divinely inspired, when he says that David was inspired by the Holy
Spirit when writing Psalm 110. We can see from here that Jews found it difficult
to interpret the beginning of the Psalm. Jesus shows the messianic sense of the
words "The Lord said to my Lord" : the second "Lord" is the Messiah, with
whom Jesus implicitly identifies himself. The mysteriously transcendental
character of the Messiah is indicated by the paradox of his being the son, the
descendant, of David, and yet David calls him his Lord. Cf. note on Mt
22:41-46.

ᵃOr *himself, in*

Jesus censures the scribes

Mt 23:6-7
Lk 20:45-47

³⁸And in his teaching he said, "Beware of the scribes, who like to go about in long robes, and to have salutations in the market places ³⁹and the best seats in the synagogues and the places of honour at feasts, ⁴⁰who devour widows' houses and for a pretence make long prayers. They will receive the greater condemnation."

The widow's mite

Lk 21:1-4
2 Kings 12:10

⁴¹And he sat down opposite the treasury, and watched the multitude putting money into the treasury. Many rich people put in large sums. ⁴²And a poor widow came, and put in two copper coins, which make a penny. ⁴³And he called his disciples to him, and said to them, "Truly, I say to you, this poor widow has put in more than all those who

---

iam audebat eum interrogare. ³⁵Et respondens Iesus dicebat docens in templo: "Quomodo dicunt scribae Christum filium esse David? ³⁶Ipse David dixit in Spiritu Sancto: '*Dixit Dominus Domino meo: Sede a dextris meis, donec ponam inimicos tuos sub pedibus tuis.*' ³⁷Ipse David dicit eum Dominum, et unde est filius eius?" Et multa turba eum libenter audiebat. ³⁸Et dicebat in doctrina sua: "Cavete a scribis, qui volunt in stolis ambulare et salutari in foro ³⁹et in primis cathedris sedere in synagogis et primos discubitus in cenis; ⁴⁰qui devorant domos viduarum et ostentant prolixas orationes. Hi accipient amplius iudicium." ⁴¹Et sedens contra gazophylacium aspiciebat quomodo turba iactaret aes in gazophylacium; et multi divites iactabant multa. ⁴²Et cum venisset una vidua pauper, misit duo minuta, quod est quadrans. ⁴³Et convocans discipulos suos ait illis: "Amen dico vobis: Vidua haec pauper plus omnibus misit, qui

---

38-40. Our Lord reproves disordered desire for human honours : "We should notice that salutations in the marketplace are not forbidden, nor people taking the best seats if that befits their position; rather, the faithful are warned to avoid, as they would evil men, those who set too much store by such honours" (St Bede, *In Marci Evangelium expositio, in loc.*). See also notes on Mt 23:2-3, 5, 11 and 14.

41-44. Our Lord uses this little event to teach us the importance of things which apparently are insignificant. He puts it somewhat paradoxically; the poor widow has contributed more than all the rich. In God's sight the value of such an action lies more in upright intention and generosity of spirit than in the quantity one gives. "Didn't you see the light in Jesus' eyes as the poor widow left her little alms in the temple? Give him what you can: the merit is not in whether it is big or small, but in the intention with which you give it" (J. Escrivá, *The Way*, 829).

are contributing to the treasury. ⁴⁴For they all contributed
out of their abundance; but she out of her poverty has put
in everything she had, her whole living."

13

THE ESCHATOLOGICAL DISCOURSE

Introduction

¹And as he came out of the temple, one of his disciples said
to him, "Look, Teacher, what wonderful stones and what

miserunt in gazophylacium: ⁴⁴omnes enim ex eo, quod abundabat illis, miserunt; haec vero de penuria sua omnia, quae habuit, misit, totum victum suum."

¹Et cum egrederetur de templo, ait illi unus ex discipulis suis: "Magister, aspice
quales lapides et quales structurae." ²Et Iesus ait illi: "Vides has magnas
aedificationes? Hic non relinquetur lapis super lapidem, qui non destruatur."
³Et cum sederet in montem Olivarum contra templum, interrogabat eum

By the same token, our actions are pleasing to God even if they are not as
perfect as we would like. St Francis de Sales comments : "Now as among the
treasures of the temple, the poor widow's mite was much esteemed, so the least
little good works, even though performed somewhat coldly and not according
to the whole extent of the charity which is in us, are agreeable to God, and
esteemed by him; so that though of themselves they cannot cause any increase
in the existing love [. . .] yet divine providence, counting on them and, out of
his goodness, valuing them, forthwith rewards them with increase of charity
for the present, and assigns to them a greater heavenly glory for the future" (St
Francis de Sales, *Treatise on the Love of God*, book 3, chap. 2).

1. The temple of Jerusalem was the pride of the Jews, awe-inspiring in scale
and magnificence. Its enormous blocks of cut stone gave it an overwhelming
sense of permanence. Using here, as always, everyday incidents as examples
to engrave his teaching on people's minds, Jesus Christ prophesied that soon
the Temple would be toppled, leaving not one stone upon another. The contrast
between reality and prophecy left the Apostles dumbfounded.

The prophecy was fulfilled to the letter in the year 70, when Titus conquered
Jerusalem. The Roman soldiers set fire to the temple. Titus, who wanted to
preserve it, tried to put out the blaze, but when he failed to do so he ordered its
total destruction. The walls which exist today were the foundations of the
building and part of the exterior wall : of the sanctuary itself not one stone
remained standing on another. In the reign of Julian the Apostate (A.D. 363)
some Jews tried in vain to rebuild the temple; since then no such attempts have
been made.

wonderful buildings!" ²And Jesus said to him, "Do you see these great buildings? There will not be left here one stone upon another, that will not be thrown down."

Signs of the destruction of Jerusalem

³And as he sat on the Mount of Olives opposite the temple, Peter and James and John and Andrew asked him privately, ⁴"Tell us, when will this be, and what will be the sign when these are all to be accomplished?" ⁵And Jesus began to say to them, "Take heed that no one leads you astray. ⁶Many will come in my name, saying, 'I am he!' and they will lead many astray. ⁷And when you hear of wars and rumours of wars, do not be alarmed; this must take place, but the end is not yet. ⁸For nation will rise against nation, and kingdom against kingdom; there will be earthquakes in various places, there will be famines; this is but the beginning of the sufferings.

Mt 24:4-14
Lk 21:8-19

Is 19:2
2 Chron 15:6

---

separatim Petrus et Iacobus et Ioannes et Andreas: ⁴"Dic nobis, quando ista erunt, et quod signum erit, quando haec omnia incipient consummari." ⁵Iesus autem coepit dicere illis: "Videte, ne quis vos seducat! ⁶Multi venient in nomine meo dicentes: 'Ego sum', et multos seducent. ⁷Cum audieritis autem bella et opiniones bellorum, ne timueritis; oportet fieri sed nondum finis. ⁸Exsurget

---

4. The prophecy of the destruction of the temple went clean contrary to the nationalistic ideas of the Jews. To their minds such a catastrophe could only happen as part of the end of the world (cf. Mt 24:3). After remaining silent for a while (cf. Mk 13:2-3), the Apostles ask when will this happen and what signs will indicate that the temple is about to be destroyed.

This destruction, Jesus explains, prefigures the end of the world, but does not imply that the latter is imminent; each event has characteristics of its own. Thus, the destruction of the temple will have its own signals and will happen in the next generation. The end of the world, however, is a secret known to God alone, and not even the Son wishes to reveal when this final event will happen (cf. Mk 13:32-33; Mt 24:36).

The Apostles ask Jesus about the end of the temple of Jerusalem and he notifies them of something more important : a time is approaching when they will need to be on the alert, in order not to be led into temptation or be deceived by false prophets.

Jesus replies to his disciples' questions in the form of a sermon, called the "eschatological discourse," which takes up all chapter 13 of St Mark. It is also called the "synoptic apocalypse," because it deals, mainly, with the last days of history, which will be marked by great catastrophes. Jesus uses this style of language to encourage us to be vigilant.

9"But take heed to yourselves; for they will deliver you up to councils, and you will be beaten in synagogues; and you will stand before governors and kings for my sake, to bear testimony before them. 10And the gospel must first be preached to all nations. 11And when they bring you to trial

Mt 10:17-22
Lk 21:12-17

Mk 16:15

enim gens super gentem, et regnum super regnum, erunt terrae motus per loca, erunt fames. Initium dolorum haec. 9Videte autem vosmetipsos. Tradent vos conciliis et in synagogis vapulabitis et ante praesides et reges stabitis propter me in testimonium illis. 10Et in omnes gentes primum oportet praedicari evangelium. 11Et cum duxerint vos tradentes, nolite praecogitare quid

9. Jesus prophesies to the Apostles that they will undergo persecutions because they preach the Gospel. These will be set in motion by the Jews (cf. Acts 4:5ff; 5:21ff; 6:12ff; 22:30; 23:1ff; 2 Cor 11:24), whose synagogues Tertullian called "fountains of persecution" (*Scorpiace*, X, 143), and continued by the Gentiles. These words of Jesus came true even in the lifetime of the Apostles. Appearance before the courts gave Christians a very valuable opportunity to bear witness to the Gospel (Acts 4:1-21; 5:17-42) and sometimes stirred the conscience of those who wielded authority, as the imprisonment of St Paul clearly shows (Acts 16:19-38; 22:24-26; 28:30-31).

10. This is one of the occasions on which our Lord proclaims that the Gospel, the good news of salvation, is destined to spread all over the world; and indeed, before the destruction of Jerusalem, the Apostles had already preached it all over the known world. Similarly, before the end of time all peoples will have heard the news and been given an opportunity to be converted, through the preaching of the Church; but this does not mean that everyone will accept and remain faithful to Christ's teaching. In any event, persecutions and difficulties should not lessen the apostolic zeal of his disciples but rather urge it on, for Christ's promise should always act as an effective stimulus. Our Lord, in fact, counts on us to engage in the truly apostolic task of spreading the Gospel.

The Second Vatican Council lays stress on the missionary character of the Church: "Even in the secular history of mankind the Gospel has acted as a leaven in the interests of liberty and progress, and it always offers itself as a leaven with regard to brotherhood, unity and peace. So it is not without reason that Christ is hailed by the faithful as 'the hope of the nations and their saviour' (Antiphon, 23 December). The period, therefore, between the first and second comings of the Lord is the time of missionary activity, when, like the harvest, the Church will be gathered from the four winds into the kingdom of God. For the Gospel must be preached to all peoples before the Lord comes" (*Ad gentes*, 8-9).

11. The natural fear this prophecy causes in the disciples provides our Lord with an opportunity to encourage them, by promising them the help of the Holy Spirit, who will suggest to them what to say in these circumstances.

and deliver you up, do not be anxious beforehand what you are to say; but say whatever is given you in that hour, for it is not you who speak, but the Holy Spirit. ¹²And brother will deliver up brother to death, and the father his child, and children will rise against parents and have them put to death; ¹³and you will be hated by all for my name's sake. But he who endures to the end will be saved.

loquamini, sed, quod datum vobis fuerit in illa hora, id loquimini: non enim estis vos loquentes sed Spiritus Sanctus. ¹²Et tradet frater fratrem in mortem et pater filium; et consurgent filii in parentes et morte afficient eos; ¹³et eritis odio omnibus propter nomen meum. Qui autem sustinuerit in finem, hic salvus erit.

The lives of the martyrs are full of examples of how ordinary people find words of wisdom far above their natural ability.

Supported by Jesus' promise, so often fulfilled, we should never be afraid, no matter what difficulties arise; on the contrary, we should have a holy daring, leading us to confess, spread and defend the faith, thereby fulfilling our obligation to be apostolic in our own environment.

13. In the first three centuries of the Church the mere fact of being a Christian was reason enough to be hauled before the courts. St Justin (2nd century) went as far as saying that "in our case you use the mere name as proof against us" (*Apologia*, 4, 44). There have been, and are, countless Christians whose lives, reputations and property have been attacked out of hatred of the Gospel; in them are fulfilled these words of Jesus : "Blessed are those who are persecuted for righteousness' sake, for theirs is the kingdom of heaven. Blessed are you when men revile you and persecute you and utter all kinds of evil against you falsely on my account" (Mt 5:10-11; cf. Acts 5:41; 1 Pet 4:12-14). Nothing compares with the glory which will be the reward of those who persevere (cf. Rom 8:18).

Our Lord's final words in Mark 13:13 are an exhortation to persevere to the very end : "He who endures to the end will be saved." For each person this "end" is the moment of death. As the Magisterium of the Church teaches, each person, *immediately* after dying, passes on to enjoy his or her eternal reward or to suffer eternal punishment—though some must undergo purification in purgatory before entering the joy of heaven : "We make the following definition: In the usual providence of God the souls of all the saints who departed from this world before the Passion of our Lord Jesus Christ, and also those of the holy Apostles, martyrs, confessors, virgins, and others of the faithful who died after receiving the Baptism of Christ—provided that they had no need of purification at the time of their death, or will not have such need when they die at some future time; [. . .] and that the souls of children who have been reborn with the Baptism of Christ [. . .] when they die before attaining the use of free will : all these souls immediately after death, or in the case of those needing it, after the purification we have mentioned, have been, are, and will

The destruction of Jerusalem

¹⁴"But when you see the desolating sacrilege set up where it ought not to be (let the reader understand), then let those who are in Judea flee to the mountains; ¹⁵let him who is on the housetop not go down, nor enter his house, to take anything away; ¹⁶and let him who is in the field not turn back to take his mantle. ¹⁷And alas for those who are with child and for those who give suck in those days! ¹⁸Pray that it may not happen in winter. ¹⁹For in those days there will

Dan 9:27
12:4, 10

Mt 24:15-25
Lk 21:20-24

Dan 12:1
Joel 2:2

---

¹⁴Cum autem videritis *abominationem desolationis* stantem, ubi non debet, qui legit intellegat, tunc, qui in Iudaea sunt, fugiant in montes, ¹⁵qui autem super tectum, ne descendat nec introeat, ut tollat quid de domo sua, ¹⁶et qui in agro erit, non revertatur retro tollere vestimentum suum. ¹⁷Vae autem praegnantibus et nutrientibus in illis diebus! ¹⁸Orate vero, ut hieme non fiat; ¹⁹erunt enim dies

---

be in heaven [. . .] with Christ, joined to the company of the holy angels [. . .]. We also define that [. . .] the souls of those who die in actual mortal sin go down into hell soon after their death, and there suffer the pains of hell. Nevertheless, on the Day of Judgment, all men will appear with their bodies before the tribunal of Christ to render an account of their personal deeds, that 'each one may receive good or evil, according to what he has done in the body' (2 Cor 5:10)" (Benedict XII, *Benedictus Deus*).

14-19. From v.14 on, the discourse refers to the events which will happen at the time of the destruction of Jerusalem. For interpretation of this passage cf. note on Mt 24:15-20.

14. "The desolating sacrilege", the "abomination of desolation", a phrase taken from Daniel (9:27), is normally used to designate any idolatrous and sacrilegious person, thing or act outrageous to the religious faith and worship of the Jewish people (1 Mac 1:5).

From the parallel passage in St Matthew (24:25) we can see that Jesus explicitly cited the prophecy of Daniel 9:27. Hence, the phrase "let the reader understand", which occurs in both Gospels, should be seen as an exhortation by Jesus to attentively read the prophetic text in the light of his words. Cf. note on Mt 24:15.

19-20. V. 19 evokes a passage in Daniel (12:1). In this way Jesus moves on to describe the signals of the imminent end of the world, and the great distress that will obtain at the time. This distress, although it covers the entire history of the Church from its beginnings, will become especially severe at the time of the End. Despite being fearsome times, these are times of salvation, arranged by divine providence for the good of those who love God (cf. Rom 8:28). Therefore, they have to be faced with total confidence in God : he will shorten these days and will save us.

be such tribulation as has not been from the beginning of the creation which God created until now, and never will be. [20]And if the Lord had not shortened the days, no human being would be saved; but for the sake of the elect, whom he chose, he shortened the days.

Signs of the end of the world and the coming of the Son of man

[21]"And then if any one says to you, 'Look, here is the Christ!' or 'Look, there he is!' do not believe it. [22]False Christs and false prophets will arise and show signs and wonders, to lead astray, if possible, the elect. [23]But take heed; I have told you all things beforehand.

[24]"But in those days, after that tribulation, the sun will

Deut 13:1

Is 13:10
Is 34:4

---

illi *tribulatio talis, qualis non fuit ab initio creaturae*, quam condidit Deus, *usque nunc*, neque fiet. [20]Et nisi breviasset Dominus dies, non fuisset salva omnis caro. Sed propter electos, quos elegit, breviavit dies. [21]Et tunc, si quis vobis dixerit: 'Ecce hic est Christus, ecce illic', ne credideritis: [22]exsurgent enim pseudochristi et pseudoprophetae et dabunt signa et portenta ad seducendos, si potest fieri, electos. [23]Vos autem videte; praedixi vobis omnia. [24]Sed in illis diebus post tribulationem illam sol contenebrabitur, *et luna non*

21-22. Life is a testing-time to prove our fidelity to God, and fidelity consists in acting on foot of this capital truth : there is no Saviour other than Jesus Christ (cf. Acts 4:12; 1 Tim 2:5). Anyone else who puts himself forward as a saviour sent by God is a liar or a fool : whether he be a person, an ideology or a political system. Forewarned by what Jesus says here, a Christian knows that these false messiahs who try to take God's place can be successfully resisted by clinging to revealed Truth, which is guarded by the Magisterium of the Church.

23. "Not only did he foretell the good things which his saints and faithful would attain, but also the many bad experiences they would undergo in this life; his purpose being to give us a surer hope of reaching the good things which will come at the end of time, despite the evils which must precede them" (St Augustine, *Letter* 127).

24-25. It would seem that at the end of time even irrational creatures will shrink before the Supreme Judge, Jesus Christ, coming in the majesty of his glory, thus fulfilling the prophecies of the Old Testament (cf., e.g., Is 13:10; 34:4; Ezek 32:7). Some Fathers, such as St Jerome (*Comm. in Matth., in loc.*) and St John Chrysostom (*Hom. on St Matthew*, 77) understand "the powers in the heavens" to mean the angels, who will be in awe at these events. This interpretation is supported by the liturgical use of describing the angels, taken together, as "virtutes caelorum" (cf. *Roman Missal*, Preface of Martyrs). But

be darkened, and the moon will not give its light, 25and the stars will be falling from heaven, and the powers in the heavens will be shaken. 26And they they will see the Son of man coming in clouds with great power and glory. 27And then he will send out the angels, and gather his elect from the four winds, from the ends of the earth to the ends of heaven.

Dan 7:13

Zech 2:6
Deut 30:4
Mt 13:41

The time of the destruction of Jerusalem

28"From the fig tree learn its lesson: as soon as its branch becomes tender and puts forth its leaves, you know that summer is near. 29So also, when you see these things taking place, you know that he is near, at the very gates. 30Truly,

---

dabit splendorem suum, 25*et erunt stellae de caelo decidentes, et virtutes, quae sunt in caelis,* movebuntur. 26Et tunc videbunt *Filium hominis venientem in nubibus* cum virtute multa et gloria.27Et tunc mittet angelos et congregabit electos suos a quattuor ventis, a summo terrae usque ad summum caeli. 28A ficu autem discite parabolam: cum iam ramus eius tener fuerit et germinaverit folia, cognoscitis quia in proximo sit aestas. 29Sic et vos, cum videritis haec fieri, scitote quod in proximo sit in ostiis. 30Amen dico vobis: Non transiet generatio

---

many other commentators think the phrase, like the preceding words in the text, could mean "cosmic forces" or "stars of the firmament."

26-27. Christ here describes his second coming, at the end of time, as announced by the prophet Daniel (7:13). He discloses the deeper meaning of the words of the ancient prophet : the "one like a son of man", whom Daniel saw and to whom "was given dominion and glory and kingdom, that all peoples, nations and languages should serve him," is Jesus Christ himself, who will gather the saints around him.

28-30. As already pointed out in the note on Mark 13:4, Jesus' disciples, following the ideas current among Jews at the time, could not conceive the destruction of Jerusalem as separate from the end of the world; and, also, there is a connexion between the two events, in that the former is a prefigurement of the latter. Our Lord answers his disciples in Mark 13:20 by saying that the destruction of Jerusalem will happen in the lifetime of their generation (as in fact occurred in the year 70, at the hands of the Roman legions). For further explanation of the ruin of Jerusalem as a figure of the end of the world, cf. note on Mt 24:32-35.

31. With this sentence our Lord adds a special solemnity to what he is saying: all this will definitely come to pass.

God has only to speak and his words come true, only he who is Lord of the

I say to you, this generation will not pass away before all these things take place. [31]Heaven and earth will pass away, but my words will not pass away.

Mt 24:36

[32]"But of that day or that hour no one knows, not even the angels in heaven, nor the Son, but only the Father. [33]Take heed, watch and pray;[a] for you do not know when the time will come. [34]It is like a man going on a journey,

Mt 25:14
Lk 19:12

when he leaves home and puts his servants in charge, each with his work, and commands the doorkeeper to be on the

Lk 12:38

watch. [35]Watch therefore—for you do not know when the master of the house will come, in the evening, or at midnight, or at cockcrow, or in the morning—[36]lest he come suddenly and find you asleep. [37]And what I say to you I say to all: Watch."

---

haec, donec omnia ista fiant. [31]Caelum et terra transibunt, verba autem mea non transibunt. [32]De die autem illo vel hora nemo scit, neque angeli in caelo neque Filius nisi Pater. [33]Videte, vigilate; nescitis enim, quando tempus sit. [34]Sicut homo, qui peregre profectus reliquit domum suam et dedit servis suis potestatem, unicuique opus suum, ianitori quoque praecepit, ut vigilaret. [35]Vigilate ergo; nescitis enim quando dominus domus veniat, sero an media nocte an galli cantu an mane, [36]ne cum venerit repente, inveniat vos dormientes. [37]Quod autem vobis dico, omnibus dico: vigilate!"

Universe has all existence in his power, and Jesus has received from the Father all power over heaven and earth (cf. Mt 11:27 and 28:18).

32. Referring to this verse, St Augustine explains (*On the Psalms*, 36:1): "Our Lord Jesus Christ was sent to be our Master, yet he declared that even the Son of Man was ignorant of that day, because it was not part of his office as Master to acquaint us with it."

Regarding the knowledge Christ had during his life on earth, see the note on Lk 2:52.

33-37. "Watch" : since we do not know when the Lord will come, we must be prepared. Vigilance is, above all, love. A person who loves keeps the commandments and looks forward to Christ's return; for life is a period of hope and waiting. It is the way towards our encounter with Christ the Lord. The first Christians often tenderly repeated the aspiration : "Come, Lord Jesus" (1 Cor 16:22; Rev 22:20). By expressing their faith and charity in this way, those Christians found the interior strength and optimism necessary for fulfilling their family and social duties, and interiorly detached themselves from earthly goods, with the self-mastery that came from hope of eternal life.

[a]Other ancient authorities omit *and pray*

PASSION, DEATH AND RESURRECTION OF JESUS

14

The conspiracy against Jesus

[1]It was now two days before the Passover and the feast
of Unleavened Bread. And the chief priests and the scribes
were seeking how to arrest him by stealth, and kill him; [2]for
they said, "Not during the feast, lest there be a tumult of the
people."

Mt 26:1-5
Lk 22:1-2

The anointment at Bethany and the treachery of Judas

[3]And while he was at Bethany in the house of Simon the

Mt 26:6-13
Jn 12:1-8
Lk 7:36

---

[1]Erat autem Pascha et Azyma post biduum. Et quaerebant summi sacerdotes et
scribae, quomodo eum dolo tenerent et occiderent; [2]dicebant enim: "Non in die
festo, ne forte tumultus fieret populi." [3]Et cum esset Bethaniae in domo Simoni
leprosi et recumberet, venit mulier habens alabastrum unguenti nardi puri

---

1. The Passover was the main national and religious festival. It lasted one
week, during which the eating of leavened bread was forbidden, which is why
the period was known as the Azymes, the feast of the Unleavened Bread. The
celebration opened with the passover meal on the night of the 14th to 15th of
the month of Nisan. The essential rite of the meal consisted in eating the paschal
lamb sacrificed in the temple the afternoon before. During the meal the
youngest member of the family asked what was the meaning of the ceremony;
and the head of the household explained to those present that it commemorated
God's liberation of the Israelites when they were slaves in Egypt, and
specifically the passing of the angel of Yahweh, doing no harm to the firstborn
of the Hebrews but destroying the firstborn of the Egyptians (cf. Ex 12).

2. The chief priests and the scribes sought by every means to ensure the
condemnation and death of the Lord prior to the Passover, for during the festival
Jerusalem would be thronged with pilgrims and they feared that Jesus' popu-
larity might cause the complications referred to in the Gospel text. Cf. note on
Mt 26:3-5.

3-9. It was a custom at the time to honour distinguished guests by offering
them scented water. This woman treated the Lord with exquisite refinement by
pouring a flask of nard over his head; and we can see that he was very
appreciative. Three hundred denarii was approximately what a worker would
earn in a year: so her action was very generous. Breaking the flask to allow the

leper, as he sat at table, a woman came with an alabaster jar of ointment of pure nard, very costly, and she broke the jar and poured it over his head. ⁴But there were some who said to themselves indignantly, "Why was the ointment thus wasted? ⁵For this ointment might have been sold for more than three hundred denarii,ᵇ and given to the poor." And they reproached her. ⁶But Jesus said, "Let her alone; why do you trouble her? She has done a beautiful thing to me.

Deut 15:11

⁷For you always have the poor with you, and whenever you will, you can do good to them; but you will not always have

Acts 3:6

me. ⁸She has done what she could; she has anointed my body beforehand for burying. ⁹And truly, I say to you, wherever the gospel is preached in the whole world, what she has done will be told in memory of her.

---

pretiosi; fracto alabastro, effudit super caput eius. ⁴Erant autem quidam indigne ferentes intra semetipsos: "Ut quid perditio ista unguenti facta est? ⁵Poterat enim unguentum istud veniri plus quam trecentis denariis et dari pauperibus." Et fremebant in eam. ⁶Iesus autem dixit: "Sinite eam; quid illi molesti estis? Bonum opus operata est in me. ⁷Semper enim pauperes habetis vobiscum et, cum volueritis, potestis illis bene facere; me autem non semper habetis. ⁸Quod habuit, operata est: praevenit ungere corpus meum in sepulturam. ⁹Amen autem

---

last drop to flow, so that no one else could use it, implies that Jesus merited everything.

It is important to notice the significance our Lord gave to this gesture : it was an anticipation of the pious custom of embalming bodies prior to burial. This woman would never have thought that her action would become famous throughout the world, but Jesus knew the transcendence and universal dimension of even the smallest episodes in the Gospel story. His prophecy has been fulfilled: "Certainly we hear her story told in all the churches. . . . Wherever in the world you may go, everyone respectfully listens to the story of her good service. . . . And yet hers was not an extraordinary deed, nor was she a distinguished person, nor was there a large audience, nor was the place one where she could easily be seen. She made no entrance onto a theatre stage to perform her service but did her good deed in a private house. Nevertheless ..., today she is more illustrious than any king or queen; no passage of years has buried in oblivion this service she performed" (St John Chrysostom, *Adversus Iudaeos*, V, 2).

This episode teaches us the refinement with which we should treat the holy humanity of Jesus; it also shows that generosity in things to do with sacred worship is always praiseworthy, for it is a sign of our love for the Lord. Cf. note on Mt 26:8-11.

ᵇThe denarius was a day's wage for a labourer

¹⁰Then Judas Iscariot, who was one of the twelve, went
to the chief priest in order to betray him to them. ¹¹And
when they heard it they were glad, and promised to give
him money. And he sought an opportunity to betray him.

Mt 26:14-16
Lk 22:3-6

The Last Supper

¹²And on the first day of Unleavened Bread, when they
sacrificed the passover lamb, his disciples said to him,
"Where will you have us go and prepare for you to eat the
passover?" ¹³And he sent two of his disciples, and said to
them, "Go into the city, and a man carrying a jar of water
will meet you; follow him, ¹⁴and wherever he enters, say to

Mt 26:17-19
Lk 22:7-13

Mk 11:3

---

dico vobis: Ubicumque praedicatum fuerit evangelium in universum mundum,
et, quod fecit haec, narrabitur in memoriam eius." ¹⁰Et Iudas Iscarioth, unus de
Duodecim, abiit ad summos sacerdotes, ut proderet eum illis. ¹¹Qui audientes
gavisi sunt et promiserunt ei pecuniam se daturos. Et quaerebat quomodo illum
opportune traderet. ¹²Et primo die Azymorum, quando Pascha immolabant,
dicunt ei discipuli eius: "Quo vis eamus et paremus, ut manduces Pascha?" ¹³Et
mittit duos ex discipulis suis et dicit eis: "Ite in civitatem, et occurret vobis
homo lagoenam aquae baiulans; sequimini eum, ¹⁴et, quocumque introierit,
dicite domino domus: 'Magister dicit: Ubi est refectio mea, ubi Pascha cum

10-11. In contrast with the generous anointing by the woman, the Gospel
now reports Judas' sad treachery. Her magnaminity highlights the covetousness
of Jesus' false friend. "O folly, or rather ambition, of the traitor, for ambition
spawns every kind of evil and enslaves souls by every sort of device; it causes
forgetfulness and mental derangement. Judas, enslaved by his mad ambition,
forgot all about the years he had spent alongside Jesus, forgot that he had eaten
at his table, that he had been his disciple; forgot all the counsel and persuasion
Jesus had offered him" (St John Chrysostom, *Hom. de prodit. Judae*).

Judas' sin is always something Christians should be mindful of : "Today
many people are horrified by Judas' crime—that he could be so cruel and so
sacrilegious as to sell his Master and his God; and yet they fail to realize that
when they for human reasons dismiss the rights of charity and truth, they are
betraying God, who is very charity and truth" (St Bede, *Super qui audientes
gavisi sunt*).

12-16. At first sight our Lord's behaviour described here seems quite out
of character. However, if we think about it, it is quite consistent : probably Jesus
wanted to avoid Judas knowing in advance the exact place where the Supper
will be held, to prevent him notifying the Sanhedrin. And so God's plans for
that memorable night of Holy Thursday were fulfilled : Judas was unable to
advise the Sanhedrin where they could find Jesus until after the celebration of
the passover meal (during which Judas left the Cenacle): cf. Jn 13:30.

the householder, 'The Teacher says, Where is my guest room, where I am to eat the passover with my disciples?' [15]And he will show you a large upper room furnished and ready; there prepare for us." [16]And the disciples set out and went to the city, and found it as he had told them; and they prepared the passover.

[17]And when it was evening he came with the twelve. [18]And as they were at table eating, Jesus said, "Truly, I say to you, one of you will betray me, one who is eating with me." [19]They began to be sorrowful, and to say to him one after another, "Is it I?" [20]He said to them, "It is one of the twelve, one who is dipping bread in the same dish with me. [21]For the Son of man goes as it is written of him, but woe to that man by whom the Son of man is betrayed! It would have been better for that man if he had not been born."

Mt 26:20-29
Lk 22:14-23
Jn 13:21-26
Ps 41:10

The institution of the Eucharist

1 Cor 11:23-25

[22]And as they were eating, he took bread, and blessed,

---

discipulis meis manducem?' [15]Et ipse vobis demonstrabit cenaculum grande stratum paratum; et illic parate nobis." [16]Et abierunt discipuli et venerunt in civitatem et invenerunt, sicut dixerit illis, et paraverunt Pascha. [17]Et vespere facto venit cum Duodecim. [18]Et discumbentibus eis et manducantibus, ait Iesus: "Amen dico vobis: Unus ex vobis me tradet, qui manducat mecum." [19]Coeperunt contristari et dicere ei singillatim: "Numquid ego?" [20]Qui ait illis: "Unus ex Duodecim, qui intingit mecum in catino. [21]Nam Filius quidem hominis vadit, sicut scriptum est de eo. Vae autem homini illi, per quem Filius hominis traditur! Bonum est ei, si non esset natus homo ille." [22]Et manducantibus illis,

---

St Mark describes in more detail than the other evangelists the place where the meal took place : he says it was a large, well- appointed room—a dignified place. There is an ancient Christian tradition that the house of the Cenacle was owned by Mary the mother of St Mark, to whom, it seems, the Garden of Olives also belonged.

17-21. Jesus shows that he knows in advance what is going to happen and is acting freely and deliberately, identifying himself with the will of his Father. The words of vv. 18 and 19 are a further call to Judas to repent; our Lord refrained from denouncing him publicly, so making it easier for him to change his mind. But he did not want to remain silent about the incipient treachery; they should realize that the Master knew everything (cf. Jn 13:23ff).

22. The word "this" does not refer to the act of breaking the bread but to the "thing" which Jesus gives his disciples, that is, something which looked

and broke it, and gave it to them, and said, "Take; this is my body." ²³And he took a cup, and when he had given thanks he gave it to them, and they all drank of it. ²⁴And he said to them, "This is my blood of the^c covenant, which is

accepit panem et benedicens fregit et dedit eis et ait: "Sumite; hoc est corpus meum." ²³Et accepto calice, gratias agens dedit eis, et biberunt ex illo omnes. ²⁴Et ait illis: "Hic est sanguis meus novi testamenti, qui pro multis effunditur.

like bread and which was no longer bread but the body of Christ. "This is my body. That is to say, what I am giving you now and what you are taking is my body. For the bread is not only a symbol of the body of Christ; it becomes his very body, as the Lord has said : the bread which I shall give for the life of the world is my flesh. Therefore, the Lord conserves the appearances of bread and wine but changes the bread and wine into the reality of his flesh and his blood" (Theophylact, *Enarratio in Evangelium Marci, in loc.*). Therefore, any interpretation in the direction of symbolism or metaphor does not fit the meaning of the text. The same applies to the "This is my blood" (v. 24). On the realism of these expressions, cf. first part of note on Mt 26:26- 29.

24. The words of consecration of the chalice clearly show that the Eucharist is a sacrifice : the blood of Christ is poured out, sealing the new and definitive Covenant of God with men. This Covenant remains sealed forever by the sacrifice of Christ on the cross, in which Jesus is both Priest and Victim. The Church has defined this truth in these words : "If anyone says that in the Mass a true and proper sacrifice is not offered to God, or that to be offered is nothing else but that Christ is given us to eat, let him be anathema" (Council of Trent, *De S. Missae sacrificio*, chap. 1, can. 1).

These words pronounced over the chalice must have been very revealing for the Apostles, because they show that the sacrifices of the Old Covenant were in fact a preparation for and anticipation of Christ's sacrifice. The Apostles were able to grasp that the Covenant of Sinai and the various sacrifices of the temple were merely an imperfect pre-figurement of the definitive sacrifice and definitive Covenant, which would take place on the cross and which they were anticipating in this Supper.

A clear explanation of the sacrificial character of the Eucharist can be found in the inspired text in chapters 8 and 9 of the Letter to the Hebrews. Similarly, the best preparation for understanding the real presence and the Eucharist as food for the soul is a reading of chapter 6 of the Gospel of St John.

In the Last Supper, then, Christ already offered himself voluntarily to his Father as a victim to be sacrificed. The Supper and the Mass constitute with the Cross one and the same unique and perfect sacrifice, for in all these cases the victim offered is the same—Christ; and the priest is the same—Christ. The only difference is that the Supper, which takes place prior to the Cross, anticipates

^cOther ancient authorities insert *new*

poured out for many. ²⁵Truly, I say to you, I shall not drink again of the fruit of the vine until that day when I drink it new in the kingdom of God."

The disciples will abandon Jesus

Mt 26:30-35
Lk 22:31-34, 39
Ps 113-118

²⁶And when they had sung a hymn, they went out to the Mount of Olives. ²⁷And Jesus said to them, "You will all fall away; for it is written. 'I will strike the shepherd, and

Zech 13:7

the sheep will be scattered.' ²⁸But after I am raised up, I

Mk 16:7

will go before you to Galilee." ²⁹Peter said to him, "Even

---

²⁵Amen dico vobis: Iam non bibam de genimine vitis usque in diem illum, cum illud bibam novum in regno Dei." ²⁶Et hymno dicto, exierunt in montem Olivarum. ²⁷Et ait eis Iesus: "Omnes scandalizabimini, quia scriptum est: *'Percutiam pastorem, et dispergentur oves.'* ²⁸Sed posteaquam resurrexero, praecedam vos in Galilaeam." ²⁹Petrus autem ait ei: "Et si omnes scandalizati

---

the Lord's Death in an unbloody way and offers a victim soon to be immolated; whereas the Mass offers, also in an unbloody manner, the victim already immolated on the cross, a victim who exists forever in heaven.

25. After instituting the Holy Eucharist, our Lord extends the Last Supper in intimate conversation with his disciples, speaking to them once more about his imminent death (cf. Jn, chap. 13-17). His farewell saddens the Apostles, but he promises that the day will come when he will meet with them again, when the Kingdom of God will have come in all its fullness : he is referring to the beatific life in heaven, so often compared to a banquet. Then there will be no need of earthly food or drink; instead there will be a new wine (cf. Is 25:6). Definitively, after the Resurrection, the Apostles and all the saints will be able to share the delight of being with Jesus.

The fact that St Mark brings in these words after the institution of the Eucharist indicates in some way that the Eucharist is an anticipation here on earth of possession of God in eternal blessedness, where God will be everything to everyone (cf. 1 Cor 15:28). "At the Last Supper," Vatican II teaches, "on the night he was betrayed, our Saviour instituted the eucharistic sacrifice of his body and blood. This he did in order to perpetuate the sacrifice of the Cross throughout the ages until he should come again, and so to entrust to his beloved Spouse, the Church, a memorial of his death and resurrection: a sacrament of love, a sign of unity, a bond of charity, a paschal banquet in which Christ is consumed, the mind is filled with grace, and a pledge of future glory is given to us" (*Sacrosanctum Concilium*, 47).

26. "When they had sung a hymn" : it was a custom at the passover meal to recite prayers, called "Hallel", which included Psalms 113 to 118; the last part was recited at the end of the meal.

though they all fall away, I will not." ³⁰And Jesus said to Jn 13:38
him, "Truly, I say to you, this very night, before the cock
crows twice, you will deny me three times." ³¹But he said Jn 11:16
vehemently, "If I must die with you, I will not deny you.".
And they all said the same.

The agony in the garden
Mt 26:36-46
³²And they went to a place which was called Geth- Lk 22:40-46
Jn 18:1

---

fuerint, sed non ego." ³⁰Et ait illi Iesus: "Amen dico tibi: Tu hodie, in nocte hac,
priusquam bis gallus vocem dederit, ter me es negaturus." ³¹At ille amplius
loquebatur: "Et si oportuerit me commori tibi, non te negabo." Similiter autem
et omnes dicebant. ³²Et veniunt in praedium, cui nomen Gethsemani, et ait

---

30-31. Only St Mark gives us the exact detail of the two cockcrows (v. 30),
and Peter's insistence that he would never betray Jesus (v. 31). This is another
sign of the connexion between St Mark's Gospel and St Peter's preaching; only
Peter, full of contrition and humility, would so deliberately tell the first
Christians about these episodes in which his presumption and failures con-
trasted with Jesus' mercy and understanding. The other evangelists, surely out
of respect for the figure of Peter, pass over these incidents more quickly.

This account shows us that our Lord takes into account the weaknesses of
those whom he calls to follow him and be his Apostles. Peter is too self-
confident; very soon he will deny him. Jesus knows this well and, in spite of
everything, chooses him as head of the Church. "They [the disciples] remain
just like that until they are filled with the Holy Spirit and thus become pillars
of the Church. They are ordinary men, complete with defects and shortcomings,
more eager to say than to do. Nevertheless, Jesus calls them to be fishers of
men, co- redeemers, dispensers of the grace of God. Something similar has
happened to us. . . . But I also realize that human logic cannot possibly explain
the world of grace. God usually seeks out deficient instruments so that the work
can more clearly be seen to be his" (J. Escrivá, *Christ is passing by*, 2 and 3).

32-42. The very human way Jesus approaches his passion and death is
noteworthy. He feels everything any man would feel in those circumstances.
"He takes with him only the three disciples who had seen his glorification on
Mount Tabor, that these who saw his power should also see his sorrow and
learn from that sorrow that he was truly man. And, because he assumed human
nature in its entirety, he assumed the properties of man— fear, strength, natural
sorrow; for it is natural that men approach death unwillingly" (Theophylact,
Enarratio in Evangelium Marci, in loc.).

Jesus' prayer in the garden shows us, as nothing else in the Gospel does, that
he prayed the prayer of petition—not only for others, but also for himself. For,
in the unity of his Person there were two natures, one human and one divine;
and, since his human will was not omnipotent, it was appropriate for Christ to

175

Jn 12:27
Ps 43:5

semane; and he said to his disciples, "Sit here, while I pray."
³³And he took with him Peter and James and John, and
began to be greatly depressed and troubled. ³⁴And he said
to them, "My soul is very sorrowful, even to death; remain
here, and watch."ᵈ ³⁵And going a little farther, he fell on the

---

discipulis suis: "Sedete hic, donec orem." ³³Et assumit Petrum et Iacobum et
Ioannem secum et coepit pavere et taedere ³⁴et ait illis: "Tristis est anima mea
usque ad mortem; sustinete hic et vigilate." ³⁵Et cum processisset paululum,

---

ask the Father to strengthen that will (cf. St Thomas Aquinas, *Summa theologiae*, III, q. 21, a. 1).

Once more, Jesus prays with a deep sense of his divine sonship (cf. Mt 11:25; Lk 23:46; Jn 17:1). Only St Mark retains in the original language his filial exclamation to the Father : "Abba", which is how children intimately addressed their parents. Every Christian should have a similar filial trust, especially when praying. At this moment of climax, Jesus turns from his private dialogue with his Father to ask his disciples to pray so as not to fall into temptation. It should be noted that the evangelists, inspired by the Holy Spirit, give us both Jesus' prayer and his commandment to us to pray. This is not a passing anecdote, but an episode which is a model of how Christians should act : prayer is indispensable for staying faithful to God. Anyone who does not pray should be under no illusions about being able to cope with the temptations of the devil: "If our Lord had said only *watch*, we might expect that our own power would be sufficient, but when he adds *pray*, he shows that *if he keeps not* our souls in time of temptation, in vain shall they watch who keep them" (cf. Ps 127:1) (St Francis de Sales, *Treatise on the Love of God*, book 11, chap. 1).

34. "But when he had gone on a little way, he suddenly felt such a sharp and bitter attack of sadness, grief, fear, and weariness that he immediately uttered, even in their presence, those anguished words which gave expression to his overburdened feelings : 'My soul is sad unto death.' For a huge mass of troubles took possession of the tender and gentle body of our most holy Saviour. He knew that his ordeal was now imminent and just about to overtake him : the treacherous betrayer, the bitter enemies, binding ropes, false accusations, slanders, blows, thorns, nails, the cross, and horrible tortures stretched out over many hours. Over and above these, he was tormented by the thought of his disciples' terror, the loss of the Jews, even the destruction of the very man who so disloyally betrayed him, and finally the ineffable grief of his beloved Mother. The gathered storm of all these evils rushed into his most gentle heart and flooded it like the ocean sweeping through broken dikes" (St Thomas More, *De tristitia Christi, in loc.*).

35. "Therefore, since he foresaw that there would be many people of such

ᵈOr *Keep awake*

ground and prayed that, if it were possible, the hour might
pass from him. ³⁶And he said, "Abba, Father, all things are
possible to thee; remove this cup from me; yet not what I

---

procidebat super terram et orabat, ut, si fieri posset, transiret ab eo hora, ³⁶et
dicebat "Abba, Pater! Omnia tibi possibilia sunt. Transfer calicem hunc a me;

---

a delicate constitution that they would be convulsed with terror at any danger
of being tortured, he chose to enhearten them by the example of his own sorrow,
his own sadness, his own weariness and unequalled fear, lest they should be so
disheartened as they compare their own fearful state of mind with the boldness
of the bravest martyrs that they would yield freely what they fear will be won
from them by force. To such a person as this, Christ wanted his own deed to
speak out (as it were) with his own living voice: 'O faint of heart, take courage
and do not despair. You are afraid, you are sad, you are stricken with weariness
and dread of the torment with which you have been cruelly threatened. Trust
me; I conquered the world, and yet I suffered immeasurably more from fear; I
was sadder, more afflicted with weariness, more horrified at the prospect of
such cruel suffering drawing eagerly nearer and nearer. Let the brave man have
his high-spirited martyrs, let him rejoice in imitating a thousand of them. But
you, my timorous and feeble little sheep, be content to have me alone as your
shepherd; follow my leadership. If you do not trust yourself, place your trust
in me. See, I am walking ahead of you along this fearful road. Take hold of the
border of my garment and you will feel going out from it a power which will
stay your heart's blood from issuing in vain fears, and will make your mind
more cheerful, especially when you remember that you are following closely
in my footsteps (and I am to be trusted and will not allow you to be tempted
beyond what you can bear, but I will give together with the temptation a way
out that you may be able to endure it) and likewise when you remember that
this light and momentary burden of tribulation will prepare for you a weight of
glory which is beyond all measure. For the sufferings of this time are not worthy
to be compared with the glory to come which will be revealed in you. As you
reflect on such things, take heart, and use the sign of my cross to drive away
this dread, this sadness, and weariness like vain spectres of the darkness.
Advance successfully and press through all obstacles, firmly confident that I
will champion your cause until you are victorious and then in turn will reward
you with the laurel crown of victory'" (St Thomas More, *De tristitia Christi*,
in loc.).

36. "Jesus prays in the garden. *Pater mi* (Mt 26:39), *Abba Pater!* (Mk
14:36). God is my Father, even though he may send me suffering. He loves me
tenderly, even while wounding me. Jesus suffers, to fulfil the Will of the Father.
. . . And I, who also wish to fulfil the most holy Will of God, following the
footsteps of the Master, can I complain if I too meet suffering as my travelling
companion?

will, but what thou wilt." [37]And he came and found them sleeping, and he said to Peter, "Simon, are you asleep?

Rom 7:5

could you not watch[d] one hour? [38]Watch[d] and pray that you may not enter into temptation; the spirit indeed is willing, but the flesh is weak." [39]And again he went away and

Mk 9:6

prayed, saying the same words. [40]And again he came and found them sleeping, for their eyes were very heavy; and they did not know what to answer him. [41]And he came a third time, and said to them, "Are you still sleeping and taking your rest: It is enough; the hour has come; the Son

Jn 14:31

of man is betrayed into the hands of sinners. [42]Rise, let us be going; see, my betrayer is at hand."

Mt 26:47-58
Lk 22:47-55
Jn 18:2-18

The arrest

[43]And immediately, while he was still speaking, Judas

---

sed non quod ego volo, sed quod tu." [37]Et venit et invenit eos dormientes et ait Petro: "Simon, dormis? Non potuisti una hora vigilare? [38]Vigilate et orate, ut non intretis in tentationem; spiritus quidem promptus, caro vero infirma." [39]Et iterum abiens oravit, eundem sermonem dicens. [40]Et veniens denuo invenit eos dormientes; erant enim oculi illorum ingravati, et ignorabant quid responderent ei. [41]Et venit tertio et ait illis: "Dormite iam et requiescite? Sufficit, venit hora: ecce traditur Filius hominis in manus peccatorum. [42]Surgite, eamus; ecce, qui me tradit, prope est." [43]Et confestim, adhuc eo loquente, venit Iudas unus ex

---

"It will be a sure sign of my sonship, because God is treating me as he treated his own divine Son. Then I, just as he did, will be able to groan and weep alone in my Gethsemane; but, as I lie prostrate on the ground, acknowledging my nothingness, there will rise up to the Lord a cry from the depths of my soul: *Pater mi, Abba, Pater, . . . fiat!*" (J. Escrivá, *The Way of the Cross*, I, 1).

41-42. "See now, when Christ comes back to his apostles for the third time, there they are, buried in sleep, though he commanded them to bear up with him and to stay awake and pray because of the impending danger; but Judas the traitor at the same time was so wide awake and intent on betraying the Lord that the very idea of sleep never entered his mind.

"Does not this contrast between the traitor and the apostles present to us a clear and sharp mirror image (as it were), a sad and terrible view of what has happened through the ages from those times even to our own? [. . .] For very many are sleepy and apathetic in sowing virtues among the people and maintaining the truth, while the enemies of Christ in order to sow vices and uproot the faith (that is, insofar as they can, to seize Christ and cruelly crucify him once again) are wide awake—so much wiser (as Christ says) are the sons of darkness in their generation than the sons of light (cf. Lk 16:8)" (St Thomas More, *De tristitia Christi, in loc.*).

came, one of the twelve, and with him a crowd with swords and clubs, from the chief priests and the scribes and the elders. ⁴⁴Now the betrayer had given them a sign, saying, "The one I shall kiss is the man; seize him and lead him away safely." ⁴⁵And when he came, he went up to him at once, and said, "Master!"ᵉ And he kissed him. ⁴⁶And they laid hands on him and seized him. ⁴⁷But one of those who stood by drew his sword, and struck the slave of the high priest and cut off his ear. ⁴⁸And Jesus said to them, "Have you come out as against a robber, with swords and clubs to capture me? ⁴⁹Day after day I was with you in the temple teaching, and you did not seize me. But let the scriptures be fulfilled. ⁵⁰And they all forsook him, and fled.

⁵¹And a young man followed him, with nothing but a linen cloth about his body; and they seized him, ⁵²but he left the linen cloth and ran away naked.

Jn 16:32

Duodecim, et cum illo turba cum gladiis et lignis a summis sacerdotibus et scribis et senioribus. ⁴⁴Dederat autem traditor eius signum eis dicens; "Quemcumque osculatus fuero, ipse est; tenete eum et ducite caute." ⁴⁵Et cum venisset, statim accedens ad eum ait: "Rabbi", et osculatus est eum. ⁴⁶At illi manus iniecerunt in eum et tenuerunt eum. ⁴⁷Unus autem quidam de circumstantibus educens gladium percussit servum summi sacerdotis et amputavit illi auriculum. ⁴⁸Et respondens Iesus ait illis: "Tamquam ad latronem existis cum gladiis et lignis comprehendere me? ⁴⁹Cotidie eram apud vos in templo docens et non me tenuistis; sed adimpleantur Scripturae." ⁵⁰Et relinquentes eum omnes

---

43-50. The Gospel reports the arrest of our Lord in a matter-of-fact sort of way. Jesus, who was expecting it, offered no resistance, thereby fulfilling the prophecies about him in the Old Testament, particularly this passage of the poem of the Servant of Yahweh in the Book of Isaiah : "like a lamb that is led to the slaughter, and like a sheep that before its shearers is dumb, so he opened not his mouth . . . because he poured out his soul to death . . ." (Is 53:7 and 12).

Dejected only moments earlier at the beginning of his prayer in Gethsemane Jesus now rises up strengthened to face his passion. These mysteries of our Lord, true God and true man, are really impressive.

51-52. This detail about the young man in the linen cloth is found only in St Mark. Most interpreters see in it a discreet allusion to Mark himself. It is probable that the Garden of Olives belonged to Mark's family, which would explain the presence there at night-time of the boy, who would have been awakened suddenly by the noise of the crowd.

ᵉOr *Rabbi*

Jesus before the Sanhedrin

⁵³And they led Jesus to the high priests, and all the chief priests and the elders and the scribes were assembled. ⁵⁴And Peter had followed him at a distance, right into the courtyard of the high priest; and he was sitting with the

fugerunt. ⁵¹Et adulescens quidam sequebatur eum amictus sindone super nudo, et tenent eum; ⁵²at ille, reiecta sindone, nudus profugit. ⁵³Et adduxerunt Iesum ad summum sacerdotem, et conveniunt omnes summi sacerdotes et seniores et scribae. ⁵⁴Et Petrus a longe secutus est eum usque intro in atrium summi

"One sees rich men—less often, it is true, than I would like—but still, thank God, one sometimes sees exceedingly rich men who would rather lose everything they have than keep anything at all by offending God through sin. These men have many clothes, but they are not tightly confined by them, so that when they need to run away from danger, they escape easily by throwing off their clothes. On the other hand we see people—and far more of them than I would wish—who happen to have only light garments and quite skimpy outfits and yet have so welded their affections to those poor riches of theirs that you could sooner strip skin from flesh than separate them from their goods. Such a person had better get going while there is still time. For once someone gets hold of his clothes, he will sooner die than leave his linen cloth behind. In summary, then, we learn from the example of this young man that we should always be prepared for troubles that arise suddenly, dangers that strike without warning and might make it necessary for us to run away; to be prepared, we ought not be so loaded with various garments, or so buttoned up in even one, that in an emergency we are unable to throw away our linen cloth and escape naked" (St Thomas More, *De tristitia Christi, in loc.*).

53-65. This meeting of the Sanhedrin in the house of the high priest was quite irregular. The normal thing was for it to meet during the daytime and in the temple. Everything suggests that the rulers arranged this session secretly, probably to avoid opposition from the people, which would have thwarted their plans. The direct intervention of the high priest and the ill- treatment of the prisoner before sentence were also illegal. The Jewish authorities had for some time past been of a mind to do away with Jesus (cf., e.g., Mk 12:12; Jn 7:30; 11:45-50). Now all they are trying to do is give their actions an appearance of legality—that is, looking for concurring witnesses to accuse him of capital crimes. Because they do not manage to do this, the chief priest goes right to the key issue : was Jesus the Messiah, yes or no? Jesus' affirmative answer is regarded as blasphemy. Appearances are saved; they can now condemn him to death and ask the Roman procurator to ratify the sentence (cf. note on Mt 27:2). Despite the irregularities and even though not all the members of the Sanhedrin were present, the significance of this session lies in the fact that the Jewish authorities, the official representatives of the chosen people, reject Jesus as Messiah and condemn him to death.

guards, and warming himself at the fire. ⁵⁵Now the chief priests and the whole council sought testimony against Jesus to put him to death, but they found none. ⁵⁶For many bore false witness against him, and their witness did not agree. ⁵⁷And some stood up and bore false witness against him saying, ⁵⁸"We heard him say, 'I will destroy this temple that is made with hands, and in three days I will build another, not made with hands.'" ⁵⁹Yet not even so did their testimony agree. ⁶⁰And the high priest stood up in the midst, and asked Jesus, "Have you no answer to make? What is it that these men testify against you?" ⁶¹But he was silent and

Mt 26:59-68
Lk 22:63-71
Jn 18:19-24

Jn 2:19
2 Cor 5:1

Mk 15:5
Is 53:7

---

sacerdotis, et sedebat cum ministris et calefaciebat se ad ignem. ⁵⁵Summi vero sacerdotes et omne concilium quaerebant adversus Iesum testimonium, ut eum morte afficerent, nec inveniebant. ⁵⁶Multi enim testimonium falsum dicebant adversus eum, et convenientia testimonia non erant. ⁵⁷Et quidam surgentes falsum testimonium ferebant adversus eum dicentes: ⁵⁸"Nos audivimus eum dicentem: 'Ego dissolvam templum hoc manu factum et intra triduum aliud non manu factum aedificabo.' " ⁵⁹Et ne ita quidem conveniens erat testimonium illorum. ⁶⁰Et exsurgens summus sacerdos in medium interrogavit Iesum dicens; "Non respondes quidquam ad ea, quae isti testantur adversum te?" ⁶¹Ille autem

---

57-59. From the Gospel of St John (2:19) we know the words of Jesus which gave rise to this accusation : "Destroy the temple, and in three days I will raise it up." Now they accuse him of having said three things : that he is going to destroy the temple; that the temple of Jerusalem is the work of human hands, not something divine; and that in three days he will raise up another one, not made by hands of men. As can be seen, this is not what our Lord said. First they change his words : Jesus did not say he was going to destroy the temple; and, secondly, they apply what he said to the temple of Jerusalem, not understanding that Jesus was speaking about his own body, as is made plain in St John (2:21-22). After the Resurrection, the Apostles understood the depth of Jesus' words (Jn 2:22): the temple of Jerusalem, where God's presence was manifested in a special way and where he was offered due worship, was but a sign, a prefiguring of the humanity of Christ, in which the fullness of divinity, God, dwelt (cf. Col 2:9).

The same accusation is made at the martyrdom of St Stephen : "We have heard him say that this Jesus of Nazareth will destroy this place, and will change the customs which Moses delivered to us" (Acts 6:14). In fact, St Stephen knew that the true temple was no longer that of Jerusalem but Jesus Christ; but once again they misinterpreted his meaning and accused him as they had our Lord.

61. As at other points during his passion, Jesus kept completely silent. He appeared defenceless before the false accusations of his enemies. "God our Saviour," St Jerome says, "who has redeemed the world out of mercy, lets

Dan 7:13
Ps 110:1

made no answer. Again the high priest asked him, "Are you the Christ, the Son of the Blessed?" ⁶²And Jesus said, "I am; and you will see the Son of man sitting at the right hand of Power, and coming with the clouds of heaven." ⁶³And the high priest tore his mantle, and said, "Why do we still

---

tacebat et nihil respondit. Rursum summus sacerdos interrogabat eum et dicit ei: "Tu es Christus filius Benedicti?" ⁶²Iesus autem dixit: "Ego sum, et *videbitis Filium hominis a dextris sedentem Virtutis et venientem cum nubibus caeli.*" ⁶³Summus autem sacerdos scindens vestimenta sua ait: "Quid adhuc necessarii

---

himself be led to death like a lamb, not saying a word; he does not complain, he makes no effort to defend himself. Jesus' silence obtains forgiveness for Adam's protest and excuse" (*Comm. in Marcum, in loc.*). This silence is another motive and encouragement to us to be silent at times in the face of calumny or criticism. "In quietness and in trust shall be your strength," says the prophet Isaiah (30:15).

"'Jesus remained silent, *Jesus autem tacebat.*' Why do you speak, to console yourself, or to excuse yourself?

"Say nothing. Seek joy in contempt: you will always receive less than you deserve.

"Can you, by any chance, ask: '*Quid enim mali feci,* what evil have I done?'" (J. Escrivá, *The Way,* 671).

61-64. The high priest was undoubtedly trying to corner Jesus : if he replied that he was not the Christ, it would be equivalent to his contradicting everything he had said and done; if he answered yes, it would be interpreted as blasphemy, as we shall see later. Strictly speaking it was not blasphemy to call oneself the Messiah, or to say one was the Son of God, taking that phrase in a broad sense. Jesus' reply not only bore witness to his being the Messiah; it also showed the divine transcendence of his messianism, by applying to him the prophecy of the Son of Man in Daniel (7:13-14). By making this confession, Jesus' reply opened the way for the high priest to make his theatrical gesture : he took it as a mockery of God and as blasphemy that this handcuffed man could be the transcendent figure of the Son of man. At this solemn moment Jesus defines himself by using the strongest of all the biblical expressions his hearers could understand—that which most clearly manifested his divinity. We might point out that had Jesus said simply "I am God" they would have thought it simply absurd and would have regarded him as mad : in which case he would not have borne solemn witness to his divinity before the authorities of the Jewish people.

63. The rending of garments was a custom in Israel to express indignation and protest against sacrilege and blasphemy. The rabbis had specified exactly how it should be done. Only a kind of seam was torn, to prevent the fabric being damaged. With this tragi-comic gesture Caiaphas brings the trial to an end,

need witnesses? 64You have heard his blasphemy. What is
your decision?" And they all condemned him as deserving
death. 65And some began to spit on him, and to cover his
face, and to strike him, saying to him, "Prophesy!" And the
guards received him with blows.

Peter's denial

66And as Peter was below in the courtyard, one of the
maids of the high priest came; 67and seeing Peter warming
himself, she looked at him, and said, "You also were with
the Nazarene, Jesus." 68But he denied it, saying, "I neither
know nor understand what you mean." And he went out
into the gateway.f 69And the maid saw him, and began
again to say to the bystanders, "This man is one of them."
70But again he denied it. And after a little while the bystanders said to Peter, "Certainly you are one of them; for
you are a Galilean." 71But he began to invoke a curse on
himself and to swear, "I do not know this man of whom you
speak." 72And immediately the cock crowed a second time.

---

sunt nobis testes? 64Audistis blasphemiam; quid vobis videtur?" Qui omnes
condemnaverunt eum esse reum mortis. 65Et coeperunt quidam conspuere eum
et velare faciem eius et colaphis eum caedere et dicere ei: "Prophetiza"; et
ministri alapis eum caedebant. 66Et cum esset Petrus in atrio deorsum, venit una
ex ancillis summi sacerdotis 67et, cum vidisset Petrum calefacientem se,
aspiciens illum ait: "Et tu cum hoc Nazareno, Iesu, eras." 68At ille negavit
dicens: "Neque scio neque novi quid tu dicas." Et exiit foras ante atrium, et
gallus cantavit. 69Et ancilla, cum vidisset illum, rursus coepit dicere circumstantibus: "Hic ex illis est." 70At ille iterum negabat. Et post pusillum rursus,
qui adstabant, dicebant Petro: "Vere ex illis es, nam et Galilaeus es." 71Ille
autem coepit anathematizare et iurare: "Nescio hominem istum, quem dicitis."
72Et statim iterum gallus cantavit. Et recordatus est Petrus verbi, sicut dixerat
ei Iesus: "Priusquam gallus cantet bis, ter me negabis", et coepit flere.

---

cleverly sabotaging any later procedure that might favour the prisoner and show
up the truth.

64. Through Luke 23:51 and John 7:25-33 we know that not all the
members of the Sanhedrin condemned Jesus, for Joseph of Arimathea did not
consent in this act of deicide. It may be supposed, therefore, that they were not
present at this meeting of the council, either because they had not been
summoned or because they absented themselves.

fOr forecourt. Other authorities add and the cock crowed

And Peter remembered how Jesus had said to him, "Before the cock crows twice, you will deny me three times." And he broke down and wept.

15

Jesus before Pilate

Mt 27:1-2
Lk 22:66; 23:1
Jn 18:28

¹And as soon as it was morning the chief priests, with the elders and scribes, and the whole council held a con-

Mt 27:11-30
Lk 23:2-25
Jn 18:29-19:16

sultation; and they bound Jesus and led him away and delivered him to Pilate. ²And Pilate asked him, "Are you

---

¹Et confestim mane consilium facientes summi sacerdotes cum senioribus et scribis, id est universum concilium, vincientes Iesum duxerunt et tradiderunt

---

66-72. Although the accounts given by the three Synoptic Gospels are very alike, St Mark's narrative does have its own characteristics : the sacred text gives little details which add a touch of colour. He says that Peter was "below" (v. 66), which shows that the council session was held in an upstairs room; he also mentions the two cockcrows (v. 72), in a way consistent with our Lord's prophecy described in v. 30.

On the theological and ascetical implications of this passage, cf. note on Mt 26:70-75.

1. At daybreak the Sanhedrin holds another meeting to work out how to get Pilate to ratify the death sentence. And then Christ is immediately brought before Pilate.

It is not known for certain where the governor was residing during these days. It was either in Herod's palace, built on the western hill of the city, south of the Jaffa Gate, or the Antonia fortress, which was on the north-east of the temple esplanade. It is more than likely that, for the Passover, Pilate lived in the fortress. From there he could have a full view of the whole outside area of the temple, where unrest and riots were most likely to occur. In the centre of this impressive building there was a perfectly paved courtyard of about 2,500 square metres (approx. half an acre). This may well have been the yard where Pilate judged our Lord and which St John (19:13) called The Pavement (*Lithostrotos*, in Greek).

Philo, Josephus and other historians depict Pilate as having the defects of the worst type of Roman governor. The evangelists emphasize his cowardice and his sycophancy bordering on wickedness.

2. Jesus' reply, as given in St Mark, can be interpreted in two ways. It may mean : You say that I am king; I say nothing; or else : I am a king. The second

the King of the Jews?" And he answered him, "You have said so." ³And the chief priests accused him of many things. ⁴And Pilate again asked him, "Have you no answer to make? See how many charges they bring against you." ⁵But Jesus made no further answer, so that Pilate wondered.

⁶Now at the feast he used to release for them one prisoner whom they asked. ⁷And among the rebels in prison, who had committed murder in the insurrection, there was a man called Barabbas. ⁸And the crowd came up and began to ask Pilate to do as he was wont to do for them. ⁹And he answered them, "Do you want me to release for you the King of the Jews?" ¹⁰For he perceived that it was out of

Pilato. ²Et interrogavit eum Pilatus: "Tu es rex Iudaeorum?" At ille respondens ait illi: "Tu dicis." ³Et accusabant eum summi sacerdotes in multis. ⁴Pilatus autem rursum interrogabat eum dicens: "Non respondes quidquam? Vide in quantis te accusant." ⁵Iesus autem amplius nihil respondit, ita ut miraretur Pilatus. ⁶Per diem autem festum dimittere solebat illis unum ex vinctis, quem peterent. ⁷Erat autem qui dicebatur Barabbas, vinctus cum seditiosis, qui in seditione fecerant homicidium. ⁸Et cum ascendisset turba, coepit rogare, sicut

interpretation is the more common and logical, since in other Gospel passages he affirms his kingship quite categorically (cf. Mt 27:37 and par.; Jn 18:36- 38).

In St John's Gospel (18:33-38) Jesus tells Pilate that he is a King and explains the special nature of his kingship : his Kingdom is not of this world; it transcends this world (cf. note on Jn 18:35-37).

3-5. On three occasions the evangelists specify that Jesus remained silent in the face of these unjust accusations : before the Sanhedrin (14:61); here, before Pilate; and later on, before Herod (Lk 23:9). From the Gospel of St John we know that our Lord did say other things during this trial. St Mark says that he made no further reply, since he is referring only to the accusations made against our Lord : being false, they deserved no reply. Besides, any attempt at defence was futile, since they had decided in advance that he should die. Nor did Pilate need any further answer, since he was more concerned to please the Jewish authorities than, correctly, to find Jesus innocent.

6-15. Instead of simply coming to the rescue of this innocent prisoner, as was his duty and as his conscience advised him, Pilate wants to avoid a confrontation with the Sanhedrin; so he tries to deal with the people and have them set Jesus free. Since it was customary to release a prisoner of the people's choice to celebrate the Passover, Pilate offers them the chance of selecting Jesus. The priests, seeing through this manoeuvre, incite the crowd to ask for Barabbas. This was not difficult to do, since many felt disillusioned about Jesus because he had not set them free of the foreign yoke. Pilate could not oppose

185

envy that the chief priests had delivered him up. [11]But the chief priests stirred up the crowd to have him release for them Barabbas instead. [12]And Pilate again said to them, "Then what shall I do with the man whom you call the King of the Jews?" [13]And they cried out again, "Crucify him." [14]And Pilate said to them, "Why, what evil has he done?" But they shouted all the more, "Crucify him." [15]So Pilate, wishing to satisfy the crowd, released for them Barabbas; and having scourged Jesus, he delivered him to be crucified.

Acts 3:13

---

faciebat illis. [9]Pilatus autem respondit eis et dixit: "Vultis dimittam vobis regem Iudaeorum?" [10]Sciebat enim quod per invidiam tradidissent eum summi sacerdotes. [11]Pontifices autem concitaverunt turbam, ut magis Barabbam dimitteret eis. [12]Pilatus autem iterum respondens aiebat illis: "Quid ergo vultis faciam regi Iudaeorum?" [13]At illi iterum clamaverunt: "Crucifige eum." [14]Pilatus vero

---

their choice; and so it became even more difficult for him to give a just decision. All he can do now is appeal to the people on behalf of "the King of the Jews". The humble and helpless appearance of Jesus exasperates the crowd : this is not the sort of king they want, and they ask for his crucifixion.

In the course of the trial Pilate was threatened with being reported to the emperor if he interfered in this affair (cf. Jn 19:12); he now accedes to their shouting and signs the warrant for death by crucifixion, to protect his political career.

15. Scourging, like crucifixion, was a degrading form of punishment applied only to slaves. The whip or *flagellum* used to punish serious crimes was strengthened with small sharp pieces of metal at the end of the thongs, which had the effect of tearing the flesh and even fracturing bones. Scourging often caused death. The condemned person was tied to a post to prevent him collapsing. People condemned to crucifixion were scourged beforehand.

These sufferings of Jesus have a redemptive value. In other passages of the Gospel our Lord made carrying the cross a condition of following him. Through self-denial a Christian associates himself with Christ's passion and plays a part in the work of redemption (cf. Col 1:24).

"Bound to the pillars. Covered with wounds.

"The blows of the lash sound upon his torn flesh, upon his undefiled flesh, which suffers for your sinful flesh. More blows. More fury. Still more . . . It is the last extreme of human cruelty.

"Finally, exhausted, they untie Jesus. And the body of Christ yields to pain and falls limp, broken and half dead.

"You and I cannot speak. Words are not needed. Look at him, look at him ... slowly.

"After this ... can you ever fear penance?" (J. Escrivá, *Holy Rosary*, second sorrowful mystery).

The crowning with thorns

16And the soldiers led him away inside the palace (that is, the praetorium); and they called together the whole battalion. 17And they clothed him in a purple cloak, and plaiting a crown of thorns they put it on him. 18And they began to salute him, "Hail, King of the Jews!" 19And they struck his head with a reed, and spat upon him, and they knelt down in homage to him. 20And when they had mocked him, they stripped him of the purple cloak, and put his own clothes on him. And they led him out to crucify him.

The crucifixion and death of Jesus

Mt 27:32-56
Lk 23:26-49
Jn 19:17-30

21And they compelled a passer-by, Simon of Cyrene,

---

dicebat eis: "Quid enim mali fecit?" At illi magis clamaverunt: "Crucifige eum." 15Pilatus autem, volens populo satisfacere, dimisit illis Barabbam et tradidit Iesum flagellis caesum, ut crucifigeretur. 16Milites autem duxerunt eum intro in atrium, quod est praetorium, et convocant totam cohortem. 17Et induunt eum purpuram et imponunt ei plectentes spineam coronam, 18et coeperunt salutare eum: "Ave, rex Iudaeorum", 19et percutiebant caput eius arundine et conspuebant eum et ponentes genua adorabant eum. 20Et postquam illuserunt ei, exuerunt illum purpuram et induerunt eum vestimentis suis. Et educunt

---

16-19. The soldiers make Jesus an object of mockery; they accuse him of pretending to be a king, and crown him and dress him up as one.

The image of the suffering Jesus, scourged and crowned with thorns, with a reed in his hands and an old purple cloak around his shoulders, has become a vivid symbol of human pain, under the title of the "Ecce homo".

But, as St Jerome teaches, "his ignominy has blotted out ours, his bonds have set us free, his crown of thorns has won for us the crown of the Kingdom, his wounds have cured us" (*Comm. in Marcum, in loc.*).

"You and I . . . , haven't we crowned him anew with thorns and struck him and spat on him?" (J. Escrivá, *Holy Rosary*, third sorrowful mystery).

21. "Jesus is exhausted. His footsteps become more and more unsteady, and the soldiers are in a hurry to be finished. So, when they are going out of the city through the Judgment Gate, they take hold of a man who was coming in from a farm, a man called Simon of Cyrene, the father of Alexander and Rufus, and they force him to carry the Cross of Jesus (cf. Mk 15:21).

"In the whole context of the Passion, this help does not add up to very much. But for Jesus, a smile, a word, a gesture, a little bit of love is enough for him to pour out his grace bountifully on the soul of his friend. Years later, Simon's sons, Christians by then, will be known and held in high esteem among their brothers in the faith. And it all started with this unexpected meeting with the Cross.

who was coming in from the country, the father of

---

illum, ut crucifigerent eum. [21]Et angariant praetereuntem quempiam Simonem Cyrenaeum venientem de villa, patrem Alexandri et Rufi, ut tolleret crucem

---

"*I went to those who were not looking for me; I was found by those who sought me not* (Is 65:1).

"At times the Cross appears without our looking for it: it is Christ who is seeking us out. And if by chance, before this unexpected Cross which, perhaps, is therefore more difficult to understand, your heart were to show repugnance . . . don't give it consolations. And, filled with a noble compassion, when it asks for them, say to it slowly, as one speaking in confidence: 'Heart: heart on the Cross! Heart on the Cross!' " (J. Escrivá, *The Way of the Cross*, V). St Mark stops for a moment to say who this Simon was : he was the father of Alexander and Rufus. It appears that Rufus, years later, moved with his mother to Rome; St Paul sent them affectionate greetings in his Letter to the Romans (16:13). It seems reasonable to imagine that Simon first felt victimized at being forced to do such unpleasant work, but contact with the Holy Cross—the altar on which the divine Victim was going to be sacrificed—and the sight of the suffering and death of Jesus, must have touched his heart; and the Cyrenean, who was at first indifferent, left Calvary a faithful disciple of Christ : Jesus had amply rewarded him. How often it happens that divine providence, through some mishap, places us face to face with suffering and brings about in us a deeper conversion.

When reading this passage, we might reflect that, although our Lord has rescued us voluntarily, and although his merits are infinite, he does seek our cooperation. Christ bears the burden of the cross, but we have to help him carry it by accepting all the difficulties and contradictions which divine providence presents us with. In this way we grow in holiness, at the same time atoning for our faults and sins.

From the Gospel of St John (19:17) we know that Jesus bore the cross on his shoulders. In Christ burdened by the Cross St Jerome sees, among other meanings, the fulfilment of the figure of Abel, the innocent victim, and particularly of Isaac (cf. Gen 22:6), who carried the wood for his own sacrifice (cf. St Jerome, *Comm. in Marcum, in loc.*). Later, weakened from the scourging, Jesus can go no further on his own, which is why they compel this man from Cyrene to carry the cross.

"If anyone would follow me . . . Little friend, we are sad, living the Passion of our Lord Jesus. See how lovingly he embraces the Cross. Learn from him. Jesus carries the Cross for you: you . . . carry it for Jesus.

"But don't drag the Cross . . . . Carry it squarely on your shoulder, because the Cross, if you carry it like that, will not be just any Cross. . . . It will be the Holy Cross. Don't carry your Cross with resignation : resignation is not a generous word. Love the Cross. When you really love it, your Cross will be ... a Cross without a Cross.

"And surely you will find Mary on the way, just as Jesus did" (J. Escrivá, *Holy Rosary*, fourth sorrowful mystery).

Alexander and Rufus, to carry his cross. [22]And they brought
him to the place called Golgotha (whch means the place of
a skull). [23]And they offered him wine mingled with myrrh; $\quad$ Ps 69:22
but he did not take it. [24]And they crucified him, and divided $\quad$ Ps 22:19

---

eius. [22]Et perducunt illum in Golgotha locum, quod est interpretatum Calvariae
locus. [23]Et dabant ei myrrhatum vinum, ille autem non accepit. [24]Et crucifigunt
eum et *dividunt vestimenta eius, mittentes sortem super eis* quis quid tolleret.

22. There is no doubt about where this place was : it was a small, bare hill,
at that time outside the city, right beside a busy main road.

23. Following the advice of Proverbs (31:6), the Jews used to offer dying
criminals wine mixed with myrrh or incense to drug them and thus alleviate
their suffering.

Jesus tastes it (according to Mt 27:34), but he does not drink it. He wishes
to remain conscious to the last moment and to keep offering the chalice of the
Passion, which he accepted at the Incarnation (Heb 10:9) and did not refuse in
Gethsemane. St Augustine (*On the Psalms*, 21: 2 and 8) explains that our Lord
wanted to suffer to the very end in order to purchase our redemption at a high
price (cf. 1 Cor 6:20).

Faithful souls have also experienced this generosity of Christ in embracing
pain : "Let us drink to the last drop the chalice of pain in this poor present life.
What does it matter to suffer for ten years, twenty, fifty . . . if afterwards there
is heaven for ever, for ever . . . for ever?

"And, above all rather than because of the reward, 'propter retributionem'
what does suffering matter if we suffer to console, to please God our Lord, in
a spirit of reparation, united to him on his Cross; in a word: if we suffer for
Love? . . ." (J. Escrivá, *The Way*, 182).

24-28. Crucifixion, as well as being the most degrading of punishments,
was also the most painful. By condemning him to death, Jesus' enemies try to
achieve the maximum contrast with his triumphant entry into Jerusalem some
days previously. Usually, the bodies of people crucified were left on the gibbet
for some days as a warning to people. In the case of Christ they also sought
death by crucifixion as the most convincing proof that he was not the Messiah.

Cruxifixion took various forms. The usual one, and perhaps the one applied
to Jesus, consisted of first erecting the upright beam and then positioning the
cross-beam with the prisoner nailed to it by his hands; and finally nailing his
feet to the lower part of the the the upright.

According to St John's Gospel (19:23-25) the seamless tunic—that is,
woven in a piece—was wagered for separately from the rest of his clothes,
which were divided into four lots, one for each soldier. The words of this verse
reproduce those of Psalm 22:19. Any Jew versed in the Scriptures reading this
passage would immediately see in it the fulfilment of a prophecy. St John
expressly notes it (cf. 19:24). St Mark, without losing the thread of his account

his garments among them, casting lots for them, to decide what each should take. ²⁵And it was the third hour, when they crucified him. ²⁶And the inscription of the charge against him read, "The King of the Jews." ²⁷And with him

---

²⁵Erat autem hora tertia, et crucifixerunt eum. ²⁶Et erat titulus causae eius inscriptus: "Rex Iudaeorum." ²⁷Et cum eo crucifigunt duos latrones, unum a

---

of the Passion, implicitly argues that Jesus Christ is the promised Messiah, for in him this prophecy is fulfilled.

Looking at Jesus on the cross, it is appropriate to recall that God "decreed that man should be saved through the wood of the Cross. The tree of man's defeat became his tree of victory; where life was lost, there life has been restored" (*Preface of the Holy Cross*).

25. "The third hour" : between nine o'clock and noon. St Mark is the only evangelist who specifies the time at which our Lord was nailed to the cross. For the relationship between our clock and the Jewish system in that period, cf. note on Mt 20:3.

26. This inscription was usually put in a prominent place so that everyone could see what the prisoner was guilty of. Pilate ordered them to write "Jesus the Nazarene, King of the Jews," in Latin, Greek and Hebrew; St Mark summarizes the inscription.

Motivated by malice, the Jews accuse Jesus of a political crime, when all his life and preaching left it quite clear that his mission was not political but supernatural. On the meaning of the inscription over the cross and the circumstances surrounding it, see John 19:19-22 and note.

27. Jesus is thus put to further shame; his disciples will also experience the humiliation of being treated like common criminals.

But in the case of Jesus this was providential, for it fulfilled the Scripture which prophesies that he would be counted among the evildoers. The Vulgate, following some Greek codexes adds: "And the scripture was fulfilled which says, 'He was reckoned with the transgressors'" (v.28; cf. Lk 22:37). "Positioned between the evildoers," St Jerome teaches, "the Truth places one on his left and one on his right, as will be the case on the day of judgment. So we see how distinct the end of similar sinners can be. One precedes Peter into Paradise, the other enters hell before Judas : a brief confession brings eternal life, a momentary blasphemy is punished with eternal death" (*Comm. in Marcum, in loc.*).

The Christian people have from early on given various names to these thieves. The commonest in the West is Dismas for the good thief and Gestas for the bad thief.

they crucified two robbers, one on his right and one on his left.g 29And those who passed by derided him, wagging their heads, and saying, "Aha! You who would destroy the temple and build it in three days, 30save yourself, and come down from the cross!" 31So also the chief priests mocked him to one another with the scribes, saying, "He saved others; he cannot save himself. 32Let the Christ, the King of Israel, come down now from the cross, that we may see and believe." Those who were crucified with him also reviled him.

Ps 22:8
109:25
Mk 14:58

Mt 16:1, 4

33And when the sixth hour had come, there was darkness

Amos 8:9

---

dextris et alium a sinistris eius. (28) 29Et praetereuntes blasphemabant eum *moventes capita* sua et dicentes: "Vah, qui destruit templum et in tribus diebus aedificat, 30salvum fac temetipsum descendens de cruce." 31Similiter et summi sacerdotes ludentes ad alterutrum cum scribis dicebant: "Alios salvos fecit, seipsum non potest salvum facere. 32Christus rex Israel descendat nunc de cruce, ut videamus et credamus." Etiam qui cum eo crucifixi erant, conviciabantur ei. 33Et, facta hora sexta, tenebrae factae sunt per totam terram usque

---

29-32. Christ's suffering did not finish with the crucifixion : there now follows a form of mockery worse (if possible) than the crowning with thorns. He is mocked by passersby, by the priests chanting insults with the scribes, and even by the two crucified thieves (cf., however, the clarification in Lk 23:39-43). They combine to reproach him for his weakness, as if his miracles had been deceptions, and incite him to manifest his power.

The fact that they ask him to work a miracle does not indicate that they have any desire to believe in him. For faith is a gift from God which only those receive who have a simple heart. "You ask for very little," St Jerome upbraids the Jews, "when the greatest event in history is taking place before your very eyes. Your blindness cannot be cured even by much greater miracles than those you call for" (*Comm. in Marcum, in loc.*).

Precisely because he was the Messiah and the Son of God he did not get down from the cross; in great pain, he completed the work his Father had entrusted to him. Christ teaches us that suffering is our best and richest treasure. Our Lord did not win victory from a throne or with a sceptre in his hand, but by opening his arms on the cross. A Christian, who, like any other person, will experience pain and sorrow during his life, should not flee it or rebel against it, but offer it to God, as his Master did.

33. The evangelist reports this as a miraculous phenomenon signalling the magnitude of the crime of deicide which was taking place. The phrase "over the whole land" means over all the immediate horizon, without specifying its

gOther ancient authorities insert verse 28, *And the scripture was fulfilled which says, "He was reckoned with the transgressors"*

Ps 22:2

over the whole land[h] until the ninth hour. [34]And at the ninth hour Jesus cried out with a loud voice, "Eloi, Eloi, lama sabachthani?" which means, "My God, my God, why hast thou forsaken me?" [35]And some of the bystanders hearing

Ps 69:22

it said, "Behold, he is calling Elijah." [36]And one ran and,

---

in horam nonam. [34]Et hora nona exclamavit Iesus voce magna: *"Heloi, heloi, lema sabacthani?"*, quod est interpretatum: *"Deus meus, Deus meus, ut quid dereliquisti me?"* [35]Et quidam de circumstantibus audientes dicebant: "Ecce Eliam vocat." [36]Currens autem unus et implens spongiam aceto

---

limits. The normal interpretation of the meaning of this event is dual and complementary; Origen (*In Matth. comm.*, 143) sees it as an expression of the spiritual darkness which overtook the Jewish people as a punishment for having rejected—crucified—him who is the true light (cf. Jn 1:4-9). St Jerome (*Comm. in Matth., in loc.*) explains the darkness as expressing, rather, the mourning of the universe at the death of its Creator, nature's protest against the unjust killing of its Lord (cf. Rom 8:19-22).

34. These words, spoken in Aramaic, are the start of Psalm 22, the prayer of the just man who, hunted and cornered, feels utterly alone, like "a worm, and no man; scorned by men and despised by the people" (v. 7). From this abyss of misery and total abandonment, the just man has recourse to Yahweh: "My God, my God, why art thou so far from helping me. . . . Since my mother bore me thou has been my God. . . . But thou, O Lord, be not far off! O thou my help, hasten to my aid!" (vv. 2, 10 and 19). Thus, far from expressing a moment of despair, these words of Christ reveal his complete trust in his heavenly Father, the only one on whom he can rely in the midst of suffering, to whom he can complain like a Son and in whom he abandons himself without reserve : "Father, into thy hands I commit my spirit" (Lk 23:46; Ps 31:6).

One of the most painful situations a person can experience is to feel alone in the face of misunderstanding and persecution on all sides, to feel completely insecure and afraid. God permits these tests to happen so that, experiencing our own smallness and world-weariness, we place all our trust in him who draws good from evil for those who love him (cf. Rom 8:28).

"So much do I love Christ on the Cross that every crucifix is like a loving reproach from my God: '. . . I suffering, and you . . . a coward. I loving you, and you forgetting me. I begging you, and you . . . denying me. I, here, with arms wide open as an Eternal Priest, suffering all that can be suffered for love of you . . . and you complain at the slightest misunderstanding, over the tiniest humiliation . . .'" (J. Escrivá, *The Way of the Cross*, XI, 2).

35-36. The soldiers near the cross, on hearing our Lord speak, may have thought, wrongly, that he was calling on Elijah for help. However, it seems it

[h]Or *earth*

filling a sponge full of vinegar, put it on a reed and gave it
to him to drink, saying, "Wait, let us see whether Elijah will
come to take him down." 37And Jesus uttered a loud cry,
and breathed his last. 38And the curtain of the temple was

circumponensque calamo potum dabat ei dicens: "Sinite, videamus, si veniat
Elias ad deponendum eum." 37Iesus autem, emissa voce magna, exspiravit. 38Et

is the Jews themselves who, twisting our Lord's words, find another excuse for
jeering at him. There was a belief that Elijah would come to herald the Messiah,
which is why they used these words to continue to ridicule Christ on the cross.

37. The evangelist recalls it very succinctly : "Jesus uttered a loud cry, and
breathed his last." It is as if he did not dare make any comment, leaving it to
the reader to pause and meditate. Although the death of Christ is a tremendous
mystery, we must insist : Jesus Christ died; it was a real, not an apparent, death;
nor should we forget that our sin was what caused our Lord's death. "The abyss
of malice, which sin opens wide, has been bridged by his infinite charity. God
does not abandon men. His plans foresee that the sacrifices of the Old Law were
insufficient to repair our faults and re-establish the unity which has been lost:
a man who was God must offer himself up. To help us grasp in some measure
this unfathomable mystery, we might imagine the Blessed Trinity taking
counsel together in its uninterrupted intimate relationship of infinite love. As
a result of its eternal decision, the only- begotten Son of God the Father takes
on our human condition and bears the burden of our wretchedness and sorrows,
to end up sewn with nails to a piece of wood. . . . Let us meditate on our Lord,
wounded from head to foot out of love for us" (J. Escrivá, *Christ is passing by*,
95).

"...Now it is all over. The work of our Redemption has been accomplished.
We are now children of God, because Jesus has died for us and his death has
ransomed us.

"*Empti enim estis pretio magno!* (1 Cor 6:20), you and I have been bought
at a great price.

"We must bring into our lives, to make them our own, the life and death of
Christ. We must die through mortification and penance, so that Christ may live
in us through Love. And then follow in the footsteps of Christ, with a zeal to
co-redeem all mankind.

"We must give our lives for others. That is the only way to live the life of
Jesus Christ and to become one and the same thing with him" (J. Escrivá, *The
Way of the Cross*, XIV).

38. The strictly sacred precinct of the temple of Jerusalem had two parts:
the first, called "the Holy Place," where only priests could enter for specific
liturgical functions; the second, called "the Holy of Holies" (*Sancta Sanctorum*). This was the most sacred room where once the Ark of the Covenant
stood, containing the tablets of the Law. Above the Ark was the "propitiatory"

Mt 4:3

torn in two, from top to bottom. [39]And when the centurion, who stood facing him, saw that he thus[i] breathed his last, he said, "Truly this man was the Son[x] of God!"

Lk 8:2-3
Mk 6:3

[40]There were also women looking on from afar, among whom were Mary Magdalene, and Mary the mother of James the younger and of Joses, and Salome, [41]who, when he was in Galilee, followed him, and ministered to him; and also many other women who came up with him to Jerusalem.

Mt 27:57-61
Lk 23:50-55
Jn 19:38-42

The burial

[42]And when evening had come, since it was the day of

---

velum templi scissum est in duo a sursum usque deorsum. [39]Videns autem centurio, qui ex adverso stabat, quia sic clamans exspirasset, ait: "Vere homo hic Filius Dei erat." [40]Erant autem et mulieres de longe aspicientes, inter quas et Maria Magdalene et Maria Iacobi minoris et Iosetis mater et Salome, [41]quae, cum esset in Galilaea, sequebantur eum et ministrabant ei, et aliae multae, quae simul cum eo ascenderant Hierosolymam. [42]Et cum iam sero esset factum, quia

---

with figures of two cherubim. Only once a year did the high priest have access to the Holy of Holies, on the great Day of Atonement, to perform the rite of purification of the people. The curtain of the temple was the great curtain which separated the Holy of Holies from the Holy Place (cf. 1 Kings 6:15f).

The prodigy of the tearing of the curtain of the temple—apparently of no great importance—is full of theological meaning. It signifies dramatically that with Christ's death the worship of the Old Covenant has been brought to an end; the temple of Jerusalem has no longer any *raison d'être*. The worship pleasing to God—in spirit and truth (cf. Jn 4:23)—is rendered him through the humanity of Christ, who is both Priest and Victim.

39. Regarding this passage St Bede says that this miracle of the conversion of the Roman officer is due to the fact that, on seeing the Lord die in this way, he could not but recognize his divinity; for no one has the power to surrender his spirit but he who is the Creator of souls (cf. St Bede, *In Marci Evangelium expositio, in loc.*). Christ, indeed, being God, had the power to surrender his spirit; whereas in the case of other people their spirit is taken from them at the moment of death. But the Christian has to imitate Christ, also at this supreme moment : that is, we should accept death peacefully and joyfully. Death is the point planned by God for us to leave our spirit in his hands; the difference is that Christ yielded up his spirit when he chose (cf. Jn 10-18), whereas we do so when God so disposes.

[i]Other ancient authorities insert *cried out and*
[x]Or *a son*

Preparation, that is, the day before the sabbath, [43]Joseph of Arimathea, a respected member of the council, who was also himself looking for the kingdom of God, took courage and went to Pilate, and asked for the body of Jesus. [44]And Pilate wondered if he were already dead; and summoning the centurion, he asked him whether he was already dead.[j] [45]And when he learned from the centurion that he was dead, he granted the body to Joseph. [46]And he brought a linen shroud, and taking him down, wrapped him in the linen shroud, and laid him in a tomb which had been hewn out of the rock; and he rolled a stone against the door of the tomb. [47]Mary Magdalene and Mary the mother of Joses saw where he was laid.

---

erat Parasceve, quod est ante sabbatum, [43]venit Ioseph ab Arimathaea nobilis decurio, qui et ipse erat exspectans regnum Dei, et audacter introivit ad Pilatum et petiit corpus Iesu. [44]Pilatus autem miratus est si iam obisset, et, accersito centurione, interrogavit eum si iam mortuus esset, [45]et, cum cognovisset a centurione, donavit corpus Ioseph.[46]Is autem mercatus sindonem et deponens eum involvit sindone et posuit eum in monumento, quod erat excisum de petra, et advolvit lapidem ad ostium monumenti. [47]Maria autem Magdalene et Maria Iosetis aspiciebant, ubi positus esset.

"Don't be afraid of death. Accept it from now on, generously . . . when God wills it, where God wills it, as God wills it. Don't doubt what I say: it will come in the moment, in the place and in the way that are best: sent by your Father-God. Welcome be our sister death!" (J. Escrivá, *The Way*, 739).

43-46. Unlike the Apostles, who fled, Joseph of Arimathea, who had not consented to the decision of the Sanhedrin (cf. Lk 23:51), had the bold and refined piety of personally taking charge of everything to do with the burial of Jesus. Christ's death had not shaken his faith. It is worth noting that he does this immediately after the debacle of Calvary and before the triumph of the glorious resurrection of the Lord. His action will be rewarded by his name being written in the Book of Life and recorded in the Holy Gospel and in the memory of all generations of Christians.

Joseph of Arimathea put himself at the service of Jesus, without expecting any human recompense and even at personal risk : he ventured his social position, his own as yet unused tomb, and everything else that was needed. He will always be a vivid example for every Christian of how one ought to risk money, position and honour in the service of God.

[j]Other ancient authorities read *whether he had been some time dead*

16

The Resurrection

Mt 28:1-8
Lk 24:1-12
Jn 20:1-10

¹And when the sabbath was past, Mary Magdalene, and Mary the mother of James, and Salome, bought spices, so that they might go and anoint him. ²And very early on the first day of the week they went to the tomb when the sun had risen. ³And they were saying to one another. "Who will roll away the stone for us from the door of the tomb?" ⁴And looking up, they saw that the stone was rolled back; for it was very large. ⁵And entering the tomb, they saw a young

---

¹Et cum transisset sabbatum, Maria Magdalene et Maria Iacobi et Salome emerunt aromata, ut venientes ungerent eum. ²Et valde mane, prima sabbatorum, veniunt ad monumentum, orto iam sole. ³Et dicebant ad invicem: "Quis revolvet nobis lapidem ab ostio monumenti?" ⁴Et respicientes vident revolutum lapidem; erat quippe magnus valde. ⁵Et introeuntes in monumentum viderunt iuvenem sedentem in dextris, coopertum stola candida, et obstupuerunt. ⁶Qui dicit illis: "Nolite expavescere! Iesum quaeritis Nazarenum crucifixum. Surrexit, non est hic; ecce locus, ubi posuerunt eum. ⁷Sed ite, dicite

---

1. The sabbath rest was laid down in the Law of Moses as a day when the Israelites should devote themselves to prayer and the worship of God, and also as a form of protection for workers. As time went by the rabbis specified in miniscule detail what could and could not be done on the sabbath. This was why the holy women were unable to organize things on the sabbath for anointing the dead body of our Lord, and why they had to wait until the first day of the week.

From the earliest days of the Church, this first day is called the "dies Domini", the Lord's Day, because, St Jerome comments, "after the sorrow of the sabbath, a joyful day breaks out, the day of greatest joy, lit up by the greatest light of all, for this day saw the triumph of the risen Christ" (*Comm. in Marcum, in loc.*). This is why the Church has designated Sunday as the day specially consecrated to the Lord, a day of rest on which we are commanded to attend Holy Mass.

3-4. On the structure of Jewish tombs and the stone covering the entrance, cf. note on Mt 27:60.

5. Like so many other passages of the Gospel this one shows the extreme sobriety with which the evangelists report historical facts. From the parallel passage of St Matthew (28:5) we know that this person was an angel. But both Mark and Luke are content to report what the women say, without any further interpretation.

man on the right side, dressed in a white robe; and they were
amazed. ⁶And he said to them, "Do not be amazed; you seek   Mt 2:23
Jesus of Nazareth, who was crucified. He has risen, he is

---

discipulis eius et Petro: 'Praecedit vos in Galilaeam. Ibi eum videbitis, sicut
dixit vobis.' " ⁸Et exeuntes fugerunt de monumento; invaserat enim eas tremor
et pavor, et nemini quidquam dixerunt, timebant enim. ⁹Surgens autem mane,
prima sabbati, apparuit primo Mariae Magdalenae, de qua eiecerat septem

6. These women's sensitive love urges them, as soon as the Law permits,
to go to anoint the dead body of Jesus, without giving a thought to the difficulties
involved. Our Lord rewarded them in kind : they were the first to hear news of
his resurrection. The Church has always invoked the Blessed Virgin "pro devota
femineo sexu", to intercede for devout womanhood. And it is indeed true that
in the terrible moments of the passion and death of Jesus women proved
stronger than men : "Woman is stronger than man, and more faithful, in the
hour of suffering: Mary of Magdala and Mary of Cleophas and Salome!

"With a group of valiant women like these, closely united to our Lady of
Sorrows, what work for souls could be done in the world!" (J. Escrivá, *The
Way*, 982).

"Jesus of Nazareth, who was crucified" : the same name as written on the
inscription on the cross is used by the angel to proclaim the glorious victory of
the resurrection. In this way St Mark bears witness explicitly to the crucified
man and the resurrected man being one and the same. Jesus' body, which was
treated so cruelly, now has immortal life.

"He has risen" : the glorious resurrection of Jesus is the central mystery of
our faith. "If Christ has not been raised, then our preaching is in vain and your
faith is in vain" (1 Cor 15:14). It is also the basis of our hope : "if Christ has
not been raised, your faith is futile and you are still in your sins. . . . If for this
life only we have hoped in Christ, we are of all men most to be pitied" (1 Cor
15:17 and 19). The Resurrection means that Jesus has overcome death, sin, pain
and the power of the devil.

The Redemption which our Lord carried out through his death and
resurrection is applied to the believer by means of the sacraments, especially
by Baptism and the Eucharist : "We were buried with him by baptism and death,
so that as Christ was raised from the dead by the glory of the Father, we might
walk in newness of life" (Rom 6:4). "He who eats my flesh and drinks my blood
has eternal life, and I will raise him up at the last day" (Jn 6:54). The resurrection
of Christ is also the rule of our new life : "If you have been raised with Christ,
seek the things that are above, where Christ is seated at the right hand of God.
Set your minds on things that are above, not on things that are on earth" (Col
3:1-2). Rising with Christ through grace means that "just as Jesus Christ through
his resurrection began a new immortal and heavenly life, so we must begin a
new life according to the Spirit, once and for all renouncing sin and everything
that leads us to sin, loving only God and everything that leads to God" (*St Pius
X Catechism*, 77).

Mk 14:28 not here; see the place where they laid him. ⁷But go, tell his disciples and Peter that he is going before you to Galilee; there you will see him, as he told you." ⁸And they went out and fled from the tomb; for trembling and astonishment had come upon them; and they said nothing to any one, for they were afraid.

Jesus appears to Mary Magdalene and to two disciples

Lk 8:2
Jn 20:11-18 ⁹Now when he rose early on the first day of the week, he appeared first to Mary Magdalene, from whom he had cast out seven demons. ¹⁰She went and told those who had been with him, as they mourned and wept. ¹¹But when they heard that he was alive and had been seen by her, they would not believe it.

Lk 24:13-35 ¹²After this he appeared in another form to two of them,

---

daemonia. ¹⁰Illa vadens nuntiavit his, qui cum eo fuerant, lugentibus et flentibus; ¹¹et illi audientes quia viveret et visus esset ab ea, non crediderunt. ¹²Post

---

7. The designation of the Apostle Peter by name is a way of focussing attention on the head of the Apostolic College, just at this time when the Apostles are so discouraged. It is also a delicate way of indicating that Peter's denials have been forgiven, and of confirming his primacy among the Apostles.

11-14. When reporting these first appearances of the risen Jesus, St Mark stresses the disciples' disbelief and their reluctance to accept the fact of the Resurrection, even though Jesus foretold it (cf. Mk 8:31; 9:31; 10:34). This resistance shown by the Apostles is a further guarantee of the truth of Jesus' resurrection : they were to be direct, specially-appointed witnesses to the risen Christ, yet they were reluctant to accept this role until they had personal, direct proof of the truth of the Resurrection.

However, our Lord will say : "Blessed are those who have not seen and yet believe" (Jn 20:29). In the Apostles' case, they needed, in addition to faith in the risen Christ, clear evidence of his resurrection, for they were to be the eye-witnesses, key witnesses who would proclaim it as an irrefutable fact. In this connexion St Gregory the Great comments : "The reason why the disciples were slow to believe in the Resurrection was not so much due to their weakness as to our future firmness in the faith; what other purposes does this have (the very Resurrection being demonstrated by many arguments to those who were in doubt) than that our faith should be strengthened by their doubt?" (*In Evangelia homiliae*, 16).

12. Our Lord's appearance to these two disciples is reported more fully by St Luke (cf. 24:13-35).

as they were walking into the country. ¹³And they went back and told the rest, but they did not believe them.

Jesus appears to the Eleven. The Apostles' mission

¹⁴Afterwards he appeared to the eleven themselves as they sat at table; and he upbraided them for their unbelief and hardness of heart, because they had not believed those who saw him after he had risen. ¹⁵And he said to them, "Go

Lk 24:36-49
Jn 20:19-23
1 Cor 15:5

Mt 28:18-20

---

haec autem duobus ex eis ambulantibus ostensus est in alia effigie euntibus in villam; ¹³et illi euntes nuntiaverunt ceteris, nec illis crediderunt. ¹⁴Novissime recumbentibus illis Undecim apparuit, et exprobravit incredulitatem illorum et duritiam cordis, quia his, qui viderant eum resuscitatum, non crediderant. ¹⁵Et dixit eis: "Euntes in mundum universum praedicate evangelium omni creaturae.

---

15. This verse contains what is called the "universal apostolic mandate" (parallelled by Mt 28:19-20 and Lk 24:46-48). This is an imperative command from Christ to his Apostles to preach the Gospel to the whole world. This same apostolic mission applies, especially, to the Apostles' successors, the bishops in communion with Peter's successor, the Pope.

But this mission extends further : the whole "Church was founded to spread the kingdom of Christ over all the earth for the glory of God the Father, to make all men partakers in redemption and salvation. . . . Every activity of the mystical body with this in view goes by the name of 'apostolate'; the Church exercises it through all its members, though in various ways. In fact, the Christian vocation is, of its nature, a vocation to the apostolate as well. In the organism of a living body no member plays a purely passive part, sharing in the life of the body it shares at the same time in its activity. The same is true for the body of Christ, the Church: 'the whole body achieves full growth in dependence on the full functioning of each part' (Eph 4:16). Between the members of this body there exists, further, such a unity and solidarity (cf. Eph 4:16) that a member who does not work at the growth of the body to the extent of his possibilities must be considered useless both to the Church and to himself.

"In the Church there is diversity of ministry but unity of mission. To the apostles and their successors Christ has entrusted the office of teaching, sanctifying and governing in his name and by his power. But the laity are made to share in the priestly, prophetical and kingly office of Christ; they have therefore, in the Church and in the world, their own assignment in the mission of the whole people of God" (Vatican II, *Apostolicam actuositatem*, 2).

It is true that God acts directly on each person's soul through grace, but it must also be said that it is Christ's will (expressed here and elsewhere) that men should be an instrument or vehicle of salvation for others.

Vatican II also teaches this : "On all Christians, accordingly, rests the noble obligation of working to bring all men throughout the whole world to hear and accept the divine message of salvation" (*ibid.*, 3).

into all the world and preach the gospel to the whole
creation. [16]He who believes and is baptized will be saved;
but he who does not believe will be condemned. [17]And

---

[16]Qui crediderit et baptizatus fuerit, salvus erit; qui vero non crediderit,
condemnabitur. [17]Signa autem eos, qui crediderint haec sequentur: in nomine

---

16. This verse teaches that, as a consequence of the proclamation of the
Good News, faith and Baptism are indispensable pre-requisites for attaining
salvation. Conversion to the faith of Jesus Christ should lead directly to
Baptism, which confers on us "the first sanctifying grace, by which original sin
is forgiven, and which also forgives any actual sins there may be; it remits all
punishment due for these sins; it impresses on the soul the mark of the Christian;
it makes us children of God, members of the Church and heirs to heaven, and
enables us to receive the other sacraments" (*St Pius X Catechism*, 553).

Baptism is absolutely necessary for salvation, as we can see from these
words of the Lord. But physical impossibility of receiving the rite of Baptism
can be replaced either by martyrdom (called, therefore, "baptism of blood") or
by a perfect act of love of God and of contrition, together with an at least implicit
desire to be baptized : this is called "baptism of desire" (cf. *ibid.*, 567-568).

Regarding infant Baptism, St Augustine taught that "the custom of our
Mother the Church of infant Baptism is in no way to be rejected or considered
unnecessary; on the contrary, it is to be believed on the ground that it is a
tradition from the Apostles" (*De Gen. ad litt.*, 10, 23, 39). The new *Code of
Canon Law* also stresses the need to baptize infants : "Parents are obliged to
see that their infants are baptized within the first few weeks. As soon as possible
after the birth, indeed even before it, they are to approach the parish priest to
ask for the sacrament for their child, and to be themselves duly prepared for it"
(can. 867).

Another consequence of the proclamation of the Gospel, closely linked with
the previous one, is that *the Church is necessary*, as Vatican II declares: "Christ
is the one mediator and way of salvation; he is present to us in his body which
is the Church. He himself explicitly asserted the necessity of faith and baptism
(cf. Mk 16:16; Jn 3:5), and thereby affirmed at the same time the necessity of
the Church which men enter through baptism as through a door. Hence they
could not be saved who, knowing that the Church was founded as necessary by
God through Christ, would refuse to enter it, or to remain in it" (*Lumen gentium*,
14; cf. *Presbyterorum ordinis*, 4; *Ad gentes*, 1-3; *Dignitatis humanae*, 11).

17-18. In the early days of the Church, public miracles of this kind happened
frequently. There are numerous historical records of these events in the New
Testament (cf., e.g., Acts 3:1- 11; 28:3-6) and in other ancient Christian
writings. It was very fitting that this should be so, for it gave visible proof of
the truth of Christianity. Miracles of this type still occur, but much more seldom;
they are very exceptional. This, too, is fitting because, on the one hand, the truth
of Christianity has been attested to enough; and, on the other, it leaves room

these signs will accompany those who believe: in my name
they will cast out demons; they will speak in new tongues;
[18]they will pick up serpents, and if they drink any deadly
thing, it will not hurt them; they will lay their hands on the
sick, and they will recover."

The Ascension

[19]So then the Lord Jesus, after he had spoken to them, Lk 24:50-53
Acts 1:4-11; 7:55
was taken up into heaven, and sat down at the right hand of 2 Kings 2:11
God.

The Apostles go forth and preach

[20]And they went forth and preached everywhere, while Heb 2:4
Acts 14:3

---

meo daemonia eicient, linguis loquentur novis, [18]serpentes tollent, et, si morti-
ferum quid biberint, non eos nocebit, super aegrotos manus imponent et bene
habebunt." [19]Et Dominus quidem Iesus, postquam locutus est eis, assumptus

---

for us to merit through faith. St Jerome comments: "Miracles were necessary
at the beginning to confirm people in the faith. But, once the faith of the Church
is confirmed, miracles are not necessary" (*Comm. in Marcum, in loc.*). However, God still works miracles through saints in every generation, including our
own.

19. The Lord's ascension into heaven and his sitting at the right hand of the
Father is the sixth article of faith confessed in the Creed. Jesus Christ went up
into heaven body and soul, to take possession of the Kingdom he won through
his death, to prepare for us a place in heaven (cf. Rev 3:21) and to send the Holy
Spirit to his Church (cf. *St Pius X Catechism*, 123).

To say that he "sat at the right hand of God" means that Jesus Christ,
including his humanity, has taken eternal possession of heaven and that, being
the equal of his Father in that he is God, he occupies the place of highest honour
beside him in his human capacity (cf. *St Pius V Catechism*, I, 7, 2-3). Already
in the Old Testament the Messiah is spoken of as seated at the right hand of the
Almighty, thereby showing the supreme dignity of Yahweh's Anointed (cf. Ps
110:1). The New Testament records this truth here and also in many other
passages (cf. Eph 1:20-22; Heb 1:13).

As the *St Pius V Catechism* adds, Jesus went up to heaven by his own power
and not by any other. Nor was it only as God that he ascended, but also as man.

20. Inspired by the Holy Spirit, the evangelist attests that the words of Christ
have already begun to be fulfilled by the time of writing. The Apostles, in other
words, were faithfully carrying out the mission our Lord entrusted to them.
They began to preach the Good News of salvation throughout the known world.
Their preaching was accompanied by the signs and wonders the Lord had

the Lord worked with them and confirmed the message by the signs that attended it. Amen.[k]

---

est in caelum et sedit a dextris Dei. [20]Illi autem profecti praedicaverunt ubique, Domino cooperante et sermonem confirmante, sequentibus signis.

---

promised, which lent authority to their witness and their teaching. Yet, we know that their apostolic work was always hard, involving much effort, danger, misunderstanding, persecution and even martyrdom—like our Lord's own life.

Thanks to God and also to the Apostles, the strength and joy of our Lord Jesus Christ has reached as far as us. But every Christian generation, every man and woman, has to receive the preaching of the Gospel and, in turn, pass it on. The grace of God will always be available to us: "Non est abbreviata manus Domini" (Is 59:1), the power of the Lord has not diminished.

---

[k]Other ancient authorities omit verses 9-20. Some ancient authorities conclude Mark instead with the following: *But they reported briefly to Peter and those with him all that they had been told. And after this, Jesus himself sent out by means of them, from east to west, the sacred and imperishable proclamation of eternal salvation*

Headings added to the Gospel text
for this edition

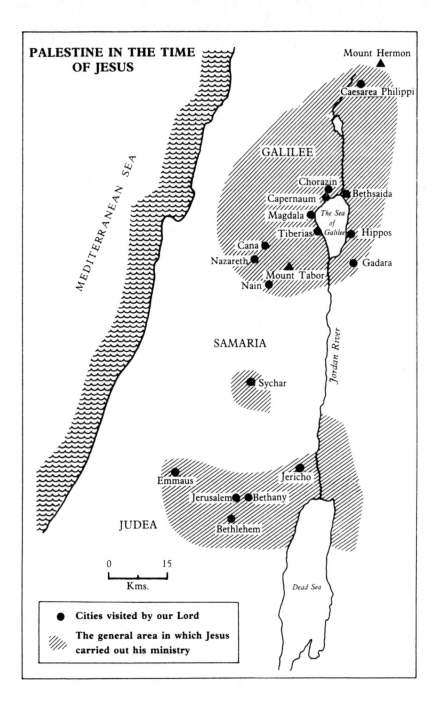

205

The Navarre Bible (New Testament)

St Matthew's Gospel
St Mark's Gospel
St Luke's Gospel
St John's Gospel
Acts of the Apostles
Romans and Galatians
Corinthians
Hebrews
Captivity Epistles
Thessalonians and Pastoral Epistles
Catholic Epistles
Revelation

ESSAYS ON BIBLICAL SUBJECTS

In addition to special introduction(s) in each volume, the following essays etc. are published in the series:

St Mark	General Introduction to the Bible; Introduction to the Books of the New Testament; Introduction to the Holy Gospels; and The Dates in the Life of our Lord Jesus Christ
St Luke	Index to the Four Gospels
Acts	The History of the New Testament Text
Romans & Galatians	Introduction to the Epistles of St Paul
Corinthians	Divine Inspiration of the Bible
Captivity Epistles	The Canon of the Bible
Thessalonians	The Truth of Sacred Scripture
Hebrews	Interpretation of Sacred Scripture and the Senses of the Bible; Divine Worship in the Old Testament
Catholic Epistles	Rules for Biblical Interpretation
Revelation	Index to the New Testament